In Green and Red
The Lives of Frank Ryan

ADRIAN HOAR

IN GREEN AND RED

The Lives of Frank Ryan

First published in 2004 by Brandon
an imprint of Mount Eagle Publications
Dingle, Co. Kerry, Ireland, and
Unit 3, Olympia Trading Estate, Coburg Road,
London N22 6TZ, England

2   4   6   8   10   9   7   5   3   1

Copyright © Adrian Hoar 2004

The author has asserted his moral rights.

ISBN 0 86322 332 X

Cover design by id communications, Tralee, Co. Kerry
Typesetting by Red Barn Publishing, Skeagh, Skibbereen
Printed in the UK

CONTENTS

Prologue

In June 1979, four Irishmen travelled to Dresden in the German Democratic Republic to collect the remains of a man who had died there thirty-five years previously. The exhumation of Frank Ryan's remains was done with full military honours and attended by men, Irish and German, who had fought with the Republican forces during the Spanish civil war, as well as representatives of the Irish and East German governments.[1] Two days later his remains were brought to Dublin, where the deceased's sister Eilís and nephew John Ryan were waiting. The removal of the coffin, which Niall Andrews, TD, draped with an Irish tricolour, was to White-friars Street Carmelite Church where the deceased had gone to mass as a young man. The prayers were all in Irish, as were the requiem mass and the prayers at the graveside the following day. The mass was concelebrated by three priests, including Father Tom Walsh, chaplain to the Old IRA. The cortège passed through the centre of Dublin, stopping briefly outside the GPO in acknowledgement of Ryan's reverence for the heroes of 1916, and wound its way on to the republican plot in Glasnevin cemetery, where he was finally laid to rest.

Among the thousands of mourners were friends and colleagues of Ryan from the first half of the century as well as those who, ever since, looked to Frank Ryan as a visionary ideologue and an exemplary political activist. Wreaths were laid by the IRA and the Basque separatist organisation ETA. The first secretary of the West German Embassy was in attendance, while the East German representative claimed that Ryan "would always remain a link" between Ireland and the Soviet Union's satellite (even though Dublin had not granted it recognition). Indeed, groups carrying the banners of the various

mutations of Irish republicanism, communism and democratic socialism all crowded the cemetery as legitimate heirs of
Frank Ryan's political "vision".[2]

That such a broad spectrum of political opinion could
claim Ryan as an ideological ancestor was a consequence of
his never having followed a single, coherent political vision.
He was at various times a diehard republican, a physical force
revolutionary, an anti-imperialist, a labour and rent strike agitator, a socialist and a democrat. Carrying the torch of the
various causes to which he was committed, he served as a
street-brawler, a major in a foreign army and a political advi-
sor in the pay of his enemies. Ryan possessed many talents for
propaganda, as journalist and orator, all of which he spent to
serve his ideals. His absolute dedication to the furtherance of
his beliefs was questioned by no one. In books and newspapers can be found myriad testimonies to Frank Ryan's resolute character, his conviviality and generosity, his rectitude
and capacity for selfless resolve. His friend Budge Mulcahy
was prompted to describe him as a "friend of humanity.
Everybody was his friend, even his enemies were friends."[3]
Éamon de Valera was a case in point. The two men were sparring partners more often than not. Yet Ireland's premier
statesman during the century of Ryan's life freely conceded
that "Frank Ryan was a man for whom I have always held
the highest regard."[4]

Yet Ryan's actions in the last few years of his life beg questions that still cause discomfort to his champions. Some histo-
rians less than sympathetic to Ryan's struggles through his
ideological labyrinth have defamed him as an ideological naif
or else as guilty of "propaganda and stool pigeon work for the
Nazis".[5]

It is true that he was an idealist who possessed some notions
bordering on the fantastic and that in the 1940s he was in a
compromising position, one that he had placed himself in.
Ryan was in Germany because of a gamble he took that did
not pay off, which is not to claim that he was an innocent. He
was dogmatic, intransigent and an apologist for political murders. Ryan's fanaticism deemed that his proposal at the 1933
IRA Convention to have "objectionable people removed" left
his conscience unruffled. However, the combination of his zeal
and the ideological polarisations that held sway between 1916

and the Second World War helps to explain why Ryan's sallies into Irish and international affairs led frequently into cul de sacs and why his broadsides scored more misses than hits. The tumultuous times through which he lived and his frustration at the political knots he laboured to unravel were bound to ignite a man so packed with idealism and ardour. Thus primed, Ryan was, unfortunately, not the best judge of how to reap maximum reward from the potency he possessed.

Further, while overlooking the complexities of Ryan's position can lead to a misreading of the man and his activities, it is, paradoxically, quite simple to see how he came to lend himself to German intelligence in 1940. To point out that the label of "collaborator" does not discriminate between those who worked for a Nazi victory and those who foresaw in it primarily the advancement of their own cause is not to exonerate Ryan of an ethically dubious opportunism. Of that, he was certainly guilty.[6] But his work for Irish neutrality, favoured by the vast number of Irish men and women, was, and is, undervalued.

This prologue makes the irresistible mistake of eclipsing Ryan's life's work by his final years in Germany. The years of tireless work he undertook for the poor in Ireland, his conversion to democratic politics and the bravery he showed in risking his life for Republican Spain have all been overshadowed by his time in the shelter of Nazism. Consequently, his reputation has not enjoyed a smooth ascent since his death. Things would have been easier had the Gestapo done away with him rather than leaving him to die in his bed. As Enda Staunton has pointed out, "in such circumstances, while his end might have been less peaceful, his posthumous reputation would be infinitely more secure".[7]

At his reinterment in 1979, Ryan's reputation among the faithful was not secure but lauded. He would have been pleased to be heralded as a "staunch anti-fascist" despite suggestions to the contrary. He would have been more pleased, however, that a wish expressed from the battlefields of Spain had finally been granted: "I don't want my bones to lie in any foreign cemetery. When I die I want it to be in Ireland but, at least, I want my bones in Ireland."[8]

Notes to Prologue

1. The Irish veterans were Frank Edwards, Peter O'Connor and Michael O'Riordan. Niall Andrews, TD, whose father was a friend and workmate of Ryan's, represented the Irish government.
2. Eilís Ryan was infuriated by what she perceived as an attempt by the Communist Party of Ireland to hijack the funeral for political purposes. Niall Andrews was so disgusted that he left early.
3. Interview with the author.
4. *Irish Times,* 11 April 1975.
5. Robert Stradling, "A War of Ideals? Irish Volunteers in the Spanish Civil War", *Cathair na Mart*, no. 15, 1995. For a critical assessment of the politics of Ryan and fellow republican socialists in Ireland, see Richard English, *Radicals and the Republic: Socialist Republicanism in the Irish Free State* (Oxford: Clarendon Press, 1994).
6. An interesting assessment of the extent to which Ryan can be called a collaborator is provided in Enda Staunton, "Frank Ryan and Collaboration: A Reassessment", *History Ireland*, Autumn 1997.
7. *Ibid.*, p. 51.
8. Quoted in Seán Cronin, *Frank Ryan: The Search for the Republic* (Dublin: Repsol, 1980), p. 89.

PART ONE

CHAPTER 1

From the Cradle to the Civil War

The townland of Bottomstown lies close to the village of Elton in the rich grasslands of east Limerick, a few miles from Knocklong and adjacent to the Tipperary border. At the turn of the twentieth century, the small national school in Bottomstown was run by Vere and Ann Ryan, a respectable couple of modest means. Vere Ryan was from Sallybank in Limerick, where his own father had been a schoolteacher, who had named his son after the educationalist Vere Foster. Ann Ryan was a Slattery from near Kilfenora in County Clare. They had met whilst teaching in the same school near the Burren. Ann used to arrive at the school from Kilfenora every Monday morning by horse and car, driven by an elder brother. The Ryans were to have nine children; their seventh child and fifth son, Francis Richard, was born on 11 September 1902.

Vere Ryan was a strict father who neither smoked nor drank. However, like his namesake, he had progressive ideas about teaching, insisting for example that at least one of his daughters forsake the conventional needlework classes to study maths with the boys.[1] The reputation he enjoyed as an excellent teacher was surpassed only by his renown for severity and, unencumbered by any tolerance for what he considered to be the flaws of his pupils or their parents, he was remembered for years afterwards as a classroom tyrant. Pupils were beaten and parents were harangued.

The schoolteachers' house was one filled with books. Shakespeare, Goldsmith, Sir Walter Scott, Dickens and collections of Irish literature, including nationalist writing, crowded the

13

shelves. According to Frank's sister, no dust settled on them: "We were all readers, especially Frank."[2] Frank, who was the youngest son, loved to romp through the fields near his home and was a roughneck from an early age, albeit one also recognised to be the brains among the children. A happy, laughing child, big and strong, he was so frustrated by being shackled to the school desk that he once escaped his father's lesson by climbing out through the window and leading his pursuers a merry dance through neighbouring gardens.

The children passed idyllic summers with their mother's family, the Slatterys, at their farm at Ballygownan, near Kilfenora. It was here that Frank's elder brother Vincent enjoyed exercising his talents in Irish, still the first language of some of the locals. This love of the language was passed down to Frank. Experiencing Irish as a daily, living language rather than as grammar book drudgery seduced the young boy, and the language was a reserve of novel entertainment, as Vincent "used to hunt out old stories and songs" that he doubtless repeated to his younger brother.[3]

A mysterious childhood illness resulted in a hearing problem that was to persist and gradually worsen throughout Frank's life. The local doctors had been ignorant of it, and it was only noticed by his mother when she tried to teach him to play the piano, as she did with all of her children. Frank was brought to specialists whose treatment gave him temporary reprieve but no more.

In 1916, following in the footsteps of his brother Maurice (Moss), Frank went to the prestigious St Colman's College in Fermoy, County Cork, run by the Holy Ghost fathers. His enrolment was unorthodox. He travelled with his father to drop off Moss, but after a conversation with a priest it was suggested that he simply stay. He did so, and his belongings were sent from home in Elton after him. The priest must have been impressed with the young Ryan, who transpired to be "a student of more than average ability",[4] despite acquiring "a rich and varied experience of flogging" for fighting, smoking and truancy.[5] He improved on his experiences in national school to become a frequent escapee from St Colman's, but he was sufficiently in attendance to gain honours at Junior and Intermediate Grades, winning a First Class Prize in the latter, as well as coming first in English and French in a class of forty-four students. The following year he also obtained honours, as well as winning an overall Distinction First Prize in literature, coming second in English, history and French out of thirty-three students.

Frank Ryan thought he heard the call of a religious vocation, and so transferred to the Holy Ghost Fathers at Rockwell College near Cashel in Tipperary, where young men were prepared for a priesthood with the missions. His time there was brief. Apparently he was expelled for leading a protest against the poor quality of the food. If God gave up on the adolescent rabble-rouser, St Colman's did not. Returned there, in his final Senior Grade in 1920 he passed his matriculation but with no distinction. This relatively poor showing could have been due to his extracurricular activities: he was by this time a member of a local IRA battalion and used to slip out of the grounds after dark for drilling and exercises. He had also brought no small measure of outrage to the school when a revolver belonging to him was found hidden in the toilets.

It seems that the young Ryan possessed a flourishing multiformity that rendered him all things to all men: an appreciable academic, a schoolboy Spartacus and a valued sportsman. Towering over his classmates and brimming with vigour, he had a natural advantage on the playing fields that complemented his passion for Gaelic games, and he was a member of the St Colman's football team that won the Junior Cup, beating the North Monastery. A sociable boy, happy with the companionship of others, Ryan equally savoured his free time alone, walking through the fields near his home and rambling through the foothills of the mountains a few miles distant. Adventurous but with a curious and contemplative nature, he explored the boreens, the green roads and the copses of east Limerick. On his expeditions, Ryan particularly liked to dally by the ruins of old homesteads and castles, to explore the abandoned fairy forts of the popular imagination. He drank deeply of the local history and lore that clung to these monuments from the past, and this fired his imagination and fed the romantic spirit within him.

Despite the fairly scanty amount of information pertaining to Ryan's schooldays, the man that he was to become is foreshadowed by the boy that he was. Until his death, he remained a voracious reader (circumstances allowing) of history and literature. A visitor to the Gaeltacht during his teens, he was already an avid proponent of the Irish language, and when at home on holidays from school, he spoke Irish constantly to his younger sister, re-christening Elizabeth as Eilís. The name stuck. He would frequently adopt the Irish version of his own name, Proinnsias Ó Riain. As for his vocation for the priesthood, although it was perhaps a symptom of confused adolescent fervour, unlike most of his later associates Ryan was to remain a church-going Catholic for the rest of his life.

As for matters less spiritual or cerebral, young Ryan's stand against the poor food at school could not give a clearer indication of the man he would become. His rebellious nature was doubtless encouraged by his ability to induce others to follow him. At St Colman's, "fellow students remembered Frank as a student of fiery disposition who didn't react well to discipline",[6] and Eilís Ryan's complaint that "they always picked him out as the leader, whether he was or not", is foreboding despite its implication of his innocence.[7]

During his teenage years, Ryan nurtured a faith in political ends being achieved by violent means, despite the political moderation that pervaded his home. His father was a strong Parnellite, but not active in politics; his mother had no interest in politics at all. Despite being schoolteachers, neither instilled any profound sense of history into their children, yet it was a deep appreciation of Irish history that formed the basis of much of Ryan's republicanism. East Limerick was not excessively nationalist before 1921 and latterly never a haven of republicanism, but the family's summer retreat near Kilfenora was always an enclave of republicanism with accordant politics that perhaps influenced Ryan.[8]

The accepted explanation for Ryan's burgeoning extremism is that a Father Roche at St Colman's was a "mad Republican" and the fourteen-year-old Ryan, who joined the college only months after the Easter Rising, fell under his sway. A brilliant mathematician, Father Roche left the college in 1919, but three years would have been time aplenty to win over a mind as emotionally charged as Ryan's.

This is perfectly plausible, but Ryan's short time at Rockwell College also had an effect on him. In 1916, the former Dean of Studies, Father John Byrne, became president of the college, making no secret of his distinctly nationalistic outlook and his strong republican affiliations. He injected fervour into the study of Irish and the elevation of Gaelic games and culture, arguing that they gave "a new moral uplift to the whole life of the school".[9] Students and staff who had been under Father Byrne's academic republicanism included Éamon de Valera, Fionán Lynch and, executed the year his former teacher assumed the school's presidency, Thomas MacDonagh.[10]

Eilís Ryan believes Father Roche's hold on young Frank was only possible thanks to Ryan's being, at that age, unduly impressionable. Moss, too, flirted with republicanism, but "Frank was very easily influenced, he did what he was told . . . Moss, who was with him, he wouldn't be led by anyone. That's where Frank got it . . . That was the difference, Frank was impressionable; he'd believe anything."[11]

Such an explanation for Ryan's republican zeal seems contrary to other of his character traits, yet it is unquestionable that the impressions made upon him during this period had a profound impact on him. He was thirteen years old when James Connolly and Pádraig Pearse were executed, and it was they who, throughout his life, he most revered of all political or revolutionary heroes. The doomed 1916 insurrection, according to a friend, "took irresistible hold on his imagination, which had a naturally patriotic bent . . . From that day on, he lived by the teachings of Pearse and Connolly."[12] Connolly, leader of the Irish Citizen Army (ICA) in 1916 and earlier a lieutenant of the socialist firebrand Jim Larkin, had come to Irish republicanism through his militancy in the labour movement, whereas the teacher and poet Pearse had progressed to radical republicanism after years as a cultural nationalist.

The appeal of righteous militancy and bloody glory aside, it was perhaps Pearse's mystical Catholicism and the Passion-of-Christ-drenched symbolism of an Irish resurrection at Easter, replete with sacrifices and martyrs, that particularly fascinated a boy who considered himself to have a spiritual vocation. His republican ideal became that of Pearse's: *Éire Saor Gaedhealach*.[13] That it was Pearse who initially had the more attraction for Ryan is almost inevitable in that his appeal lay in romantic nationalism and flamboyant rhetoric rather than the economic-based socialist theories of Connolly.

These were, after all, historic and turbulent times in Ireland. During Ryan's intermediate school year, 1918, Sinn Féin carried the torch of 1916 to a general election and won (by fair means and foul) a clear majority of seats. The party, with Éamon de Valera as its president, abstained from the Westminster parliament and in 1919 established its own parliament in Dublin, Dáil Éireann. The Sinn Féin government declared itself to be the only legitimate authority in the country, repudiating any connection with the British government, which had imprisoned many of its members and whose army was a very real and menacing presence in the country. In the face of the escalating War of Independence, or Black and Tan War, the newly declared Republic proclaimed it had signed its own "birth certificate . . . written with steel in the immortal blood of martyrs".[14] But proclamations were little match for the vastly superior martial power of Britain, and the IRA, the armed wing of Sinn Féin, could never hope to defeat the British army outright. From the first shots being fired in Soloheadbeg, County Tipperary, the Tan War would drag on intermittently for two and a half years.

After finishing school in the summer of 1920, Ryan returned home, where he joined up with the famous East Limerick Brigade of the IRA when the Tan War was at its height. How active a role Ryan played is uncertain, but his brigade had already earned the distinction of pioneering the use of flying columns – bodies of men fighting full-time and constantly on the move.[15] Even though Ryan had been in Fermoy, itself a barrack town where he had undoubtedly witnessed British military activity, the fighting was close to home in Elton in May 1920 when a gun battle in neighbouring Lackally left four IRA men dead. There were subsequent ambushes of British troops, particularly in December 1920, in the vicinity of the Ryan home, leaving many dead and wounded. Ryan was presumably in the area at this time, but all that is known is that he would leave the house in the evenings and be missing from the family home for long stretches at a time. Although he later claimed to have been an officer by the age of eighteen, there is nothing to suggest that his wartime exploits were particularly remarkable.

At least one of his missions was less than glorious, not to say incongruous with his professed adherence to the socialism of James Connolly; he was ordered to take his company to the creamery in Knocklong and break a strike of protesting workers. He was to evict them and have the red flag flying from the building taken down. He did so, pulling down the offending standard himself.

If Ryan's ambitions were directed towards full-time fighting within a flying column, they were thwarted by the signing of a truce in July 1921, which brought the war gasping to a close. On the other hand, the truce was a relief to Ryan. After discarding an old overcoat days before the cessation of hostilities, he realised he had left papers in its pocket revealing the names of local IRA men. An abiding memory for him was of his fear that the papers would be found and his "three days of agony lest the Tans use them before the truce and the gorgeous relief of the truce".[16]

Despite his less than exemplary record at Rockwell College and only mediocre results in his matriculation, Ryan was awarded a scholarship by Limerick County Council to study at University College, Dublin (UCD), on Earlsfort Terrace, adjacent to St Stephen's Green. His chosen subject was Celtic studies, an amalgam of Irish literature and language, history and culture. However, his increasing politicisation overrode his scholasticism; an IRA memo of the time Ryan's requests the transfer of Proinnsias Ó Riain from C Company, 4th Battalion, East Limerick Brigade to the army's Dublin Brigade, immediately upon his arrival in Dublin.[17] After only a year, his studies were suspended by the outbreak of the Irish Civil War in June 1922.

On 6 December 1921, two months after Ryan's college registration, and after months of diplomatc haggling during the truce, a treaty was signed in London between representatives of the Irish second Dáil and the British prime minister, David Lloyd George. Both sides had desperately wanted to see an end to a war that neither of them was confident of winning outright. Furthermore, the IRA was perilously short of ammunition while the British government was shamed internationally by the atrocities committed by its troops in its name. Any reluctance amongst the Irish plenipotentiaries was tempered by the conviction that they were at least getting for Ireland greater autonomy than it had won or been granted for hundreds of years. The Treaty copper-fastened Ireland's partition, with six counties in the northeast of the island remaining within Great Britain, the details of the actual boundary to be finalised by a Boundary Commission. The six counties of Ulster's nine were

selected to create a Protestant loyalist majority that would have
a home rule parliament at Stormont. For the Catholic nationalist minority stranded in the six counties, Cardinal Logue of
Armagh prophesied that "to judge by the public utterances of
those into whose hands power is fallen in this quarter of Ireland, we have times of persecution before us".[18] The remaining
twenty-six counties of Ireland would remain within the Commonwealth under an appointed governor-general, and members of its new parliament would have to swear allegiance to
"H.M. King George V, his heirs and successors by law". The
last major impediment to independent sovereignty was that the
British navy and airforce had automatic access to a handful of
strategically placed Irish ports. It seemed that "the right of the
people of Ireland to the ownership of Ireland and to the unfet-
tered control of Irish destinies", claimed in the 1916 Proclamation, was not, after all, "sovereign and indefeasible".

On 7 January 1922 the Treaty was approved in the Dáil by
a majority of 64 to 57. Of the Dáil cabinet, William Cosgrave
and three of the signatories – Arthur Griffith, Michael Collins
and Robert Barton – were in favour of the Treaty, Éamon de
Valera opposed it as a usurpation of his favoured "external
association" arrangement (effectively little different from the
terms of the Treaty), while Austin Stack and Cathal Brugha
considered anything short of an independent republic to be
treachery.[19] Éamon de Valera resigned as president and was
replaced by Arthur Griffith. As the pro-Treatyites commenced
to set up a provisional government for the new Free State, the
republicans retreated to plot its demolition.

The deepening fissure within nationalist authority trickled
down through Irish nationalism and public opinion to the
rawest foot soldiers. Marginal approval of the Treaty was
replicated in a populace grown weary of sporadic gunfire and
houseburnings, corpses found in ditches and the ever-present
threat of menaces. The pro-Treatyites were supported in their
acquiescence by the press, the Catholic Church, businessmen
and men of property; "all those", said republican Liam Mellows, "who had a stake in the country". However, for the not
insignificant minority, the Treaty concluded "the dream that
went bust", according to Seán Ó Faoláin.

Frank Ryan was one of that minority. Not pacified by the
lull of the truce, he had been attached to the Officer's Training

Corps at UCD and fomented opposition to the Free State in Dublin. He held "the signing of the Treaty of Betrayal" and its subsequent ratification by the Dáil to be "the perjury of 1921–22".[20] The fact that it was approved by the majority of the representatives of the people was immaterial; it was simply wrong, and in his rejection of the democratic wish of the people, Ryan showed that he had adopted Connolly's idea that it was the prerogative of a righteous minority to ignore the wishes of the majority.

Like Ryan, the majority of the Dublin IRA were anti-Treaty. (The anti-Treaty forces kept the IRA moniker and became commonly known as Irregulars.) Richard Mulcahy, the Dáil's Minister of Defence, initiated a recruiting drive for the new Free State army to defuse the potential threat of an organised and armed force of "out-and-outers", those determined to achieve for Ireland an independent republic. As the efforts of the two sides to organise and arm themselves escalated, so did they grow ever distant from each other. The unbearable strain reached breaking point as units, companies and brigades of men who had been welded during the Tan War rent in two. Personal ties severed. The IRA was appalled to see its membership siphoned off into the Free State army while it in turn was, with some justification, suspected of plotting a coup and military dictatorship.[21] The army that had stood steadfast against the British was irretrievably cleaved within three months.

The more militant republicans, such as Ryan, were convinced that bloodshed was inevitable, yet they were unsure as to whose blood to shed – Free State or British – and how best to go about it. At their headquarters in Dublin's Four Courts, numerous proposals were mooted, with the inevitable debates and dissensions. The assassination of Field Marshal Sir Henry Wilson, military adviser to the Stormont government, was the catalyst that overrode republican indecision and prompted Free State action. London, in demanding that the Dublin government crack down on the anti-Treatyites or else render the Treaty void, gave the Free Staters the impetus they needed.[22] At 4 a.m. on 28 June 1922, using British artillery, the Free State army bombarded the republican bastion. The Civil War had started.

After forty-eight hours the Four Courts was in blazing ruins. Within days, overt republican resistance was crushed in

Dublin. Most of those who weren't captured fled the city. Cathal Brugha, colleague of Collins and Griffith in the Dáil Cabinet when the Treaty was signed, became a hero to Ryan when he was mortally wounded trying to shoot his way out of a stand-off after ordering his men to surrender. The other leaders, including IRA Chief of Staff Liam Lynch, made their way to Munster, to regroup behind a defensive line from Waterford to Limerick, where Lynch set up his headquarters.

Frank Ryan was in the "Republic of Munster" ahead of them, free after a year in UCD and at home in Elton. He had seen no action thus far, but he remained undeterred by the defeat of his colleagues in the capital, military setbacks being no reason to abandon republican principles. He would routinely describe the Dáil as a British parliament passing British-made laws and its government as "native-born tyrants". He wrote of the Free State government that the

> . . . renegades who hold Ireland for the British empire tell you that the age-old struggle with England is ended, that we are now free. It is scarcely necessary for me to refute that lie. The British Army and Navy are still in occupation of strategic positions in Ireland, the two petty parliaments in Ireland are under the jurisdiction of the King of England.[23]

For Ryan, the Free Staters were worse than the British. Whereas the British had been murderers and tyrants, the Free Staters were not only prepared to outdo the erstwhile enemy in numbers of Irishmen killed, but were traitors as well. It was only to be expected that an imperial power would have disregard for the lives and liberty of its oppressed, but it was doubly heinous for Irishmen, former revolutionaries, to don the despot's mantle against men who refused to prostitute the republic for which they had together fought. When the Four Courts fell, Ryan had already picked up his rifle again, answering a proclamation issued by the IRA Army Executive:

> The fateful hour has come. At the dictation of our hereditary enemy our rightful cause is being treacherously assailed by recreant Irishmen. The crash of arms and the boom of artillery reverberate in this

22

supreme test of the Nation's destiny . . . We, therefore, appeal to all citizens who have withstood
unflinchingly the oppression of the enemy during the
past six years to rally to the support of the Republic
and recognise that the resistance now being offered is
but the continuance of the struggle that was suspended by the truce with the British.[24]

As Ryan's youngest sister Eilís recalls it, her brother's call to
arms had not been an overly dramatic moment: "I remember
being at home, in the garden, and two men on bicycles came
for him and he got his own bike and he went off."[25] In a stand-
off in Limerick City, a delicate truce was being observed by
IRA Chief of Staff Liam Lynch and Donnachadha O'Hannigan, OC of the city's Free State forces, who had spectacularly
led Ryan's IRA brigade during the Tan War. Presumably, this
is where Ryan was engaged; once again, his movements are
not recorded. It is only known that he had been summoned
and did not return.

The initial restraint shown by both sides soon disintegrated, giving way to light arms fire, raid and counter-raid, until
the provisional government forces, continually reinforced,
wheeled out their artillery and took the city. By the end of the
month, the Irregulars had retreated, blowing up bridges and
mining roads as they went, to dig in at Bruree and the town of
Kilmallock, a distance of perhaps five miles from the Ryan
home in Elton. From the upstairs window of their house, the
family listened to the sound of gunfire only a short distance
away.

The government advance was held off for some two weeks.
However, the republicans had little local support in east Limerick, a country of fairly prosperous farmers, and their resistance was overwhelmed. Ryan and his comrades took to their
heels into Tipperary and the Galtee Mountains, constantly
fighting a rearguard action and skirmishing with the encircling
patrols sent after them. As the days turned into weeks, they
crossed and recrossed the same country, shying away from
engaging the enemy, attempting, rather, to slip through its cordon. But the Free State troops were also constantly on the
move, snapping at the heels of their harried prey. On more
than one occasion, Ryan found himself "in a position where

your only chance of escaping death is to bob up from behind cover and fire – then get away while they are firing at where you were".[26]

There were, however, only a few safe houses to get away to. The popular support that had sustained the IRA in the Tan War was woefully sparse, and the fatigue resulting from having to sleep with one eye open, if a likely spot could be found at all, was a greater strain on the men than Free State bullets. "In 1920–21, the local people would keep sentry," remembered Ryan, "but in 1922 you had to do sentry yourself."[27] Ryan marched in his sleep, often dropping his rifle or stumbling into a ditch as he groped through the dark seeking sanctuary. A friend recalled that he led his destitute men to "a farmhouse where a girl had said 'Oh, Frank Ryan doing the rounds again.' The pleasure it was after the six weeks of unwelcome they had gone through in their travels. He was seldom so grateful for anything."[28]

Ryan's band was reduced to fifteen tired and hungry men when they came across another isolated farmhouse. Entering it in search of food for the others, Ryan was met by a fifteen-year-old boy wearing a *fáinne*,[29] who was obviously sympathetic to their plight. Knowing the local country, he offered to guide them through the tightening cordon of government troops, no doubt at great risk to himself. Having led them once more to comparative safety, the boy begged that he be allowed to join them, only to be disappointed. Grateful though he was, Ryan felt compelled to refuse the boy, letting him down easy by telling him, which was true, that they had no spare rifle to give him. Such sympathy was a rarity.

The Free State noose tightened on Ryan's men. After they had ambushed and set loose a goods train, they ran into a Free State patrol and a gunfight ensued. Caught in open fields, Ryan's men were soon pinned down by machine-gun fire and scurried between bushes and ditches for some hours as their pursuers tried to surround them. Ryan was hit and fell, lying still on the ground. The Free Staters moved toward him. When he made a movement, one of the approaching soldiers called out in alarm that he wasn't dead at all. He had been stunned by the graze of a bullet against his head. The injured Ryan was captured, along with his men.

The skirmish had taken place close to Elton, and Ryan was

transported through his native townland as a captive. The prisoners were taken to Knocklong and housed in the creamery, where Ryan's parents and siblings travelled by pony and trap to visit him. He was soon moved to Limerick jail. At first only thirty or so men were held there, but as the round-up of Irregulars gathered pace, up to a dozen men were squeezed into each cell fit for one. From there the prisoners were taken down to Cobh, County Cork, where they were placed on a government fisheries vessel, the *Murchú*, to be transported to Dublin and finally interred at the Hare Park prison camp in the Curragh.

Whilst Ryan had been on the run, President Arthur Griffith had died of a heart attack and William Cosgrave replaced him as prime minister, officially titled president of the Executive Council. In mid-October 1922, the Dáil, upon passing what republicans termed the "Murder Bill", established military courts that had the power to execute combative republicans. In December, Treatyite Dáil members Seán Hales was shot dead and colleague Padraig Ó Máille wounded when they were ambushed by the IRA on their way to the Dáil. The government's response was severe; on the much celebrated Feast of the Immaculate Conception, 8 December, it executed four prominent republicans, one from each province, and including Liam Mellows one of the sharpest political minds of the anti-Treaty side, whose fervent republicanism was tinged with socialism. This reprisal for the assassination of Dáil member Sean Hales provoked widespread revulsion amongst the public and outrage amongst republicans. Even leading churchmen who condemned the IRA remonstrated with the government. The terror that the executions were supposed to staunch only deepened. Authorised executions were followed by summary executions in the field as the infant state spiralled into an agony of self-destruction.

For the republicans, after Cork, Limerick and Waterford had fallen, the war was now reminiscent of the guerrilla war they had fought against the British, only increasingly defensive. There was little cohesion within the leadership or with the bands of men effectively on the run, skirmishing and retreating, always short of ammunition, food and sleep. Feelers sent out to the government for peace negotiations met with rebuttals as Cosgrave's men made it clear that anything less than unconditional surrender on the part of republicans was unacceptable. This in turn was unacceptable to the vast majority of republicans, even though they knew their fight was hopeless. Their cause, however, was not.

Consequently, on 24 May 1923, de Valera, president of Sinn Féin, and Liam Lynch's successor as IRA chief of staff,[30] Frank Aiken, issued an order to "Soldiers of the Republic, Legion of the Rearguard" to "dump arms". The order acknowledged that continuance of the war was in nobody's interest, declaring that "Military victory must be allowed to rest for the moment with those who have destroyed the Republic. Other means must be sought to safeguard the nation's right."[31] The war was thus terminated with neither the surrender of the Irregulars nor their recognition of the government's legitimacy.

By the time of the Civil War's quasi-conclusion, Ryan had already been interned in Hare Park for nine months. There were over 10,000 other republican prisoners in half a dozen prisons, and the absence of any reconciliation between the antagonists ensured a steady stream of new detainees. The pro-Treatyites had formed themselves into a political party, Cumann na nGaedheal, and a Public Safety Act was passed in the Dáil allowing it to enjoy emergency powers in peacetime. An election was called for late August 1923, and the IRA, despite the imprisonment of many of its members and the shattered nature of its organisation, under the banner of Sinn Féin, put forward candidates on an abstentionist ticket as they refused to recognise the legitimacy of the Dáil. There was much violent harassment of republicans, and de Valera himself was arrested. Still, he was elected to a Dáil seat he had no intention of taking, and his party won a very creditable forty-four seats against the government's poor showing of sixty-three seats and Labour's fourteen. The electorate had disowned the republican war effort but not republicanism.

Its soldiers now fought the tedium of prison life, plotting escapes and future campaigns, holding classes in languages (particularly Irish), history and literature and immersing themselves in a pervading spirit of diehard entrenchment. Ryan, despite the Spartan conditions, which aggravated his ear problem, was much inspired by the "eager discussions and mind-searching of the prisons".[32] Analysing past mistakes and plotting strategy, prison committee leaders, representing their old brigades, became "deeply concerned about organising

mass violence against the machine rather than have group violence against individuals" such as Cosgrave or Mulcahy. "The
main theme of our lives in Hare Park became more and more
organisation," wrote internee Peadar O'Donnell.[33] Substitut-
ing the prison for university, the ever-energetic and no doubt
bored Ryan started to learn his future trade of journalism. He
became editor of a journal in Irish, *An Goirrfhiodh*, the first,
and possibly sole, issue of which came out in June 1923. However, activity and optimism among the prisoners were soon
overwhelmed by frustration at the increasing numbers being
held indefinitely and usually without being charged. There
were 16,000 prisoners by October 1923, when a hunger strike
demanding unconditional release spread to Hare Park from
Mountjoy. The strike was at its height of 800 adherents in
November when Frank Ryan was released.

To fully understand Frank Ryan, the dismal consequences
of the Irish Civil War must always be borne in mind as a colossal influence. It was probably the single most significant event
in his life, a catalyst for his patriotic belligerency. He would
forever reap the bitter harvest of the seed sown in 1922–23. It
poisoned Ryan's otherwise genial disposition and instinctive
affection for his fellow Irishmen. His subsequent years were
spent fighting the war that in his mind had never finished.

The "dump arms" order had been an exhibition of defiance
in defeat, one that sustained the self-dignity of IRA men and
women. It reflected the spirit of bowed but unbroken republicanism and the acknowledgement that the republican cause
would be better served by living to fight another day. For
Ryan, the animosities engendered by the Civil War would
linger for ever. Likewise, among the vast body of Irregulars
there was precious little repentance, and remorse was reserved
not for having fought but for having lost the fight. With the
fall of Dublin to the government, there was little doubt that
victory would favour that side which had the support and
arms of Britain, greater financing, recruitment figures reaching
hundreds each week and the backing of the people. The number who met violent deaths in little under a year of fighting is
reckoned at something shy of 5,000, far more than during the
two and a half years of the Tan War. Official government executions numbered at least seventy-seven, more than triple the
number officially executed by the British leading up to the

Treaty. The cash cost to the government was estimated at £17 million, with destruction of property costing a further £30 million. The cost to the nation was the horror it had to witness and the bitter enmity instilled in so many for years to come. If the war's conclusion occasioned a widespread sense of relief, it prompted little celebration. As one combatant was to note, "In civil war, alas, there is no glory; there are no monuments to victory or victors, only to the dead."[34]

Notes to Chapter One

1. Aodh Ó Canainn, "Eilís Ryan in Her Own Words," *Saothar* 21, 1996.
2. Quoted in Seán Cronin, *Frank Ryan: The Search for the Republic* (Dublin: Repsol, 1980), p. 19.
3. Rosamond Jacob Diaries, NLI, 32/582, June 1927, p. 17.
4. In a letter from Fathers Kelleher and Forde of St Colman's College.
5. Rosamond Jacob Diaries, NLI, 32/582, January 1928, p. 56.
6. Fathers Kelleher and Forde, as above.
7. Ó Canainn, *Saothar* 21.
8. The Slatterys were to become strong de Valera supporters rather than hardliners like their nephew. There are conflicting accounts of the Slatterys' republicanism in Cronin, *Frank Ryan*, p. 19, and Ó Canainn, *Saothar* 21.
9. From information provided by Fr Edward Stirling, Archivist, Rockwell College.
10. Father Byrne's later republicanism was sufficiently well advertised that during the Civil War applications to join the school dropped markedly.
11. Ó Canainn *Saothar* 21.
12. Síghle Uí Dhonnchadha papers, UCDAD, P106/1711.
13. A Free and Gaelic Ireland.
14. From the Dáil Éireann Treaty debates, quoted in Ronan Fanning, *Independent Ireland* (Dublin: Helicon, 1983), p. 1.
15. This was an innovative and hugely successful method of guerrilla warfare, and the brigade even claimed for itself the honour of being the first truly Irish standing army for hundreds of years.
16. Rosamond Jacob Diaries, NLI, 32/582, June 1927, p. 17.
17. IRA Southern Command, UCDAD, P9/174.
18. *Irish Catholic Directory* (Dublin: Veritas, 1922), p. 552.
19. A constitutional riddle: the Treaty was therefore sanctioned by a body that it did not recognise, which morphed into the Southern parliament, which its representatives had hitherto refused to recognise.

20. Quoted in Fanning, *Independent Ireland,* p. 8.
21. *An Phoblacht,* 13 December 1930.
22. Leading republican Rory O'Connor let it be known that the IRA would, by force of arms, prevent any attempt to hold a general election. When he was asked if that meant he hoped to see the IRA establish a military, he replied, "You can take it that way if you like." Quoted in Dermot Keogh, *Twentieth Century Ireland: Nation and State* (Dublin: Gill & Macmillan, 1994), p. 4.
23. *An Phoblacht,* 10 May 1930.
24. Full text quoted in Florence O'Donoghue, *No Other Law* (Dublin: Anvil, 1986), pp. 341–2.
25. See Ó Canainn, *Saothar* 21.
26. Rosamond Jacob Diaries, NLI, 32/582, June 1927, p. 17.
27. *Ibid.,* September 1926, p. 30.
28. *Ibid.,* June 1927, p. 19.
29. A badge that denotes the wearer as a speaker of Irish.
30. Liam Lynch had been mortally wounded by Free State troops during a shoot-out in the Knockmealdown Mountains in April 1923.
31. Quoted in Dorothy Macardle, *The Irish Republic* (London: Gollancz, 1937), p. 855.
32. Figures from Fanning, *Independent Ireland,* p. 41.
33. Síghle Uí Dhonnchadha papers, UCDAD, P106/1711.
34. Peadar O'Donnell, *The Gates Flew Open* (Cork: Mercier Press, 1966), p. 104.
35. C.S. Andrews, *Dublin Made Me* (Cork: Mercier Press, 1979), pp. 243–4.

CHAPTER TWO

The Blossoming of a Revolutionary, the Emergence of a Radical

Despite being absent from college for so long, and despite engaging in a war against the government, Ryan was welcomed back to UCD and his scholarship was restored. That the vast majority of the university's teaching staff were openly or actively supportive of Cumann na nGaedheal (many of them found Ryan's strain of republicanism abhorrent) makes his readmittance even more remarkable. Still, Ryan found irreconcilable hearts aflame in the university's small but devoted Republican Club. The main aims of the club were fund-raising and nominating republican candidates for the parliamentary seats allocated to the universities, but it also played a vigorous role in political agitation in the capital. It was at this time that Ryan honed his skills as an orator and a protest organiser. As well as occupying the vanguard of student republicanism, his dedication to the college company of the IRA resulted in his becoming its officer in command.

Simultaneously, Ryan's devotion to the Irish language prompted him to run for the post of *reactaire* (auditor) in the UCD branch of An Cumann Gaedhealach,[1] which was busily encouraging the use of the Irish language amongst students. The use of Irish was seen by some as being not just symptomatic of an appreciation of Ireland's culture, but also of positively anti-English sentiment. The Gaelic League was founded in the 1890s to revive the native tongue after centuries of gagging by the English (according to many of its proponents). In the process the League inadvertently gave much shape and impetus to Irish nationalism. Anything termed Gaelic was, in the public mind, inherently Irish and Catholic, anti-English by extension and nationalist and/or republican by implication.

Consequently, the republican and language revival movements were more closely linked than some of the language purists were happy with. A colleague of Ryan's at the time recalls him "much more interested in the *Athbheocaint* [Irish language revival] than in politics" while he was a student.[2] In 1924 Ryan beat fellow republican Tadgh Forbes to the post of *reactaire* of An Cumann Gaedhealach and also became editor of the Irish language magazine *An Réalt* (The Star). In Ryan's articles for the magazine, he discussed the connection between Irish independence and the cherishing of Ireland's mother tongue, and the relationship between the universities and the Free State government. He printed a fictional piece which he had written for *An Giorrfhiodh*, "*Piobaire an Bhrianaigh*" (Piper of the O'Briens). Just as he moulded his skills in journalism through Irish, so did he develop his talent for public speaking, to the extent that Dr Douglas Hyde, founder member of the Gaelic League, awarded Ryan a gold medal for oratory. Very proud the *Reactaire* Ryan looks, too, in a photograph of the time with Hyde, de Valera and others, standing fully erect in a dress suit, chest out, a shock of hair above his face, staring almost haughtily at the camera.

In college Ryan knew many members of Cumann na mBan, a republican women's group, including Eithne Coyle, whose sister ran digs in Ranelagh where Ryan stayed for a minimal rent. He had a reputation for being always short of money but generous to the extent of borrowing cash only to help out friends poorer than himself. He was popular and gregarious, fond of both drinking with male friends and stepping out with female friends. Much of his free time at weekends was spent with a group of *Gaeilgeoirí* (Irish speakers) who organised hikes in the mountains around Dublin. Among their number was Aileen (Bobbie) Walsh, with whom Ryan fell in love, and when the group was out rambling, the two would slip off to be alone together. Ryan proposed marriage and he and Bobbie became engaged, only for her to break it off. Ryan was devastated; so much so that a friend later drew the dubious conclusion that it drove the distraught man into radical politics.[3] As well as being disappointed by Bobbie Walsh,[4] Ryan endured the torment of an unrequited love for Elgin Barry, sister of the executed and revered Tan War hero Kevin Barry. While the dejected suitor may well have become disillusioned with romance, there is nothing to suggest that politics served as its substitute; his engagement with politics was already profound and binding.

In 1925 Ryan graduated from UCD, with a second class honours BA in Celtic studies. He hoped to follow it with a master's degree, with a dissertation on John Mitchel, the Fenian whose *Jail Journals* was, and still is, *de rigueur* reading for republicans. There seems to have been some objection either from the college or his patron, Limerick County Council. In any event, the project stalled, which was perhaps inevitable as Ryan was increasingly consumed by both republican and Irish language distractions from academia, although he maintained his connections with UCD through its clubs dedicated to both. His deeply felt attachment to the two causes dovetailed in a piece he wrote berating the Gaelic League for its apolitical stance. He still placed great store by Pearse's vision of *Éire Saor Gaedhealach* (a free and Gaelic Ireland). That winter, he nonetheless started teaching an *ard rang*, or senior class, in Irish at Cúig Cúigí, the headquarters of the Gaelic League in Ely Place. His pupil and some-time lover, Rosamond Jacob, remembers him as an inspired teacher:

> He made his pupils write essays, and read poetry [in class] so as to make clear its value and something of his own deep understanding and love for Irish literature. In his class you felt that here was a bridging of the gulf between anglicised modern Ireland and its Gaelic past; here was a modern comrade of men like Raftery, or the Spailpin Fanach, or the old soldier who mourned for Padraig Sairseal.[5]

Ryan's cultural sensibilities did not preclude his subscription to more pugnacious expressions of nationalism. His faith in physical force republicanism was apparent from the aggressive speeches he gave at republican meetings and the anti-government protests that he regularly engineered. Ryan was a genial, gentle and sensitive man when in the company of his friends and quite the charmer with the ladies, but he simultaneously enjoyed a growing reputation as one of Dublin's most vociferous proponents of militant republicanism. There were, however, murmurs of disquiet within the IRA. A pragmatic minority was coming to accept that since there was no hope of their cherished thirty-two-county republic being forged by further warfare, Sinn Féin politicians had little need of an illicit army. De Valera, president of the ethereal second Dáil's Sinn Féin's government and the Irish Republic proclaimed the previous decade, was an ambitious politician whose stand against the validity of the *de facto* government may have been admirably principled, but it also meant that he was president of a republic that did not really exist. He considered his supporters' faith in military, rather than political, means to achieving a republic to be a hindrance to his and republicanism's progress. Dispirited and in poor health after many months in prison, de Valera was plotting how best to rally and further the mainstream, rather than extremist, republican sentiment of Irish men and women. Frustrated by his comrades' self-imposed prohibition from the Dáil, he was masterfully elusive when pressed about his commitment to abstentionism. The shadow-boxing between the hardline physical force men and those suspected of tip-toeing their way towards constitutional politics intensified until the IRA Convention in November 1925, during which Sinn Féin and its army divorced. Hardline republicanism had not recovered from its defeat in the Civil War and, after two disheartening years, it was clearly beginning to fracture.

That autumn threw up another major obstacle to the realisation of a thirty-two-county republic. Cumann na nGaedheal's negotiations with the governments of Stormont and Westminster regarding the drawing up of a boundary between the Free State and Northern Ireland had understandably been shelved during the Civil War. From the sidelines, Northern nationalists had looked on with growing exasperation, while unionists savoured the spectacle. The cannibalism of Southern nationalism not only weakened its ambitions to win the six counties, but vindicated unionists' claims that any republican Dublin government would be an inadequate government. The meanderings of talks held to draw up a boundary brought no appreciable results. The Stormont government treated the whole enterprise with disdain, whilst Cumann na nGaedheal seemed unable to wrest any significant concessions from the northerners on territories with Catholic majorities. Indeed, the Free State found itself in danger of losing east Donegal to the six counties. After a year, a summary of a report of the talks was leaked to the press, revealing what little progress had been made, and the "talks about talks" concluded with the Dublin and Stormont governments effectively united in distancing themselves from profitless bartering. A desperately embarrassed William Cosgrave wanted the report "burned or buried" so unflattering was it to his government's efforts. With the veil lifting on Cumann na nGaedheal's impotence during the negotiations, its representative, Eoin MacNeill, resigned. Belfast's tenacity and Dublin's ineptitude left the boundary unaltered, unionism secured and nationalism frustrated and humiliated. No longer could Cumann na nGaedheal claim that the Treaty provided for the reunification of Ireland. It would be forty years before two Irish heads of government would meet again.

In the same month that the Boundary Commission imploded, November 1925, Ryan threw his energies into an annual demonstration which would become synonymous in the public mind with his name, against the British Legion Armistice Day celebrations. The previous year, Dublin's "Poppy Day" had attracted much republican ire and had degenerated into a brawl. This year's commemoration was to be held at Earlsfort Terrace, only a stones throw from the UCD science labs, which were adroitly turned over to the production of smoke and stink bombs. Ryan and his militant repubican colleagues infiltrated the crowd and, when the call was given for two minutes' respectful silence, started lobbing their missiles. The ensuing brawl soon ended with the flight of most of the protestors in the face of thousands of Legionnaires and several CID men.[6] Ryan stood his ground; the police seized him and two others and held them until a van arrived to take them to the Bridewell garda barracks. Luckily for the three, Ryan's friend Todd Andrews had, in the scuffles, relieved a CID officer of his revolver, which he offered to return in exchange for the release of his comrades. Embarrassed at the loss of the gun, the CID agreed. Ryan, whom Andrews claimed "gained on this occasion his first experience of street brawling in which he later came adept", was set free.[7]

Very soon, the energy and talents Ryan applied to the

captaincy of running street battles branded him, paradoxically, as surely as his reputation for compassion and chivalry. He
was by now well known in republican circles outside of college, and, judging by his peers' pen-portraits of him, he
enjoyed the utmost popularity and respect. His street-corner
orations to republican mobs were imbued with bloodlust, and
the cane he brandished in (often consequent) brawls became a
familiar sight. Yet he is continually painted in memoirs subsequently written by his colleagues as genial, full of good
humour, charismatic and most attractive company for both
male and female, game for anything and highly regarded. His
integrity was never questioned. Eoghan Ó Duinnín was struck
by Ryan's sincerity: *"Nuair a bhíodh Proinsias ag labhairt faoi
éagóir éigin d'fhéadfaí macántacht a chuid feirge a aithint–ní
hionann agus fearg bhréige an pholaiteora ghairmiúil.
Labhraíodh sé le tocht ina ghlór agus faghairt ina shúile."*[8]

Ryan's voice, mellifluous then thunderous, both charmed
and inflamed republican audiences, inducing them to follow
him: "His height and straight carriage made him a conspicuous figure, and the sight of him leading an anti-Union Jack
party or speaking at a street meeting warmed the hearts of
republican crowds. His readiness to risk a fight, and to fight
when risk materialised, was a great asset, for it showed them
that he was in earnest."[9] Seán MacBride remembered him as
"a real rough and tumble character and a strong militant. He
got on well with everybody, could take a drink, danced and
sang. He had no enemies within the movement."[10] This
attribute was particularly significant in a movement plagued
by factionalism and in which paranoia was a recurrent curse.
Rosamond Jacob went so far as to say he was a "most popular figure on republican platforms . . . even the police, with
whom the movement often clashed, had undoubtedly not only
respect, but a decided soft spot".[11] Garda records indicate no
affection for the irreconcilable Limerick man, but the claim is
corroborated by another friend, Budge Mulcahy, a regular in
the republican circles that constitute Ryan's social life. She says
that it was standard behaviour for policemen to smile and
salute Ryan as he drove around town in a car so battered and
scant of windows that it was instantly recognisable.

A dissenting voice comes from Tomás Ó Maoileoin, later
commandant general of the IRA: "His only failing was that

whenever there was a scrap, he had to get into the middle of it."[12] Even Ryan's ardent admirer Rosamond Jacob was wary of his being "slightly fanatical, his insistence on everything being a waste of time that isn't preparing for a fight".[13] One IRA comrade remembered a boastful Ryan, in Belfast for a Wolfe Tone commemoration, trying to goad his more cautious listeners into action: "He made the sort of strong speech that we had come to expect from Frank Ryan. Referring to the Union Jacks flying about the city he declared: 'where I come from, if we can't pull them down, we shoot them down'".[14] For good or ill, Ryan was not a man people easily forgot.

Ryan's reputation was such that Cumann na mBan readily volunteered its members "to help him in a job he intended doing in the Abbey Theatre" in February 1926.[15] That month the third of Sean O'Casey's plays about Ireland's recent rebellion and wars, *The Plough and the Stars,* was being premiered at the Abbey Theatre. O'Casey was a disaffected member of Connolly's workers' militia, the Irish Citizen Army, but had left it before its participation in the 1916 Rising. He regularly peopled his plays with mean, petty-minded and cowardly "freedom fighters". Their motivations were sordid, and the tragic consequences of their actions were wholly void of any redeeming "terrible beauty". Set at the time of the Easter Rising, O'Casey's new drama offended the nationalism of some and the morality of others, largely because of the central role of a prostitute, Rosie Redmond, who mocks whiskey-drinking nationalists for "thinkin' of higher things than a girl's garthers".[16] That the men are familiar with the earthy likes of Rosie and bring the tricolour into the pub with them was considered an affront to the heroes of 1916.[17] Ryan, in fact, was a friend of O'Casey's, the two having played hurling together, and Síghle Uí Dhonnchadha of Cumann na mBan was "surprised that Frank approved of the protest, as I know he thought a lot of O'Casey's plays and had a much keener and deeper appreciation of literary values than most of us".[18] Literary appreciation or no, he asked Cumman na mBan to provide him with ten of their number on the play's fourth night.

As the play had already drawn some criticism from nationalists, its audience was boisterous and the air was filled with catcalls and tension until the curtain went down on the provocative Rosie Redmond. Pandemonium then broke out in the theatre. The stage was charged, Hanna Sheehy Skeffington roared out a prepared speech, seats were torn from the floor, missiles flew through the air, a lusty rendition of "The Soldier's Song" was taken up in the gallery where a tricolour was waved, and the leading man had to punch his way to safety. The police flooded in and dragged out as many protesters as they could until a semblance of calm was finally restored. W.B. Yeats, one of the directors of the Abbey, emerged from the curtain to berate the crowd: "You have disgraced yourselves again," he fumed.[19] He admonished the audience and Dublin in general for their philistinism, concluding with the absurdity "This is his [O'Casey's] apotheosis!" Ryan, meanwhile, in the good company of Cyril Cusack and the country's future president, Cearbhall Ó Dálaigh, was ejected from the theatre for making "seditious speeches".

The controversy went on for weeks. The police claimed that the house of the leading man (who later found fame under the name Barry Fitzgerald) was raided by an IRA party wanting to kidnap him, and consequently he was placed under police protection. (A socialist and republican himself, Fitzgerald's real name was William Shields. His father, Alphonsus Shields, had been responsible for bringing James Connolly to Ireland thirty years earlier.) The protests at the theatre continued, and many a policeman got to see the show for free. A wordy and public spat between O'Casey and Sheehy Skeffington, a prominent political activist and Easter 1916 widow, enlivened the letters pages of *The Irish Times*.

O'Casey's epistolic responses to "the screams and patter antagonistic to the performance" were countered by Ryan, who wrote, on behalf of Sheehy Skeffington, inviting the playwright to debate the matter with his adversary.[20] Against his better judgment, O'Casey took up the offer and arrived at the Mills Hall venue to find that the debate was to have a somewhat partial host – Francis Richard Ryan. Inexperienced at public speaking and unable to read his notes because of his near-blindness, the playwright was further overcome by such a suffocating sickness he had to sit down more than once to steady himself. Always a sickly man, "his whole being was strained with the effort" of speaking in the heat and noise of the hall; he left, "weary and scornful at the end of it all". The "bawling fools" protesting *The Plough and the Stars* had cost Ireland O'Casey's genius; he moved to London shortly afterwards.[21]

The riot's instigator, meanwhile, "evidently pleased with the affair", continued with his politics.[22] By now, spring of 1926, Ryan abandoned thoughts of further study, and his winter *ard rang* classes had finished. Although he always kept himself busy, like many an arts graduate before and since, he was foraging around for a job. He had briefly been teaching Irish at the unlikely venue of Mountjoy School, a Protestant school very much associated with the old ruling order. The job, perhaps inevitably, had come to an end soon after Ryan had taken a day off sick. Unfortunately, that same day he was seen by one of his students leading the Armistice Day protest. Through Todd Andrews, Ryan got work writing and carrying out editorial duties for the Irish Tourist Association, working on brochures and an omnibus guide to Ireland. Although he undoubtedly had a flair for teaching, journalism was his real vocation, and it was one that could well serve his republicanism.

The republican newspaper *An Phoblacht* was being rejuvenated, and Ryan was given the job of touring the country to collect monies owed and take orders for the paper's imminent renaissance. Its new editor was to have a considerable influence on Ryan's politics and beliefs. An avid reader of Marx, Peadar O'Donnell was soon to become not merely the leading figurehead of Irish republican socialism, but its living embodiment. O'Donnell was an IRA man and Civil War internee, who drew his politics from the rural land agitation in his native Donegal as much as from rejection of the Treaty. His interest in the labour movement nourished his faith in Connolly's notion that capitalist structures had been imposed on Ireland by the English ruling class, so it followed that to properly sever the link with England, those structures must be eradicated. O'Donnell still adhered to Liam Mellows' gospel that the support of the people would be won only with a social and economic programme, rather than a republicanism which "could only judge of a situation in terms of guns and men".[23]

O'Donnell had therefore pinned his revolutionary hopes on land agitation, by leading a campaign directing farmers to withhold their land annuity payments, which were collected by the Irish government and passed on to Westminster. O'Donnell saw his opportunity. He planned to mobilise a mass movement against the government, which would be propelled by an anti-English, anti-landlord consciousness that had long been established within the rural community.

Ryan, having acquitted himself well in his organisational work for *An Phoblacht,* and having proved his abilities as a journalist and his trustworthiness as a militant republican, was given O'Donnell's old job of editing *An t-Óglach* (The Volunteer), a four-page monthly news-sheet, for the IRA. Despite his respectable day job at the Irish Tourist Association, Ryan's spare time was given over to publishing the underground paper, helped by sympathetic printers while under the constant strain of CID surveillance. But Ryan's association with O'Donnell educated him in more than propaganda and illegal activity. As yet, Ryan's appreciation of Irish socialist republicanism was crude. He later admitted that O'Donnell "has a habit of hitting you between the two eyes with some fact that you have never realised 'that way' before, and you kick yourself for not having seen it already".[24] But the gestation of Ryan's socialism would prove lengthy, and in 1926 he considered himself to be a soldier, not a politician. As such, he won promotion to the rank of adjutant in the Dublin IRA.

Ryan's hybrid socialist/republican thinking of the time is apparent in a piece he wrote for *An Phoblacht* in the summer of that year. In "A Vindication of the Old Gaelic State" he evaluated the concept of a modern state, based on the principles, structure and mores of pre-conquest Ireland, as compared to one inclined toward the model set by the Soviet Union.

> If the ideal of the Gaelic State for which we have been striving – and for which some of us still strive – is impracticable, then, in the name of truth, let us be honest; let us admit that the Irish nation has suffered the Last Conquest; and that our nationality has gone to its grave . . . I assert that it is a question of going back to the old Gaelic State, of repairing its foundations, and of rebuilding the new state upon them, of avoiding its faults and of perfecting its virtues . . . I hold as an axiom of national faith that when the Irish

nation discards that ideal, the Irish nation will have found its grave.[25]

Ryan agrees that while an Irish counterpart of the Soviet Union would be "infinitely preferable" to a state aping England, the ideal must be an Irish one. He goes on to paint Gaelic Ireland as a collection of sub-states (as Connolly had in his *Labour in Irish History*), founded on ancient clans as medieval communes, maintaining that "Translating the term 'Gaelic State' into terms of modern Labour, we call it the 'Workers' Republic'."

For all Ryan's fascination with Irish history, the old Gaelic order's rigid class system and endemic internecine wars, replete with cynical loyalties and treacheries, prove a momentous blind spot for Ryan, blinkered as he was by a romantic reading of history that had also afflicted Connolly and, to a far greater extent, Pearse. Indeed, the article exhibits a flaw that characterises much of Ryan's early writing in that it constantly refers to Connolly and Pearse as if they were Siamese twins. One is rarely mentioned without the other's name being stuck fast to it, and the writings and speeches of the two men are drawn on as if their thought welded into a single vision for Ireland. The article's conclusion is confused, requiring a leapfrog of faith over the *non sequiturs* and missing links of its argument. Ryan's exegesis of Connolly's ideas wasn't wrong so much as argued clumsily. Still, the article is an indicator of his gradual conversion to nationalist thinking in economic, rather than purely patriotic, terms and of a twenty-three-year-old's grappling with new political ideas that he finds attractive enough to prescribe before being able to satisfactorily interpret them.

More importantly, Ryan's position was symptomatic of the conversion to left-wing thinking that was beginning to colour the ideology of the IRA. Within Ryan's new remit as adjutant was an attempt to reorganise the effectively defunct Irish Citizen Army. This in part was prompted by a need to mobilise men to replace those lost to the emigrant ships, constitutional politics or disillusion, but it equally reflected the leftist slant that the IRA was gradually adopting. There was obviously something of a contradiction here, inasmuch as the organisation was supposedly driven by a "physical force" ethos rather than political theory, and Ryan, as much as any other member, frequently voiced his distaste for political theorising which would sap the martial ambitions of the IRA. After all, the IRA's constitution did claim for itself the right, regardless of the nation's democratic wishes, to exist and act in the pursuance of a thirty-two-county sovereign republic. For most of the membership, that pursuance by arms was as far as ideology stretched.

Yet some within the movement, such as Peadar O'Donnell, were abandoning the straitjacket of non-ideology for more oblique means to satisfy the army's constitutional ambitions. In 1927 the former commander of the Dublin brigade, Michael Fitzpatrick, was among trade union leaders who went to the Soviet Union to celebrate the tenth anniversary of its revolution. At the IRA Army Convention in November of that year, delegates passed a resolution to support the Soviets should they go to war with Britain, as some suspected might soon be the case. Despite the political conservatism of the foot soldiers of the IRA and an almost xenophobic distrust of foreign ideas, the dilution of an ethos which claimed to be Irish and Gaelic and which was based on physical force rather than politics, was a price worth paying if it brought outside aid and allies. Indeed, there had always been radical and revolutionary fringes in Irish nationalism, and foreign aid had long been sought: earlier in the 1920s two IRA men had gone to Moscow seeking arms; the movement was largely funded by Irish-America; and the French and Spanish had been traditional allies of Irish freedom.

It was such a spirit that, in February 1927, prompted Ryan and a fellow IRA man, Donal O'Donoghue, being sent as delegates to an anti-imperialist congress in Brussels, a trip that would make a great impression on Ryan's political outlook. The Congress of Oppressed Nationalities, organised by the international communist organisation, the Comintern, was attended by representatives of colonised countries worldwide and resulted in the formation of an international League Against Imperialism (LAI). The Congress was, however covertly, an attempt to sow communist seed in underdeveloped countries by exploiting nationalist sentiment, and Ryan was immediately impressed by the number and calibre of the delegates. He himself gave a rousing and heartfelt speech against imperialism that won over the audience. Ryan was, in turn, enlightened by the concept of Irish nationalism in an internationalist context and from then on held that colonised peoples globally were of a fraternity. An Irish branch of the LAI was set up the following year. Ryan was an aggressive and dedicated member, and the cause of anti-imperialism, in an age when a quarter of the globe was still coloured pink in British classrooms, was to become a rallying call that Ryan would almost make his own.

Rallying crowds is what Ryan spent almost all of his time doing. He was immersed in a social circle of republicans and *Gaeilgeoirí* and, sociable as he was, he didn't stray from that circle. He was in regular contact with his family, but it is hard to imagine he met them often. His eldest brother Jeremiah Joseph was teaching in Limerick, and John had gone to America where he worked as a labourer. His two other brothers had qualified as doctors; Vincent and Moss were in England: Vincent in a TB sanatorium in Yorkshire and Moss as a GP in Liverpool. Ryan's eldest sister Catherine was in a convent in Tralee, while Mary and Ann were nuns in Cobh. Ryan was annoyed by the fact that his younger sister was in a convent, largely because the family couldn't afford to pay for her to study music. His youngest sister Eilís was sent to boarding school in Dublin – she would have met Frank frequently – and was saved from a convent only because her parents "want to keep her for our old age".[24] Ryan felt a sense of guilt; his parents had expected great things of their brightest son and couldn't understand how he had ended up living a hand-to-mouth existence as a political activist.

The previous year there had been a split within Sinn Féin. The republican boycott of all Free State institutions was frustrating the ambitions of the more pragmatic members of Sinn Féin, who were haunted by the principle of abstention from the Dáil. For de Valera, the question of signing the oath of allegiance had always been the primary obstacle to entering the Dáil; if the oath were removed, the chains of his political impotence would dissolve. This president of a mythical republic and a governing party that governed only itself was impatient to preside over something far more substantial, but in side-stepping the principled rock in the road, he risked the loss of his republican integrity.

For de Valera that risk was worth running. At the Sinn Féin

Ard Fheis, or convention, in March 1926, his premise that once the oath was removed it became a matter of policy rather than hallowed principle whether or not republicans entered the Dáil was countered by an amendment moved by the republican priest, Father Michael O'Flanagan: "That it is incompatible with the fundamental principle of Sinn Féin to send representatives into any usurping legislature set up by English law in Ireland."[27] Hardliners, the "physical force" men such as Frank Ryan, who himself claimed politics to be an "obtrusion", still remained dismissive of the value and validity of conventional politics in a revolutionary movement. Rosamond Jacob recorded that a very agitated Ryan "disapproves of the proposals but knows we couldn't get on without Dev". That the acrimonious arguments at the Ard Fheis had not spiralled into "open war" was an indication of de Valera's commendable dexterity and composure, claimed Ryan, who in the next breath flaunted his true, impetuous diehard colours "When he said something very disreputable about wanting to go out with a gun again."[28]

De Valera's suggestion that republicans might enter the Dáil was rejected and, too little consoled with the wooden spoon of the delegates voting him the greatest Irishman for a century, he resigned his presidency immediately. Within months he had founded a new party, Fianna Fáil, taking with him nineteen of the forty-four Sinn Féin Dáil deputies who had not as yet taken their seats. Ryan remained unpersuaded. Even if the new party came to power, "the Free State and all its institutions would still be there – nothing for it but the gun".[29] The consequences of the republican split would soon be felt in the less rarefied air of the public vote: a general election was called for June 1927.

Frank Ryan seemingly played an active part during the election, not for Sinn Féin but in the campaign for UCD law professor Arthur Clery as an independent republican and abstentionist candidate.[30] Clery was even more surprised than his campaigners when he won easily, beating none other than the eminent academic, pro-Treatyite and godfather of the Boundary debacle Eoin MacNeill for a Dáil seat he did not intend to take. Fianna Fáil won no less than forty-four seats (plus the support of two independent republicans), compared to governing Cumann na nGaedheal's forty-seven and Sinn Féin's pitiful five. The balance of power in the Dáil was now held by Labour, independents and others, grudgingly support-ing a government panic-stricken not only by the election results but by the assassination by the IRA of Kevin O'Hig-gins, vice-president and minister for home affairs, only two weeks after the election. The government responded with the sudden introduction of three bills intended to bolster the main-tenance of law and order by the proscription of certain organ-isations and the use of non-jury courts. Fianna Fáil deputies, emboldened by the support of their constituents and the des-peration of the government, were spurred into action. They declared that taking the oath of allegiance "is merely an empty political formula which deputies could conscientiously sign without becoming involved or without involving their nation, in obligations of loyalty to the British Crown".[31]

On 11 August, Fianna Fáil TDs entered the Dáil, their con-sciences as clean as only political consciences can be. Fancy political footwork or sell-out? Frank Ryan had "only one use for our 153 deputies – I'd gather 'em up and swap them for 153 pieces of artillery, or even three if I could get them. Then I'd live happily ever after." Politicking inspired Cosgrave to call a snap general election in September, but Ryan wanted no part of it. Although he longed desperately for any opportuni-ty to dance on the government's grave, "the price we're pay-ing for it is degrading". His flirtation with leftist radicalism, while remaining suspicious of politics in general, is evident in a letter he wrote to Rosamond Jacob at the time, venting in typically bellicose language not only his exasperation and fury, but also his confused thinking, which skips from striving for political solutions to political nihilism and back again:

> Isn't politics a dirty game? . . . Fianna Fáil policy is futile. It can never give us more than a better Free State . . . All this bother about oaths and constitution, all the promises to end tyranny, all the rattling of dead men's bones – in causes for which they never fought – and all to no purpose . . . I am more con-cerned with holding together the remnants of 100 per cent revolutionaries so there will be someone left to talk – at least – of Lalor and Connolly. Nobody in the political arena stands for the enforcement of the full

> programme of Lalor and Connolly, and that pro-
> gramme is more important than any other I know of.
> Enough of politics. I feel so mad about them that I
> want to wear a red shirt and bomb politicians of all
> degrees.[32]

The results of the election belied Ryan's prediction that Fianna Fáil would form a coalition government with Labour, peddling an anaemic socialist republicanism. Instead, Cumann na nGaedheal limped back to power. A dispirited Sinn Féin did not even contest the election. For Ryan, political tussles were now no more than a domestic spat between moderates. The election seems to have done little for him, other than to feed his rejection of democracy as a tool for progress and deepen his belief that it was the duty of the visionary minority to impose its ideals on the majority for its own betterment. His belief in democracy had always been tenuous at best, and he regretted "with sorrow" the "large sections of our people forsaking the manly policy of Irish militant nationalism for the barren and devious ways of parliamentary agitation".[33]

This aversion to constitutional politics buttressed Ryan's fidelity to the extra-constitutional ambitions of the IRA, and his loyalty did not go unnoticed. An account of a lecture given by Ryan in February 1928 on the post-Fenian secret society, the Invincibles,[34] made its way into a Department of Justice file. It noted that Ryan had quoted extensively from an account of the Invincibles written by one of its chief members, P.J. Tynan, and compared the Fenians of 1867, following their failed rising, to contemporary republicans. More specifically, it reported that Ryan "conditionally condemns the policy of the Invincibles but the whole tone of his lecture is inflammatory and . . . would seem to indicate that his disavowal of the methods of the Invincibles is not altogether honest." This conclusion is something of an understatement considering that Ryan's only criticism of the murders committed by the Invincibles was that they gained little for Irishmen. In fact, he claimed for the assassins nothing less than "as honoured a place in the history of Ireland as any other patriot". In March, the CID searched Ryan's house looking for literature intended for use by the "Ghosts", a Cumann na mBan offshoot which sent pamphlets, both beseeching and threatening, to members of the Free State army and police concerning their treasonable occupations. The author of a subsequent Department of Justice report was "reasonably certain that Frank Ryan is the author of leaflets of a most objectionable character . . . inviting the gunmen of today to copy the methods of the Invincibles".[35]

Peter Ennis, a senior CID officer, being an acquaintance of sorts due to Ryan's militant reputation and barely legal activities, called into Ryan's office at the Tourist Association with two aides in October 1928 and unearthed IRA documents relating to the organisation's trial of one of its members, along with letters addressed to Dublin Brigade officers. To the relief of Todd Andrews, Ryan's boss, who was wholly innocent of the desk's contents, the officers left with only the documents. They returned shortly afterwards, however, to take Ryan away and charge him with treason. He was brought before the judge in the Circuit Criminal Court (the authority of which Ryan refused to recognise), where the jury failed to reach an agreement. He was returned to Mountjoy to await a new trial.

Despite being mildly anxious about his trial – he was more disgruntled about missing teaching at Cúig Cúigí – he seems to have been little perturbed by his times spent in jail. He wrote to Rosamond Jacob that he had plenty of books and cigarettes in Mountjoy and was surrounded by old faces. "I'm in good humour here," he claimed, while conceding that things would be different should he be sentenced.[36] After three months and a new trial, he was found not guilty and discharged.

Republicans celebrated Ryan's acquittal as a defeat of gardaí by the hand of justice (albeit administered by those whose authority republicans refused to recognise), but there were possibly more sinister prompts to the jury's decision. A week or so after Ryan's arrest, members of the jury received letters referring to the accused and his trial, asking, "Will you assist the murderers of 1922 in their wicked vendetta against honourable citizens who scorn to betray their country in England's interests?"[37] The letters were signed "Ghosts".

Although Ryan was never found guilty of any charge, the use of his workplace as a store for IRA material occasioned the end of his career writing tour guides. Thereafter he juggled jobs and did his best for Irish language promotion, running a regular *céilí* and teaching Irish in Dún Laoghaire and for the

Gaelic League at Cúig Cúigí, as ever trying to link the language and republicanism.

Ryan was finding teaching work hard to come by, despite having excellent recommendations, and claimed that his worsening deafness hampered him in both interviews for posts and the classroom itself. He briefly edited *An Pobal*, essentially an Irish language version of *An Phoblacht*, and tried to set up a group of the same name. The few meetings of the club enabled Ryan to demonstrate that he could warmonger *as Gaeilge* as well as he could in English, "asserting we had peace now and couldn't have freedom till we had destroyed that peace".[38] Police pressure prevented the blossoming of *An Pobal*.

Being picked up by the police and released in the morning without charge, or else facing a court which he refused to recognise, on charges that no jury could find him guilty of, had by now become a fairly regular occurrence for Ryan. He was doing some writing for *Irish Freedom*, a paper supporting Sinn Féin, but he was frustrated by it, considering himself gagged by the editors. He preferred working on *An t-Óglach*, for which his editorials were neither equivocal nor understated. A standard piece declared that each volunteer "must consider himself at all times as the apostle of Republicanism and act as though the destruction of British dominance in Ireland rested solely with himself".[39]

It is as much as to be expected that Ryan should exhort all others to a zeal equal to his own. However, later passages from the same editorial, emphasising the necessary and natural alliance of nationalism and anti-imperialism, suggest the broadening of his political spectrum since his time in Brussels. Indeed, Ryan was considered a natural choice to join Seán MacBride and the British miners' leader A.J. Cook on the speakers' platform at an anti-imperialist rally at Dublin's Mansion House, but on its eve he was arrested. "The authorities feared the effect he might have," claimed Síghle Uí Dhonnchadha. "Doesn't this prove the power of Frank's oratory?"[40] In his stead, Seán MacBride read out Ryan's speech to an audience of 2,000 people. Seán MacSwiney then spoke, less on the evils of imperialism than on the harassment of Ryan, who "had been followed and touted every day for the past two years, could not leave his home or office without an escort of

'G Men', had tonight tasted some more torture, and was now lying in prison".[41]

Ryan was named as one of the directors of the Republican Press Ltd, set up by republicans to counter their difficulties in finding sympathetic publishers willing to incur the wrath of the Free State authorities. Ryan had already published the first of his political pamphlets, *Easter Week and After,* under the pen-name that he would come to use often, Seachranaidhe (Wanderer). It starts off with an impressionistic account of the Rising itself:

> Enter now the firing squads. Open now the quick-lime graves. Take your revenge now, oh, Empire! Wreck bodies you could not chain, rip hearts you could not buy. But the souls – Oh! you damn fools! – the souls escape you, and new bodies will claim them.
>
> And even now their tramp is on the hills.

In the following sections, using language only a little more temperate, Ryan berates Ireland for not being spurred by patriotism during the Great War years, leaving it to "great-souled men, Christ-like" to redeem her. Surprisingly, the Treaty signing and Civil War are dealt with in euphemisms, being a time when "war-weary men yielded to the enemy", even though "in vain did true men protest". The emphasis throughout is on the leadership and foresight of Pearse, whom he claims to have been a realist soldier figure – in his knowledge that his death would inspire others to arms – as well as an idealist. Even Ryan's discussion of a future social programme draws far more from Pearse than from Connolly, and its socialism is muted. The government is treated with splenetic eloquence, wherein it is accused of paramount treachery and deceit. "We now visit Easter graves", Ryan advises, not merely to pray but "to gain communion" with those martyred and to pledge over those graves that "we will fight to uphold the honour and guard the sovereignty of the Irish Republic".[42]

Hardly the work of a socialist, and peppered with exclamations of "Alas!" and "Nay More!", the pamphlet is worthy of little more than historical curiosity, or even sniggers, decades later, but the author's style, dripping with Pearse-isms, was obviously dictated by the readership's expected appetite. A pamphlet coloured by Connolly's socialism, rather than the romantic militancy of Pearse, would have received only a luke-warm reception, and for republicans in general, *Easter Week and After* was considered "a stirring pamphlet in those dark and confusing times".[43] The conservatism of the potential reading audience aside, it must be borne in mind that Ryan's socialism was yet callow and that he would remain a far greater admirer of Pearse than others of the socialist clique to whom he was drawn.[44] Ryan would always be prompted by nationalist sentiment as much as by the rationale of his more Marxist friends, and it was Pearse's profound attraction for him, rather than cynical populism, that shaped his first pamphlet.

His second pamphlet, published the following year as part of the 1829 Catholic Emancipation centenary celebrations, was a different affair altogether. Far more mature, it was an accomplished polemic, despite its remarkable claim that Daniel O'Connell was a one-time master of a local Orange Lodge![45] From this charge, one can safely presuppose that O'Connell is cast as the villain of the piece, titled *Emancipation,* as compared with Wolfe Tone and "the real Emancipators of Ireland – the physical force men"; indeed O'Connell "was not the Liberator but the Enslaver of his country". For Seachranaidhe, emancipation was little more than a "degrading" placebo, and the granting of religious privileges only distracted from the one, true emancipation of Ireland and its people. For Ryan, the centenary celebrations were a sham and, to make matters worse, they only perpetuated the mingling of religion and politics, which Ryan resented as much as he abhorred sectarianism. It concludes with a call to arms: "It is by Irish will, and not at English pleasure, that Emancipation can be achieved: Irishmen must emancipate themselves – in arms."[46]

By the time this pamphlet had been published, Ryan was using all his writing skills in the diffusion of his beliefs on a full-time basis, and his articles often appeared in *An Phoblacht.* During 1928 arrest had become for Peadar O'Donnell, editor of *An Phoblacht*, an almost everyday occurrence.[47] He tried to side-step suppression of *An Phoblacht* by publishing essentially the same news but in different formats, such as *Dublin News* or *War Bulletin. An Phoblacht* was suppressed for almost three months in early 1929, until Frank Ryan succeeded its beleaguered editor in May. For some reason Ryan was chosen over the assistant editor, Geoffrey Coulter, an Ulster Protestant once of Trinity College who had become an habitué of Bridewell police station. Coulter's initial resentment at the editorship being usurped by Ryan, whose bearing he remembered as being that of an "absolutely fearless young man – a trait that excites too much envy", was soon overwhelmed, as the new boss was "so darned nice, I concealed my chagrin".[48]

Fearless and nice Ryan may have been, but *An Phoblacht* was to demand of him all the energy and dedication he could muster; all too often the only readers of his battered charge were the five members of the military tribunal who would scan its pages for sedition before censoring it. Even when it was deemed fit for public consumption, weekly sales of the paper had dropped to about 4,000, having been about 18,000 in 1925. Republicanism was having enough problems without rendering itself mute. *An Phoblacht*'s sales figures mirrored the haemorrhaging of adherents from the republican cause, with membership of the IRA in 1929 standing at about 5,000, as compared to 20,000 or so in 1926. Furthermore, although Ryan's own socialist leanings were by now in mid-bloom, there were still very few like-minded political revolutionaries within or without the IRA. Ryan's opportunity to amplify the call to his favoured causes through *An Phoblacht* coincided with the acceleration of his political development. He shifted ideological gear as both a republican and a journalist. He was now in a position to hoist the colours of green and red. As editor of *An Phoblacht*, he became the country's eminent radical propagandist, and in January 1929 he was elected to the Army Executive of the IRA.

Notes to Chapter Two

1. An offshoot of the Gaelic League, or Conradh na Gaeilge, agitating to promote the use of the Irish language.
2. C.S. Andrews, *Man of No Property* (Cork: Mercier Press, 1982), p. 74.
3. *Ibid.*, pp. 74–5.
4. Walsh went on to marry Frank Edwards, who would become a friend and comrade to Ryan in Spain.
5. Rosamond Jacob papers, NLI, 33/130.
6. Republicans thought the police of the CID – Criminal

The Blossoming of a Revolutionary

Investigation Department – a particular menace since they were
armed and wore plain clothes.

7. Andrews, *Man of No Property*, p. 59.
8. "When Francis used to speak about certain injustices, you were
    able to recognise the honesty in his anger – it was not the false
    anger of the professional politician. He used to speak with a
    choking in his throat and tears in his eyes." Eoghan Ó Duinnín,
    La Niña Bonita agus An Róisín Dubh (Baile Átha Cliath: An Cló-
    chomar Tta, 1986), p. 85.
9. Síghle Uí Dhonnchadha papers, UCDAD, p. 106/1711.
10. Quoted in Uinseann Mac Eoin, *Survivors* (Dublin: Argenta Pub-
    lications, 1980), p. 123.
11. Rosamond Jacob papers, NLI, 33/132.
12. Quoted in Mac Eoin, *Survivors*, p. 101.
13. Rosamond Jacob Diaries, NLI, 32/582, February 1927, p. 72.
14. Quoted in Mac Eoin, *Survivors*, p. 308.
15. Quoted in Cronin, *Frank Ryan: The Search for the Republic*
    (Dublin: Repsol, 1980), p. 23.
16. Sean O'Casey, *Three Plays* (London: Macmillan & Co., 1970), p.
    162.
17. Perhaps cynically, it is hard not to suspect that some of the offend-
    ed, even if unconsciously, desired that the name of the Abbey be
    besmirched by republican rioting; it was now the recipient of grants
    from the despised government, and as such was a state theatre.
18. Quoted in Cronin, *Frank Ryan*, p. 23.
19. Presumably a reference to the riots that greeted J. M. Synge's *The
    Playboy of the Western World* almost twenty years earlier.
20. David Krause, ed., *The Letters of Sean O'Casey* (London: Cassell,
    1975), pp. 167–78.
21. Sean O'Casey, *Autobiographies*, Volume II (London: Macmillan
    & Co., 1963), pp. 151–3.
22. Rosamond Jacob Diaries, NLI, 32/582, February 1926, p. 50.
23. Quoted in Desmond Greaves, *Liam Mellows and the Irish Revo-
    lution* (London: Lawrence & Wishart, 1987), p. 364.
24. *Republican Congress,* 17 November 1934.
25. *An Phoblacht,* 6 August 1926.
26. Aodh Ó Canainn, "Éilis Ryan in Her Own Words" *Saothar* 21,
    1996.
27. Quoted in Conor Foley, *Legion of the Rearguard* (London: Pluto
    Press, 1992), p. 61.
28. Rosamond Jacob Diaries, NLI, 32/582, March 1926, p. 57.
29. *Ibid.,* October 1926, p. 23.
30. The UCD Republican Club had never been allied to any one
    strand of the movement, so its members could act in concert as a

united republican entity, with personal loyalties overriding political divisions.

31. Quoted in Ronan Fanning, *Independent Ireland* (Dublin: Heli-
    con, 1983), p. 98.
32. Rosamond Jacob papers, NLI, 33/130.
33. *An Phoblacht,* 2 November 1929.
34. Responsible for the 1882 murders of Chief Secretary Lord
    Cavendish and his under secretary, T.H. Burke, in the Phoenix
    Park.
35. Department of Justice files, NAI, S5631.
36. Rosamond Jacob papers, NLI, 33/130.
37. Department of Justice files, NAI, S5864.
38. Rosamond Jacob Diaries, NLI, 32/582, February 1929, p. 70.
39. *An t-Óglach,* March 1928.
40. Quoted in Cronin, *Frank Ryan*, p. 18.
41. Department of Justice files, NAI, Crime and Security Division, Jus
    8/682.
42. Copy of *Easter Week and After* in the Eithne Coyle Papers,
    UCDAD, P61/38.
43. Quoted in Cronin, *Frank Ryan*, p. 27.
44. Both George Gilmore, an advanced republican socialist, and
    Hanna Sheehy Skeffington, his close colleagues in internal IRA
    disputes and journalism respectively, were quietly dismissive of
    Pearse, the latter wondering at Ryan's reverence for him and the
    former blaming Pearse for republicanism's "muddled thinking".
45. While it hardly renders Ryan's falsity excusable, O'Connell was
    the master of a Freemason's lodge and founded a lodge in Tralee,
    which Ryan, as a Catholic, a socialist and a republican, would
    have found only slightly less odious.
46. Seachranaidhe, *Emancipation* (Dublin: The Republican Press
    Ltd., 1929).
47. O'Donnell was arrested fourteen times during the summer, and
    harassment continued unabated after a trip to America, with
    fourteen house raids without warrant occurring in fifteen days in
    early 1929. Quoted in Cronin, *Frank Ryan*, p. 25.

CHAPTER THREE

The Fusion of Green and Red
1929–1930

In the spring of 1929, Frank Ryan, free from Mountjoy after the IRA documents charge and occupying the editor's desk at *An Phoblacht,* resumed his frantic juggling of political commitments. In his role as inspecting officer for the IRA, he travelled to units around the country, establishing and maintaining contacts amongst republicans nationwide. He was particularly influential in the longer term in that he held much sway over young, potential recruits to the IRA. Among his UCD connections was the burgeoning poet and communist Charlie Donnelly, who later invited his respected elder to the inaugural meeting of a politically leftist university club he had founded, The Student Vanguard.[1] Ryan was also connected intermittently with Fianna Éireann, which can be described as either a republican boy scout movement or else an IRA nursery. When explaining the role of Fianna Éireann, Ryan would quote Pádraig Pearse: "to train the boys of Ireland to fight Ireland's battle when they are men".[2] He also gave his time and enthusiasm to left-wing groups such as the Workers' Defence League, anti-imperialist agitation and Irish language clubs, all attended to while simultaneously staying one step ahead of the law. Gardaí without a warrant frequently searched his house in Ranelagh, prompting him to receive mail, addressed to Mr O'Reilly, at Hanna Sheehy Skeffington's house. Knowing the severity of garda intimidation first hand, he was setting up a watchdog committee to deal with victimisation of republicans, drawing up lists of those held by the police without charge and others who were being dismissed from jobs for their allegiance.

Pressure was brought to bear on employers to treat republican workers equally, and notification was given to, and ignored by, the press.

Peadar O'Donnell's push within the IRA for a political appendage to the organisation that would win the disaffected but politicised over to republicanism, tentatively named Saor Éire, was received coldly at the IRA General Army Convention in 1929, for fear of diluting the movement's physical force ethos.

O'Donnell's intention had been to add on to the IRA a political dimension that would serve as a vehicle for a mass movement of the populace against the government's conservative politics and be directed towards establishing, by political agitation, the kind of thirty-two county, independent republic that the IRA strove to achieve by arms. O'Donnell hoped to channel the energy of restless IRA men and win the backing of less extreme republicans. By so doing, there was an acknowledgement amongst the proponents of Saor Éire that their aims should win the support of public opinion rather than be justified by the prerogative of the righteous minority, which had given the IRA, and the leaders of the 1916 Rising before them, their self-justification. The politics of Saor Éire, essentially a front organisation under the aegis of the IRA, was decidedly left-wing. Yet the idea of introducing politics, let alone socialist politics, into the IRA's thinking was too much for its foot soldiers, and O'Donnell had to back down.

Still, it was becoming clear to the leadership that some kind of outlet was needed to direct and utilise the pent-up zeal of thousands of diehards. By the admission of its chief of staff, Moss Twomey, the IRA was incapable of achieving any military goals and so was only treading water; not content with rhetoric, harassment of juries or the occasional shooting of a policeman or informer, the membership might well be led away by sheer ennui and frustration. This need to generate activity, uphold morale and give a coherence to republicanism gave birth, in April 1929, to Comhairle na Poblachta, a loose confederacy of republicans, radicals and anybody else disdainful of Cosgrave's conservatism and de Valera's political pirouettes. Their perceived desire to "overthrow the state by force of arms" set alarms ringing for the police.[3] However, because they had little else in common, there was no cause for alarm, and within two years Comhairle na Poblachta was moribund.

If the republican movement was stalling, it was at least starting to find its voice again. As editor, Ryan's first priority was to revive the flagging sales of *An Phoblacht,* a feat he achieved with remarkable rapidity. The potency of the press was not wasted on the man who sincerely believed that "failure to achieve the widest possible circulation for Republican Literature just now would be a national crime".[4] Ryan was well appointed and, typically, took to his task with vigour, setting up new agents for the paper on street corners, fairs and at church gates after mass. Overseas subscriptions were expanded, and in time Ryan was dispatching copies to Canada, New Zealand, Australia, South Africa and over a dozen cities in the US. In August, after three months of Ryan's tenure, the editor gratefully reported increased sales of, and agents for, the weekly, and laid out his plans to double circulation. The target was hit, then doubled and hit again.

Complementing easier access to the paper, Ryan brought dramatic changes to its layout, unveiling his true talent for publishing. Enlivened by creative use of photographs and montages, *An Phoblacht* took on a dynamic aspect that newspapers of the time lacked, its vibrancy ensuring its prominence on the news-stand among colourless competitors. "He used pictures, cartoons and make-up as they had never been used before in this country," said his assistant Geoffrey Coulter. In October 1929, with his sales having already doubled to 8,000 per week, Ryan was able to increase the paper in size from eight to sixteen pages. Coulter was impressed: "I had to admit, he taught me a great deal besides turning *An Phoblacht* from a quiet political review with organisational notes into as lively a political newspaper as I've seen." Coulter claimed that circulation grew to as much as 40,000 a week.[5]

The style of journalism changed perceptibly under Ryan.[6] Peadar O'Donnell's reportage had been that of a wordsmith, employing irony, witty barbs and light-hearted palliatives to sweeten his doctrines and denunciations. Ryan's writing, devoid of the tricks and superfluities of language, was more curt and bellicose, his sentiments devoid of garlands. It was, after all, the writing of a man who once told Rosamond Jacob, "I'm dogmatic but I bet you I'm right."[7]

He berated the predictable targets – "His Britannic Majesty's Government of the Free State" and the London government, capitalism and colonialism – but Ryan cannot be accused of employing euphemisms to win over Labour supporters, liberals or constitutional nationalists. He declared that "most of our Trade Unions are rotten. They divide instead of unifying the workers."[8] Fianna Fáil were recipients of regular vituperation, both sincerely felt in opposition to their constitutionalism (entering the "British and treaty-established Dáil" was still held to be selling out) but probably also designed to prevent republicans straying from the true diehard path.

If the style of writing in *An Phoblacht* changed, its content, largely, did not. Ryan's championing of specific causes within republicanism brought a slight shift of emphasis. As a somewhat strident *Gaeilgeoir,* Ryan frequently reminded readers that one of the four main articles of the IRA constitution was the return of the Irish language to daily parlance. However, because a sizeable percentage of the readership would have been incapable of understanding articles of any depth *as Gaeilge,* Ryan, in a rare exercise of pragmatism, published very few editorials or front page articles in Irish.[9] His dedication to the language was far from academic. Síghle Uí Dhonnchadha, a frequent visitor to the Dingle peninsula, remembered Ryan's services to the Gaeltacht and its people, particularly during a regatta festival.

> I wrote up to Proinnsias [Frank] and asked him if he could manage to come down and say a few words to the hundreds who would be gathered there. He was editor of *An Phoblacht* at the time and it was not easy to get away. It is a 225 mile drive from Dublin but once the Gaeltacht called him, Frank would not refuse them. For years afterwards people spoke of his inspiring speech. We had great difficulty in persuading him to take a hurried tea before he set out on his return journey in a car which was only held together by the grace of God. Few men would have undertaken that return journey of 450 miles in one day in such an old car, but Frank would do anything to show his genuine interest in the Gaeltacht.[10]

Considering himself an internationalist, he gave over much column space to news from abroad, particularly if it concerned colonialism. Ryan was forthright in his condemnation of Gandhi's pacifism, but he equally praised his courage and ability to organise the Indian people. *An Phoblacht* also shed light, for Irish readers, on British heavyhandedness in Palestine and South Africa, and on American interference in Nicaragua. Despite Ryan's generally universal outlook, the paper did occasionally fall into the nationalist trap of jeering at something as being "foreign" or "alien" when it suited, the importation of British newspapers being a case in point. They were condemned as being of "questionable morality . . . low intellectual level . . . by far the most potent factor in the Anglicisation of our people".[11]

Ryan's reverence for Connolly and Pearse was also apparent, his masthead displaying two quotations in bold print; Connolly's "We Shall Rise Again" and Pearse's "Ní Síothcháin go Saoirse" ("No Peace Without Freedom"). That the paper under Ryan flaunted a devotion to Pearse was sometimes frowned upon by some on the further left of its readership. Frank Edwards, a colleague of the time, recalled when Hanna Sheehy Skeffington started working on the paper with Ryan: "When Frank would be rushing off, he might direct that a blank space be filled with a quotation from Pádraig Pearse. 'I will not,' she would say, 'I have a far more appropriate one here from James Connolly.' They were great in those days for Holy Scripture!"[12]

In retrospect it is astonishing how little republicanism in the 1920s and early 1930s concerned itself with partition.[13] Unlike many who declared themselves to be socialist republicans, Ryan cultivated, in print, a fraternisation with Northern Protestant workers. By his rationale, they would naturally be drawn to separatism from Britain once they recognised that their six-county statelet was an artificial creation maintained only for the benefit of England's interests. He took aim not only at capitalism and the Orange Order for inciting sectarianism, but also at Catholic republicans who derided the majority of Northerners for their "Protestant race and religion". Ryan himself was not wholly innocent. He constantly painted historical analogies dwelling on the lost Gaelic civilisation and the planter/native dichotomy that had intruded in its stead. Knowing well that the ostentatious Catholic fervour exhibited by too many of his colleagues hampered Irish unity,

Ryan tried to recover ground with persistent castigation of religious division. He declared it an injustice perpetrated by "the agents of British Imperialism" who gladly

> . . . sow the seeds of religious hatred. Whatever fan-
> tastic notions may inflame the doped brain of the
> Orange drum-beating pogromist, it is hatred of Irish
> freedom and not Rome that buys new drums for him.
> English Catholic aristocrats are at the back of the
> Orange worker who shouts "To Hell With the Pope."[14]

Ryan, being an IRA man, had been excommunicated during the Civil War, prohibited along with all of his comrades
from receiving the sacraments. There were bitter Civil War
memories in the republican psyche of IRA men being refused
absolution, their corpses being refused entry to churches and
the hierarchy's reticence about Free State atrocities against
captured Irregulars. Yet for the vast bulk of IRA men, allegiance to the Church went arm in arm with republican faith.
Within the republican left, practising Catholics like Ryan were
something of a rarity, but it could be said of him that he possessed the "Irish capacity for opposing the clergy in politics
while considering one's self a loyal son of the Church".[15] He
almost resented the Church for its hold on him, complicating
his activism. So Ryan kept the religious content of *An
Phoblacht* to a minimum while remaining respectful of men of
the cloth – until they became involved in politics. He wrote
condemnatory articles about priests who condemned communists from the pulpit, and he engaged in some very public spats
with prominent bishops who practised political shepherdry.
He argued that, just as *An Phoblacht* never questioned the
religious authority of the Church, the pulpit should not be
used to judge the politics of lay men.

> It is not we, the revolutionary nationalists of Ireland,
> who attack religion; it is those ecclesiastics who seek
> to prostitute religion to material aims using it as it
> was used, for instance, during the war of 1922–23,
> as a lever in the national and social enslavement of
> our people. Nor shall we hesitate to attack any eccle-
> siastic who defends a social system under which a

fraction of the populace rolls in luxury at the expense
of the masses who live in penury.[16]

Double standards were at work though. Ryan's condemnation depended on the direction in which the flock was being
guided. Such clergymen as land agitator Father John Fahy of
Clonfert, and Father Michael O'Flanagan, the veteran Sinn
Féin member, received no opprobrium. "Virtually any
favourable comment from any clergyman was prominently
featured" in the paper.[17] The Church and religion were most
frequently mentioned in the context of Northern sectarianism,
and Ryan supported Catholic clergymen's condemnation of
such sectarianism, a vice that was held to be the preserve of
Protestants. Ryan undoubtedly had the editorial *nous* to know
he could only lose by engaging in slanging matches with the
Church.

However, despite all the personal touches with which Ryan
moulded *An Phoblacht*, the overall content concerned standard IRA issues, and Ryan made clear in his editorial of 26
October 1929 that the paper's primary stance remained
unchanged:

> The Gaeltacht, Land Annuities, Unemployment,
> Irish-Ireland – these and a hundred other issues are
> but subsidiary problems. They take their origin from
> the British conquest of Ireland, and until that con-
> quest is undone in its national, political, economic
> and cultural aspects not one of these other problems,
> important though they be, can find solution.

Ryan had no journalistic pretensions and admitted to his
friend Des Ryan that his was a "propagandist paper".[18] As
propaganda, the journalism in *An Phoblacht* was often predictable, repetitive and simplistic, appealing to the less refined
instincts of nationalists in a pitch occasionally hysterical and
almost always self-righteous. Despite his habit of sometimes
lapsing into romanticism or recalling long-lost heroes from
centuries past, Ryan's expressed opinions remained bald
enough: one editorial concluded that "Reform is impossible.
Must it be Revolution? . . . From the graves of our dead, from
our patriots in prison, from the thousands striving to be free –
one answer comes: IT MUST BE REVOLUTION!"[19]

Such opinions did not enhance Ryan's reputation with the forces of law and order. CID officers regularly kept the paper's office on Exchequer Street under surveillance, and their habitual attempts to arrest the editor without a warrant or a definite charge often flared into violent scenes in the street. On one typical occasion "two CID men held his arms, twisting them. A third held him by the back of the neck, twisting his collar so as to choke him. A fourth kept thumping him in the back."[20] Shots were fired at the window of Ryan's office while he worked.[21] Newsboys and agents regularly had batches of *An Phoblacht* taken from them by the police, and the Fodhla Printing Works, where the copies were run off, was often raided. Perhaps because this printer was too susceptible to raids, being run by an ex-commandant of the Dublin Brigade IRA, Oscar Traynor, a new printer was found. It too was raided and an entire issue seized. Hanna Sheehy Skeffington, who had become assistant editor, often found herself having to run the paper because Ryan had been dragged away and detained by the police. Ryan's infamy among the CID as a diehard was compounded by his perceived intrigues with left-wing radicals. A Department of Justice memo distributed by Police Commissioner Eoin O'Duffy noted that "the tone of that paper indicates some understanding with the communist movement".[22]

Ryan's convictions were not naturally given to mutation, however subtle the shading. "In the pursuit of sordid material aims, the major separatist aim is being lost sight of," Ryan wrote in 1929. "In the practise of parliamentary oratory, the nobler policy of the Fenians is being forgotten."[23] However, there was truth in O'Duffy's report. With the onset of the 1930s, Ryan was starting to fall into step behind those republicans who argued that nationalism alone, without an accompanying political agenda, would not suffice to stir the mass of the people against the existing order. Despite IRA rejection of Peadar O'Donnell's political programme Saor Éire, permission had been granted for members to join groups with political ambitions so as to cast a wider net for militant republicanism. If diehard republicanism and radical socialism individually were insufficiently attractive to the men of no property, their combination might suffice. Red was superimposed on green and vice versa, cynically in some quarters. Therefore the

60

republican left was able to draw from two wells. More importantly, it harboured some very capable and influential men.

In Europe, widespread economic depression after the Great War had allowed socialist ideas to flourish, but Ireland's politics had been distracted by ambitions of independence rather than socialism. Thus far, despite being home to some of Europe's most shameful inner city slums and rural deprivation, Ireland had suffered a paucity of left-leaning mass movements. The Labour Party was perceived as a "small party of moderate non-revolutionary men with little of James Connolly's radicalism about them", and Labour had never attracted either radicals or the middle classes and was now losing small farmers and labourers to Fianna Fáil.[24] At the time of the Treaty the Labour Party had supported Cumann na nGaedheal, whose conservatism and zeal for coercion – in the form of repression of its militant opposition – were now repellent to most Labour voters. By taking a socialist stance, the IRA could occupy a political vacuum, usurping the ground which should have been commanded by the Labour Party.

Certainly, as Cumann na nGaedheal became increasingly reactionary and dependent on repressive coercion laws, the way was eased for socialist proselytisers.[25] Repression of the IRA was perceived as excessive and the government's crying wolf about impending communist revolution while brandishing rosary beads was regarded as hysterical. Police tactics of provocative and indiscriminate harassment of republicans were coming a cropper. After IRA men started to sue their gaolers for wrongful arrest, the police were less inclined to refer cases to the courts, and the illegal activities of the gardaí increased in line with those of the IRA. Those observing the desperation of the forces of law and order might well have drawn the conclusion, just at a time when leftist alternatives were edging their way to the fore of republicanism, that rather than a new government, a new system of government was needed.

The government's lukewarm nationalism was also subject to much criticism. The Treaty had been accepted by the people as a stepping stone toward thirty-two-county sovereignty, but since Cumann na nGaedheal had fumbled the ball during the boundary negotiations, the black line dividing the island had been bolstered. Northern Catholics were a far more vulnerable prey to an entrenched Stormont than to a disinterested Westminster. The blatant failure of the Free State's constitutional politicians as saviours of their Northern kin only strengthened the appeal of radical republicans. It was often said that little had changed since the departure of the British except the colour of the letterboxes.

Under Cumann na nGaedheal's leadership since 1923, the nation had not prospered, and as the tidal wave of the Great Depression hit Ireland's shores in 1930, the poor country could only become poorer. Ireland's potential for prosperity once it had rid itself of British shackles had been a selling point of nationalism for hundreds of years. This potential had plainly not been realised. The apparent demise of capitalism engendered by the Wall Street Crash in October 1929 further strengthened the appeal of the left.

Diehards were beyond the constitutional Pale anyway, so aligning themselves with red revolutionaries was not such a huge leap. By such routes, militant republicans found themselves involved in industrial strikes, rural land agitation and tenant leagues in city slums. When the Workers' Revolutionary Party was set up in 1930, almost half of its founding committee of seventy members were IRA men, while the republican women's group Cumann na mBan was noted for being now "permeated with red ideas".[26]

The numbers of more or less communist groups attracting members of the IRA which sprang up or were revived made an exhaustive list, but the list was not as impressive as it may have seemed.[27] Not only were many groups short-lived or poorly supported, but they often shared the same membership and regularly merged. If conservatives were appalled at the prospect of foreign-influenced, dynamite-toting radicals on the rampage through God-fearing Ireland, the Department of Justice was somewhat perplexed:

> . . . the extremist movement is a strange mixture of political revolutionaries and social revolutionaries. There will be found in the same organisation intellectuals living on the dividends of the capitalist system and corner boys who have no other driving force behind them than discontent with their position in life. It is also of interest to note that much the same

people appear to be behind several organisations . . .
The number of these revolutionary organisations, all
of which have something in common, is bewildering
and each week so to speak, gives birth to the new
ones.[28]

Recognition that the membership of the groups greatly
overlapped and consequently wasn't that much greater than
the number of organisations themselves was a double-edged
sword; while it may have reassured the government of the
paucity of revolutionaries, it also suggested a conspiracy
unprecedented in its range and organisation.

Ryan was connected, either by membership or association,
with many of the new organisations, but particularly the
League Against Imperialism (LAI). In April 1929, as secretary
of the Irish chapter, he was "warmly received" at the League's
international conference in Birmingham. There he pronounced
Connolly and Pearse steadfast anti-imperialists rather than
haters of England and said that the conference "was the first
occasion when Irishmen and Englishmen met to further a
struggle for the dissolution of the British Empire. Irishmen . . .
now see that they have only succeeded in replacing English
Imperial rulers by Irish Imperial rulers and their hatred of England has altered its form to hatred of Imperialism."[29]

By November 1929, Ryan's Armistice Day demonstrations
were benefiting from his involvement in the LAI and had
become a magnet for anyone objecting to imperialism in principle, British or otherwise. In oratory and article, Ryan was
always at pains to stress that he understood fully the wishes
of those who celebrated Armistice Day as a gesture to those
lost during the Great War. Indeed, Ryan himself lamented the
sacrifice of so many Irishmen on the battlefields of France,
misled into fighting for one empire against another. What he
considered an affront was the homage paid to the British military tradition. The flaunting of medals, regimental colours
and Union Jacks sneered at those who had died or suffered at
the hands of British soldiers until so recently, and those who
continued to do so in the six counties of the North. The
demonstrations were held annually on the eve of Armistice
Day. An editorial in *An Phoblacht* had the stamp of Ryan,
giving notice to

... a small but noisy section of the British garrison which seeks each year to turn Armistice Day into an occasion of imperialist propaganda. These people think that under police protection they can safely outrage our national sentiment by flaunting the flag of our oppressor and singing the anthem of the country which holds us in subjection. We warn them once again – we are not for trouble but if they invite trouble they will get it.[30]

The 1929 Armistice and Anti-Imperialist rallies passed off without serious incident, perhaps because of the huge police presence but more probably because a cloudburst recommended postponement until the following day. Ryan remained ardent come rain or come shine. He "advised militant methods for Anti-Imperialists on Armistice Day. Imperialist blockheads, he contended, are not by nature susceptible to argument; they are susceptible to fear and must be made feel fear."[31] The speeches were concluded with the setting of a torch to a Union Jack.

India's fight against colonialism, subject of so many of Ryan's editorials, was of particular interest to the Irish branch of the LAI, and in September 1930 Ryan chaired a public meeting featuring the Indian communist, Krishna Deonarine. It attracted an audience of 1,200, from whom Ryan, at the end of the meeting, elicited three cheers for Indian freedom followed by three more for the Workers' Revolutionary Groups and a rendition of the "Red Flag". However, despite the links with international communism, Ryan did not consider himself to be driven by alien influence of Marx or Engels, but rather by the radical tradition planted and nurtured at home by Wolfe Tone and handed down through James Fintan Lalor and Connolly. The ideas and ideals rising to prominence in the IRA were far more palatable to its rank and file when dressed up as a domestic recipe for social and economic revolution.

These left-wing ideas were less palatable in America though. Many of the Irish-American fundraising clubs were now supporting Fianna Fáil, the chief exception being Clan na Gael. The Clan's figurehead, Joseph McGarrity, was unwavering in his efforts to provide money, arms and hospitality for IRA men in the US, and he was in contact regularly with senior republicans of all shades. However, repeated implications from IRA HQ that armed revolution was just over the next hill were more optimistic than they were honest, and were often bloated with self-importance. The mixture of suggestion and half-truths smacked of the messages sent over the Atlantic by the Fenians seventy years previously.

McGarrity was aware that there was a movement within the IRA to establish a political wing, but he and the majority of the Clan disapproved, having given their allegiance to the extra-constitutionalists rather than Fianna Fáil precisely because they retained faith in armed force. When he was informed, only after the event, of IRA men's sojourns in Russia, the traditionalist McGarrity was furious that the Clan had not been consulted.

Therefore the choice of Frank Ryan as the IRA's representative to America for the Clan na Gael Convention and Easter commemorations in 1930 might seem puzzling. Ryan was increasingly drawn to the leftist, ideologically based minority within the IRA, even lending his hesitant support to Saor Éire the previous year, for example. McGarrity and another venerated Clan figurehead, the octogenarian Fenian Luke Dillon, opposed this political minority. Still, Ryan was only a sympathiser rather than a leader, and it was presumably for his abilities as a speaker that he was selected. Clan members who knew him thought him "the best speaker in Ireland and he should be a great drawing card and render invaluable service to the cause here".[32] He did not disappoint.

There were in America probably tens of thousands of former IRA men and sympathisers, driven there by political disillusion, government harassment or plain poverty. Audiences and enthusiasm flooded venues for Ryan's addresses at commemorations in New York and in over a dozen other cities.[33] He started his tour in New York at the Clan na Gael convention at the Hamden Theatre, Broadway, on the night of Easter Sunday. After a reading of the Easter 1916 Proclamation, Ryan thanked Irish-America for all the support it had provided, from the days of the Fenians until the present "peace imposed by bayonets". To safeguard against the Clan's being appeased now that there was an Irish government in Dublin, the bulk of his speech was directed against "those renegades who hold Ireland for the British Empire". Members of Clan na Gael who might lean toward Fianna Fáil were told that constitutionalists were "timid" and that the only remedy for republicanism was physical force. Despondency need not be entertained thanks to "the growing strength of the physical force movement and the unmistakable signs of its extending popularity . . . We can say in truth today that in every county of Ireland, in the north-east as well as in the South, the Irish Republican Army is maintained and organised." Ryan concluded with an appeal for continued support, declaring that the "Irish race – not merely the Irish people – must be united in the great fight".

It was an impressive fund-raising speech containing nothing that might ruffle the golden goose's feathers. It was certainly true that IRA activity had been stepped up, even if it took only the form of a much heightened tit-for-tat war between itself and the police rather than revolution. But if Ryan's speech did not convey any untruths, it did not reveal the whole truth either. The closest he came to informing his audience of the ascension of left-wing ideologues in the movement was indirect, brief and cloaked by his "Pearse and Connolly" mantra:

> Our aim is the complete overthrow of the two British Governments in Ireland as a preliminary to abolishing the present social system which impoverishes Ireland and its people. That unjust system must be replaced by one on the lines laid down by Connolly and Pearse in 1916 – a system under which all citizens shall have equal rights and opportunities.[34]

Ryan had private meetings with Irish groups and made contacts with men who would be allies within the left-wing IRA for years to come.[35] He was delighted not only to meet P.J. Tynan, ex-leader of the Invincibles, but to discover that the sprightly nonagenarian was a weekly reader of *An Phoblacht*. In Springfield, Mass., Ryan laughed when he heard that only a couple of weeks earlier, a lecture by Eoin MacNeill, now minister for education, had been broken up by IRA supporters. Ryan made time to give a radio broadcast on "The Ideals of the Young Men of Ireland", referring to Kevin Barry and others who were ever an inspiration: recent commemorations had "reasserted the allegiance of Ireland's youth to the cause of the 1916 revolutionaries . . . With them, let you, exiles of Ireland, pledge yourselves." The subject, according to New York's *Irish Echo* newspaper, which published a transcript, was handled in a "masterly manner and presented a view of the present state of Ireland that the American public knows little of".[36] Hectic though his schedule was, he found time to visit his brother John, who was living then in upstate New York.

Although he expressed no desire to stay there longer than he had to – "I wouldn't live here if I was paid to" – Ryan was clearly fascinated by America. When he wrote to his family in Limerick, he told them not only about the down and outs in New York's Bowery but also about aspects of daily life that seemed to cause him much consternation:

> At meals you first chop up all your food, then eat with a fork. You eat bread too, cutting it up in your fist (You don't get a plate for it). And, mind you, that's the fashion. The newspapers here are a terrible size. You'd hardly be able to carry home the Weekend, or the Sunday editions they are so heavy . . . The drug store is another queer institution here. In it you can buy everything from a stamp to a decent meal. The chemist's part of it is only a sideline. Undertakers' places are called funeral parlors! All bodies are embalmed: men (Catholics included) are buried in dress suits and women in evening dress. The coffins are beautiful.[37]

Ryan also learned that ferrying propaganda across the Atlantic worked both ways. Back in Ireland, his articles stressed the allegiance of Irish America to diehard republicanism and claimed that "in America the timid constitutionalist has little sway". His reflections on the futility of Irish emigration to a country spinning in the vortex of economic depression were more earnest. He wrote of the destitute who "demonstrate on the street to be met with batons instead of the bread they seek. Of that multitude of the hungry, a large percentage is Irish."[38] Distinguished propagandist and silver-tongued fund-raiser that Ryan may have been, the distress he felt was sincere:

In Broadway church at early Mass one can count Irish faces by the score. Young Irish lads, some of them still wearing the clothes in which a little while ago they walked an Irish road to Sunday Mass. In the city trains you can pick them out by the dozen too, as they go to and come from work. And – oh God! the tragedy of it – one sees others of them standing stolidly in the soup lines or waiting for hours their turn for a meal. There are some Irish homes that will wait in vain for the American money that is needed to pay the rent.[39]

Despite Ryan's upset at the human fallout of the Wall Street Crash, it is not too cynical to wonder did he, in his heart of burgeoning socialist hearts, get some vindication, or even gratification, from seeing the home of capitalism reeling from such a devastating body blow. Had he still possessed any faith in free market economics it was surely quashed.

While Ryan was in the US, Peadar O'Donnell had led the fusion of the IRA and the newly established Workers' Revolutionary Party (WRP). The honeymoon was short. The communists were not long in accusing their new republican comrades of being insufficiently radical, and the war of words that soon commenced between the communist *Workers' Voice* and Ryan, via *An Phoblacht,* was typical of the fraught relationship. For, primarily, Ryan was still a physical force republican, albeit to the left of the IRA rank and file, and his lingering traditionalism limited his zeal for left-wing or political solutions to republican problems.

Peadar O'Donnell and Dave Fitzgerald drew up revised plans for Saor Éire as a more overtly political rallying point for republicanism that could counter the attraction of Fianna Fáil. During its incubation, Ryan had his reservations:

While political action, organisation and agitation would undoubtedly assist [revolutionary aims] considerably, the problem we are confronted with is essentially military. No mere agitation or expounding of theories or principles can effectively achieve the aim of overthrowing the present order and setting up the Workers' Republic.[40]

The Fusion of Green and Red 1929–1930

Republicans such as Ryan who considered themselves to be socialists were unsure that Saor Éire was a wise tactical move, as it might only drive members from the IRA and lose it the support of conservative sympathisers. However, as momentum for a political dimension to the IRA grew, so did Ryan's support. Caught in the balance, however, between approval and rejection, his position and trumpet-tongued nature ensured a stream of contradictory pronouncements regarding the viability of Saor Éire. He was shrewd enough to use *An Phoblacht* to test republican waters, and perhaps to even help himself decide which way to jump. It was under the editorship of Ryan that Saor Éire was debated and his readers encouraged to declare either "yea" or "nay". He also made pointed references to the motives of Saor Éire that were particularly consistent with IRA principles, as if bracing his readership for a change of tack. In October *An Phoblacht* declared for a workers' republic, pointing to the aims of Tone and Emmet, Mitchel and Lalor, Pearse and Connolly for justification: "In the light of present day conditions, these aims can be interpreted as a Workers' Republic for the 32 counties of Ireland, Gaelic in nature, independent of international capitalism, by virtue of the development of its own resources, in no way allied to, or committed with, the British or any other empire."[41]

In November *An Phoblacht* published the ideas of O'Donnell and Fitzgerald as filtered through IRA Chief of Staff Moss Twomey, who, writing as Manus Ó Ruairc, proposed "Suggestions for a Constitution for an Irish Republic" and invited responses from the readership for its improvement. That Twomey's proposal was forwarded under a pen-name is significant, exposing his trepidation that the proposal might be rejected wholeheartedly. The draft constitution was indeed a radical departure for the IRA. Capitalism was to be overthrown, and banks and the means of production and transport were to be commandeered by the state to be run according to the needs of the people rather than the demands of the market. The proposed Saor Éire *Constitution and Rules* claimed that malcontents of town and country would "realise that their interests are mutual and therefore they should be allies, as they are all victims of the same exploiting agency". Thus would the masses mobilise behind a "revolutionary government for the

overthrow of British imperialism in Ireland and the organisation of a workers' and working farmers' Republic".[42]

There were, predictably, not a few dissensions, from those
who derided Saor Éire as divisive and superfluous.[43] For some
IRA men the new project was a diversion from physical force,
for others it was anti-Christian and for others again, such as
Micháel Ó Faoláin, it was "too advanced . . . a declaration of
socialism in one of its most extreme forms".[44] Nevertheless, it
seemed that the majority of the IRA leadership were willing to
give Saor Éire their approval, albeit without much enthusiasm
and probably for the wrong reasons. Even the politically moderate Moss Twomey had become a convert. The wary were
persuaded that Saor Éire might win over to revolutionary
republicanism the mass support of the disaffected. This strategy essentially meant that the membership of the IRA should
support Saor Éire not for what it was in itself but for what it
might do for the Irish Republican Army; successful or not, the
strategy barely demanded loyalty to the new departure.

Despite his purported socialism, Ryan still viewed the politics of Saor Éire as being too divergent from his own brand of
unembellished republicanism. His restrained optimism for
Saor Éire precluded his becoming an architect or founder
member of the project. Besides, he was busy enough, with
more than a few demands on his time. The Armistice Day
demonstration in 1930 was the biggest yet, with a formidable
array of speakers on the platform. Described by Seán
MacBride as a "Republican *Who's Who*",[45] it included de
Valera and Ryan himself, who turned on "those in Ireland who
want to honour their king . . . From them not two minutes'
silence merely, but perpetual silence".[46] In the by now traditional rioting that followed, police fired shots to disperse a
menacing crowd that had bombarded them with missiles. The
protest culminated with "baton charges, Union Jack burnings,
bloody heads and filled jail cells".[47]

Ryan's constituency was the street. There is little in his writing to suggest that he was a distinctly original political thinker,
and the drawing up of manifestos or constitutions was left to
the brains in the back room, O'Donnell and Fitzgerald. In
Ryan's work at *An Phoblacht*, there is far more emphasis on
the need for martial prowess to regain for Ireland her four
green fields than on economics or governmental structure.

That he once told Hanna Sheehy Skeffington "my experience so far has been that intellectuals are a funky lot" indicates that he was still not enamoured of expending his time in meetings dedicated to the finer points of implementing the socialist republic he demanded.[48] Loaded rifles rather than academic resolutions were his preferred agency. Ryan was a man of action, visceral and passionate, an agitator who had the personality and oratorical dynamism that inspired in others fervency and fidelity to his causes. He retained a traditionalism, long abandoned by his leftist comrades, that kept one boot in the camp of the diehard conservatives while the other stepped on to the road of political experimentation. In December 1930 he was still deriding "quack remedies" of political agitation and "stepping stone" policies for advancement, demanding that "we rank and file republicans get down to first principles".[49] Any dilution of the republican ethos was suspect, and compromise, however expedient, always smacked of weak will. The sincerity with which Ryan held his beliefs prevented his becoming a political dilettante, and his faith in socialism could only grow steadily and slowly.

Ryan may have used his weight in IRA HQ to push Saor Éire, but who is to say that the source of its endorsement in *An Phoblacht* was not a memo from IRA leadership rather than Ryan's personal sanction? He did not own the paper, and it could be claimed – improbably, given his personality and later events – that Ryan was only the dummy for the ventriloquist leadership. It is hard to measure the depth of Ryan's approval for Saor Éire, but as an IRA officer and employed propagandist, his personal opinions were subservient to HQ's command.

At its convention in Glendalough in April 1931, the IRA Army Council adopted the programme of Saor Éire and "was on its way to becoming firmly embroiled in radical politics, bringing on the censure and condemnation of Irish conservatives".[50]

Notes to Chapter Three

1. That the meeting was disrupted by right-wingers and Blueshirts came no surprise; what was surprising was that Donnelly "managed to get the Blueshirts out of the building. They put up their knuckle-dusters and, under the protection of Frank Ryan, slipped down the stairs and away." Quoted in Joseph O'Connor, *Even the Olives Are Bleeding* (Dublin: New Island Books, 1992), p. 37.
2. *An Phoblacht,* 14 June 1930.
3. Forces Inimical to the State, Department of Justice files, NAI, Jus8/682.
4. *An Phoblacht,* 8 August 1931.
5. Quoted in Seám Cronin, *Frank Ryan: The Search for the Republic* (Dublin: Repsol, 1980), p. 25.
6. The editors wrote a large amount of copy themselves.
7. Rosamond Jacob papers, NLI, 33/130.
8. *An Phoblacht,* 1 November 1930.
9. However, as a show of defiance from a language hardliner, one of Ryan's last front pages of the newspaper was covered with an article about the importance, politically and culturally, of maintaining the language. *An Phoblacht,* 17 March 1933.
10. Quoted in Cronin, *Frank Ryan,* p. 17.
11. *An Phoblacht,* 17 January 1931.
12. Uinseann Mac Eoin, *Survivors* (Dublin: Argenta, 1980), p. 11.
13. It was more concerned with the Oath of Allegiance and Cumann na nGaedheal's perceived pandering to the Empire. By the decade's end, the stiffening of Irish-Ireland resolve following the collapse of the Boundary Commission and the shift in emphasis to an island-wide brotherhood of small farmers and urban workers provided the foundation for a bridge between Southern diehards and Northern socialists. The trade union movement was the only body that had been able to transcend the black line of partition with any degree of success.
14. *An Phoblacht,* 17 January 1931.
15. J.H. Whyte, *Church and State in Modern Ireland* (Dublin: Gill & Macmillan, 1971), p. 40.
16. *An Phoblacht,* 18 October 1930.
17. James P. McHugh, *Voices of the Rearguard: A Study of* An Phoblacht *– Irish Republican Thought in the Post-Revolutionary Era,* Unpublished MA thesis, UCD, 1986, p. 426.
18. Desmond Ryan papers, UCDAD, LA 10/Q/19 (1).
19. *An Phoblacht,* 2 November 1929.
20. *Ibid.,* 7 December 1929.
21. Ryan thought it to be the work of British *fascisti* abetted by Free Staters, possibly the police.

22. Quoted in Mary Banta, *The Red Scare in the Irish Free State*, Unpublished MA thesis, UCD, 1982, p. 20.
23. *An Phoblacht*, 20 July 1929.
24. K.B. Nowlan in F. McManus (ed.), *The Years of the Great Test 1926–1939* (Cork: Mercier, 1967), p. 9.
25. O'Higgins himself had declared that the cabinet of which he was a member comprised the world's most conservative revolutionaries.
26. Quoted in Conor Foley, *Legion of the Rearguard* (London: Pluto, 1992), p. 85.
27. Among them the Irish Working Farmers' Congress, Irish Labour Defence League, Workers International Relief, Communist Party of Ireland, Workers' Revolutionary Party, Irish National Unemployed Movement, Irish Workers' and Farmers' Republican Party and the Women's International League for Peace and Freedom.
28. Department of Justice Memorandum on Revolutionary Organizations, NAI, S 5864, 5 April 1930.
29. *The Nation*, 13 April 1929.
30. *An Phoblacht*, 9 November 1929.
31. *Ibid.*, 16 November 1929.
32. Joseph McGarrity papers, NLI, 17/467.
33. Ryan's tour included Boston, Butte, Chicago, Philadelphia, San Francisco, Buffalo, Detroit, Worcester, Minneapolis, Springfield, Waterbury, Hartford, Cleveland and Cincinnati. Even though his tour was extended, lack of time led to further dates being cancelled.
34. *An Phoblacht*, 10 May 1930.
35. Particularly IRA veterans Gerald O'Reilly from Navan and Kerryman Mike Quill, who would go on to found the Transport Workers' Union of America.
36. *An Phoblacht*, 14 June 1930. Clan na Gael must have doctored Ryan's credentials somewhat, as he was introduced over air as being from the National University of Ireland.
37. Quoted in Cronin, *Frank Ryan*, pp. 29–30.
38. *An Phoblacht*, 2 August 1930.
39. *Ibid.*, 16 August 1930.
40. *Ibid.*
41. *Ibid.*, 25 October 1930.
42. Department of the Taoiseach files, NAI, S 5864A.
43. One observer remembers that the more hostile of the IRA commanders "never missed an opportunity to sabotage the young growth. For instance, the vast majority of the Battalion OCs classified themselves as right-wing and availed themselves of the authority to call parades, courses or classes on the nights or days

when he knew that members of his battalion were wanted for work within their areas with Saor Éire." Quoted in J. Bowyer Bell, *The Secret Army; The IRA* (Dublin: Poolbeg, 1998), p. 82.

44. *An Phoblacht,* 16 May 1931.
45. Mac Eoin, *Survivors*, p. 122.
46. *An Phoblacht,* 15 November 1930.
47. Bowyer Bell, *The Secret Army*, p. 90.
48. Hanna Sheehy Skeffington papers, MS 33/607 (9).
49. *An Phoblacht,* 13 December 1930.
50. Banta, *The Red Scare*, p. 25.

CHAPTER FOUR

The Red Scare and a New Regime

Police Commissioner Eoin O'Duffy was a busy man, and by 1931 he was reaching the end of his rather short tether. Overseeing the surveillance of subversives and containing their activities had been his responsibility since 1925, but his rather breathless demands for extra powers from the Department of Justice had, as often as not, been only acknowledged and passed on to various ministers. The steady drip of O'Duffy's alarmism grew to a torrent. In a report titled "Organisations Inimical to the State", O'Duffy informed his superiors that his detectives were on the offensive against "the Irregulars and kindred organisations which were harried by continuous supervision and detentions". He claimed that rural IRA activity had decreased but, pinpointing Ryan as a prominent member, he declared that

> In Dublin a small and vicious gang is still to the fore
> . . . These men are still a nasty problem. They give
> their whole time and a great deal of energy to . . . help
> to maintain the organisation by the commission of
> acts of violence and intimidation . . . The attacks on
> jurors from an Irregular point of view has been a
> complete success.

In the same report, O'Duffy explained that impending implosion of law and order was a consequence of impotent policemen risking their lives only to be humiliated by the IRA – or far worse. During the two months prior to the report's issue, Detective Tadgh O'Sullivan in Clare had been murdered and an IRA informer had simply vanished. That Frank Ryan had been nowhere near Clare at the time did not exclude him and his journalism from culpability.

> Take *An Phoblacht*. It openly advocates a doctrine of hate and violence against the police. Ryan occupied half the paper with false and malicious reports under scare headings in regard to police methods in Clare and now he is laying the ground for even worse murders and dope. The young men who look on him as a super-patriot, and reading this doctrine, cannot be blamed if they consider it a duty to kill policemen – it is a definite incitement to crime.[1]

Ryan's oratory was also a regular feature of police reports, in which he was quoted at flattering length, particularly when he spoke of police collusion with imperialists and his determination and that of his comrades to "meet baton with baton".[2] Files documented, as far as they were able, his barely legal activities. The police continued to dog and detain Ryan, but they were frustrated by their inability to bring him before a jury, possibly intimidated, on charges, possibly trumped up, that he might be convicted of. The fleet of foot, law-savvy, left-wing diehard Irregular embodied all that was driving O'Duffy to exasperation.

In a comprehensive report titled "Revolutionary Organisations", O'Duffy once again noted of *An Phoblacht* that "the cumulative force of its constant incitements to violence" should not be under-appreciated. He fingered Ryan as being in the vanguard of Comhairle na Poblachta, which was "composed of the most virulent, active extremists in the country whose sole object is the overthrow of the state by force of arms".[3] This description of the toothless and almost defunct Comhairle was typical of O'Duffy: while the commissioner certainly had cause for concern, his case was regularly overstated regardless. O'Duffy credited the disparate strands of republicanism and socialism with more unity than they possessed, thereby facilitating his portrayal of them as a single conspiratorial entity. This made them a consummate target. Few in government likened Dublin in 1931 to St Petersburg fifteen years previously, yet there was enough evidence to suggest that O'Duffy's bloated accounts of conspiracy contained some truth.

In January 1931, Dublin IRA man P.J. Carroll was shot twice in the head and a grenade then detonated under him, blowing away half his skull. An editorial in *An Phoblacht* on 14 February explained that Carroll had been "executed by the IRA" as a traitor. Two months later Superintendent Sean Curtin was shot dead outside his home by the south Tipperary IRA after he had tried to curtail local IRA drilling and exercises through the courts. A few months later, two men called to the house of another local man, John Ryan, whom Curtin had intended calling as a witness. The three walked off together. Ryan's body was later found with a note attached: "Spies and informers beware." In April, walkers in the Dublin Mountains were shot at and wounded by an IRA patrol that thought they had been trailed by plainclothes police. A subsequent raid on the nearby home of George Gilmore unearthed a trove of armoury including a machine-gun, thirty rifles and fifteen revolvers. Gilmore, a prominent left-wing republican and close associate of Ryan's, was famous in the 1920s for organising republican prison breaks but soon found himself in Mountjoy on illegal arms charges.

The Easter IRA commemorations that year were far more conspicuous and better attended than they had been in years. Frank Ryan's graveside duties at the funeral of IRA man Mick McLaughlin in Leitrim were besieged by policemen armed with machine-guns. The government prohibited the annual Wolfe Tone commemoration at Bodenstown, cancelled the trains serving it and, on its eve, arrested the chief speaker, Sean Russell, along with any other members of IRA HQ they could get their hands on. In the face of up to 20,000 pilgrims who nonetheless arrived, the police and soldiers detailed to enforce the prohibition were powerless to do anything other than watch the parades and listen to Peadar O'Donnell's oration.

Ryan was not at Bodenstown in June, nor had he been arrested the night previously. He and Cumann na mBan had organised a protest march to Mountjoy in support of George and Charlie Gilmore and other Irregulars who had just come off a hunger strike, protesting their treatment. On the speakers' platform outside the jail, Ryan had been given enough time to greet his audience with the words "*A cháirde, táimid anseo anois – brostuigh iad!"* ("Friends, we are come together here now – rush them!") before the attendant police stormed the platform with their batons aloft, dragged off the four on it and charged the protestors. The members of Cumann na mBan held their ground before marching to Cathal Brugha Street where a gathering of thousands were told what had happened.

Ryan meanwhile was now the recipient of the kind of treatment that he had been arrested for protesting against in the first place. He refused to recognise the court, then was sentenced to one month's imprisonment for sedition and two for contempt of court, to be served concurrently. *An Phoblacht* was left in the capable but overworked hands of Hanna Sheehy Skeffington and an anxious printer.[4]

Released in August, Ryan was interviewed in his *An Phoblacht* office by the *Daily Express* journalist Lesley Randall. Randall had spent a week haggling with underground contacts before he finally met the "B.A. of Dublin and an ex-schoolmaster, whom I knew by repute as one of the most notorious rebels in Dublin". Randall could not have been more delighted with his scoop. He declared that Ryan was forthright in answers to questions that the more discreet would dodge, spoke "with a freedom that staggered me" and had no objection to his name being used. Ryan's indiscretions unleashed furies that would descend upon himself, the IRA and the whole country.

He assured his interviewer that the IRA did not undertake executions lightly and he resented their being called murders or assassinations as they were "acts of war". As such, each was justified specifically by Ryan. For example, Superintendent John Curtin, who had been shot dead outside his home in Tipperary, had "exceeded his duty. He went out of his way to persecute the IRA." John Ryan, the witness Curtin had intended to call, "was nothing but a traitor". The bomb placed under Carroll, "the *agent provocateur*", was that which he had given to an IRA colleague for his entrapment: "Who can say that Carroll did not meet with his deserts if his head was blown off with one of his own bombs." Traitors could not be tolerated, "but there are fewer in our ranks than anywhere else. Almost every day our men are offered bribes to betray us to the police."

Ryan's comments were indicative of IRA policy in that the

IRA's choice of victims was more selective than might be thought, but Ryan had inadvertently cast light on the IRA's military and strategic deficiency. The IRA was not capable of more than tit-for-tat murders; despite the chaos seeming to drown the country, it was not in a position to launch anything like a frontal assault on the Cumann na nGaedheal government.

Yet Ryan was not lacking in bravado. He claimed that unlike overly zealous Civic Guards, CID men were respected for "only doing what they are paid for". He also told Randall that

> "There are three armed detectives watching this office at the moment." Mr Ryan went over to the window and looked down into the busy street. "I have only to give the word," he said, "and every CID man would be wiped off the streets of Dublin tonight. It is not fear that holds us back." I believe that when Frank Ryan said this he was saying nothing more than what he believed to be the truth.

Ryan also touched on the shift in IRA tactics, although without describing it as such. It was no longer up to a righteous minority to act on the behalf of a vacillating majority. Ryan alleged that "we represent the majority of the Irish nation . . . one of these days there will be crowds in the street and they will not be disturbed by baton charges". His other predictions are interesting: "England will be engaged in another great war soon. Then she will try to take advantage of the provisions of the Treaty for garrisoning ports in Ireland. That will be the end of England's rule in Ireland."[5]

Exactly how accurate Randall was in his reportage of Ryan's comments is unknown. Bellicose and brash Ryan certainly could be, but stupid he was not. Even so, if the interview was not true to the literal words of the man, it was true to his spirit at the time. Ryan's comments caused a national furore, outraging the government and many others besides, and dropped the man himself into the eye of a raging storm.

A week or so later, Ryan left his office on a Friday at lunchtime, having completed the copy for the following day's edition. Its editorial had accused Justice Minister Fitzgerald

Kenny of directing "a campaign of incitement to civil war . . . Fitzgerald Kenny relies on the gun. Judging by the temper of the people it may be that he will be hoisted with his own petard."[6] Out in the street, officers from the Special Branch pounced on Ryan and dragged him to a nearby car. He was brought to Bridewell Station without warrant or charge before being brought up before a Mr Hannan, who remanded him in custody until the following Tuesday. When Hannan volunteered the information that bail would be refused, Ryan replied that he had "never given bail in my life and I am not going to begin now".[7] His objection that he could not be held without charge met with no answer, and he was taken to Mountjoy. The following week the state prosecutor's demand, at the insistence of Superintendent Peter Ennis, that Ryan be charged under the Seditious Libel Act was rejected by the judge as it would need a jury court. Frantic whisperings followed, debating what exactly Ryan could be tried for. It was not uncommon for republicans to be taken and held before an appropriate charge could be conjured up. The next tack was to have him bound over to keep the peace in the hope that, as Ryan would not recognise the court or produce sureties, he would be returned to Mountjoy. The judge refused and the prey was set free.

Under the title "*An Phoblacht Abú*", the subsequent week's editorial described how Ennis and his men had arrived at Fodhla Printers just as that edition was going to press. However, "this new attempt at police interference and censorship of the press will be met as all previous attempts at *An Phoblacht* have been met and defeated". Ryan taunted his persecutors: "If our paper breaks the British laws, why, let us be prosecuted! If we tell the truth too openly, let them suppress us!" He promised that his "readers may be reassured on this point. *An Phoblacht* carries on in spite of hog, dog or devil".[8] As evidence of police censorship, as if any were needed, the columns that had been filled with Cumann na mBan articles banned by Ennis as seditious were left blank. The mutilated copies were the only ones for sale, as all others had been seized.

There appeared to be great momentum building in the country in support of Saor Éire. Most of the public only knew of its policies in a very general way, but widespread civil disturbances were taken by the IRA to be expressions of public favour. The mass movement strategies of Mellows and O'Donnell were being vindicated. If the IRA decided that it was time for Saor Éire to emerge into the daylight of public debate, that is partly because Cumann na nGaedheal's denunciations of "the definite union of the IRA with communism in this state" demanded a counter-attack.[9] In September, Fitzgerald Kenny declared that republicans aimed to "force, by means of threats and crimes of violence, a republic of Soviet nature on this country. They are a minority but they want to ensure their Soviet views, by brute force, and we say we will not allow them."[10] It was even claimed that *An Phoblacht* was kept alive only by the injection of Muscovite roubles as it "is not a sound commercial proposition".[11] As something of a slight on Ryan's distribution and sales drives, it added insult to *An Phoblacht*'s injuries.

It was not only the government that the IRA had to protect Saor Éire, its maligned infant, from. The government decided that the enlistment of a more than willing Church hierarchy into their ranks would help quell the rising tide of disorder. On 11 September 1931, which happened to be Frank Ryan's 29th birthday, Cosgrave provided Cardinal Joseph MacRory in Armagh with clippings from *An Phoblacht* editorials to support the intelligence that those conspiring to overthrow the government were funded for by organisations "which have their headquarters in, and are controlled by, Russia". Cosgrave also handed over personal details of all those involved in the "the principle organ of this conspiracy", the full transcript of Ryan's *Daily Express* interview and intercepted Saor Éire papers. As only the guiding light of the Church "will be able to prevail in the struggle", it was respectfully suggested "whether the most effective manner for dealing with the most pernicious tendencies which are sapping the bases of all authority in this country would not be a joint Episcopal action in the form of a concise statement in the law of the Church in relation to the present issues, and the penalties attached to its violation".[12]

In the event, Cosgrave hardly needed to wait for MacRory's reply. Within days, two shootings by the IRA in Clare ignited the rage of Dr Michael Fogarty, Bishop of Killaloe. Denouncing the "Bolshevik attacks" from the pulpit, he contended that "religion is at stake".[13] Ireland's major newspapers, with the exception of the de Valera-founded *Irish Press*, beat their drums to the Church/state tune. Indeed, were it not so deferential to the government and the Church, the *Irish Independent* could have been accused of trying to upstage the two in the use of bombast. Headlines declaring "Pope Attacked at Meetings" must have alarmed the more literal-minded of its readers, who were warned of the "Anti-God Forces in Dublin". The "Irreligionists and communists have been taking advantage of the liberty granted under the Free State Constitution", claimed the paper, citing a warning to "guard against pernicious doctrines now being preached not only by foreign emissaries, but by native malcontents".[14]

The public unveiling of Saor Éire came with its first national convention on the last weekend of September 1931. Overcoming police harassment and the reluctance of hall managers to be associated with the heathen reds, a prayer led by the chairman Sean Hayes opened the convention to 120 delegates. Frank Ryan was not on the Executive, but reports of the convention in *An Phoblacht* spared no optimism or zeal for the venture. Typically, Ryan framed the principle review, "The Clarion Call of Saor Éire", around an inserted transcript of the 1916 Proclamation of Independence, simultaneously paying personal homage to his forebears while sweetening for readers a Marx-tinged interpretation of Ireland's recent history.[15]

The government reacted quickly to the public unveiling of the IRA's socialist manifesto. Prompted by Eoin O'Duffy's suggestion that certain persons should be placed "in a position uninfluenced by the constitutional rights of citizenship, where their activities can be met by suitable action", Cosgrave now effectively laid the groundwork for the introduction of martial law.[16] On 14 October, the president struck the spark to fight fire with legal fire. Article 2A was inserted into the Constitution with the introduction of a Public Safety Bill: certain organisations could be proscribed, the courts would be replaced by military tribunals with the power to impose the death penalty, and police powers against those under suspicion were greatly extended.

No doubt aware that the severity of the "coercion bill" would be challenged, Cosgrave gave a lengthy speech in the Dáil in its defence. Referring to the "widely organised conspiracy to overthrow by force the Constitution and

Government of the State", Cosgrave declared "this time the menace must be removed once and for all". He then got down to specifics, and said that anyone doubting the validity of his claim

> has only got to read the principle organ of the conspiracy, the weekly paper calling itself *An Phoblacht*, which week in and week out preaches the doctrine of the conspirators . . . These doctrines are preached with a directness, with a continuous incitement to violence and crime, which I do not believe has a parallel in any other State in the world.

Cosgrave's speech-writer must have been a more avid reader of the paper than the sturdiest diehard, as the president went on to quote from no less than nine of the paper's editorials to illustrate its truculence. The litany of Ryan's seditious incitements continued when Cosgrave moved on to the *Daily Express* and read out in full the interview Ryan had given as "an example of the ideas that spring from perverted patriotism and ignorance of fundamental Christian teaching".[17]

Ryan was well aware that his interview had stoked indignation within the government, but can he be blamed for having brought about coercion? Years later, Gerald Boland, who was minister of justice later in the decade, told the writer Tim Pat Coogan that "it was [the *Daily Express*] interview which led the Department of Justice to advise Cosgrave to reintroduce the military tribunal".[18] Extraordinary as this claim may seem, it is somewhat corroborated by a Department of Justice account of the *Daily Express* interview, which concludes: ". . . the Bill which subsequently developed into the seventeenth [Article 2A] amendment of the Constitution was then prepared".[19] Odds are, Ryan's impolitic tub-thumping had only brought forward an inevitable coercion bill and provided the government with the ammunition needed to defend it. It is going too far to suggest that Ryan hoped to provoke coercion, but he was, in retrospect and privately, probably delighted; draconian suppression would place a halo of martyrdom over extreme republicanism.

Article 2A was objected to in the Dáil by Fianna Fáil and Labour for three days before becoming law, on which day

Cosgrave again referred to Ryan's writing, this time quoting from the editorial concerning Fitzgerald Kenny's being on the less salubrious end of his own petard. Before the targets of the act had time to catch their breath, the government's ace was played. On 18 October, the day after the act became law, a joint pastoral letter was read from every parish pulpit in the country. It served as a quasi-theological echo of Cosgrave's speech in the Dáil concerning the unnamed IRA, "whose avowed object is to overthrow the State by force of arms" and the "frankly communistic" Saor Éire, which hoped to "impose upon the Catholic soil of Ireland the same material-istic régime with its fanatical hatred of God as now dominates Russia". The organisation was "sinful and irreligious . . . You cannot be a Catholic and a communist. One stands for Christ, the other for Anti-Christ." Even those churchgoers unmoved by the spiritual bankruptcy of others were nonetheless under threat of "class warfare, the abolition of private property and the destruction of family life". Of the two organisations, "no Catholic may lawfully be a member".[20] Two days later, twelve organisations were proscribed, including Saor Éire, the IRA, Cumann na mBan and Fianna Éireann.[21]

As if Ryan had anticipated the political pastoral – he sure-ly cannot have been as surprised as he was infuriated by it – the subject of the IRA and religion had featured in *An Phoblacht* the day beforehand in an attempt to preempt the colossal damage he knew the Church could inflict. Of the implication that the "IRA is an enemy of religion", Ryan claimed that "No charge could be more false." Countless IRA men "imprisoned for their opinion by the Empire and by its agent, the Free State, trooped to mass in their jails and camps. They had never a bitter word against their faith. They felt bit-terly their exclusion from the Sacraments – a strange emotion if they were Godless men!"[22]

Ryan had more secular concerns than excommunication. Surprisingly there were no mass arrests in the immediate wake of the Coercion Bill, but there was little doubt that doors would soon be kicked in. At the time of the Bill's passing, Ryan was in the Kerry Gaeltacht. As a short break it provided little balm. Staying in his brother's caravan in Baile na nGall near Dingle, the destitution of the people there in the wake of a local knitting factory's closure enraged him. The only remedy seemed to be the traditional one of emigration. For all the lip service being paid by the government to the maintenance of Irish as a living language, without material sustenance the people of the Gaeltacht would be scattered, their communities decimated and the decline of the language accelerated. The hypocrisy of the government in this respect was the subject of a scathing article Ryan wrote in *An Phoblacht* the week after the Coercion Bill; that he did so at such a pressing time gives an indication of his anxiety for the language and people of the Gaeltacht.

Indeed he was fortunate that the article saw the light of day, as the screws were being tightened even further on *An Phoblacht*. Ryan tried to print a smaller version, first of only four pages and then eight, which proved too bulky for speedy printing and distribution. A friend who thought it "rather optimistic of Frank to try eight pages and get 12,000 printed" was proven right, and it reverted to four.[23] The two subsequent issues were subject to confiscation after the Military Tribunal declared them seditious but without explaining their judgement. In the Dáil, Fitzgerald Kenny gave warning to printers handling such material. It is unlikely that anybody who knew him expected Ryan to be cowed, and indeed he was not. He wrote in *An Phoblacht*:

> For the moment a Military Dictatorship can – on the plea of "sedition"- confiscate our every issue with impunity. But if we be guilty of "sedition" then should not we be prosecuted? If they prosecute us they must define the "sedition" of which we are deemed guilty. Dare they define it? We challenge them! The masses shall be judge. LET THEM PROSE-CUTE US![24]

Brave words from Ryan reached few of his readers and were little more than bluster. Challenging the government to prosecute for sedition had little to do with the actualities of running the paper. The day the above editorial went to press, Annie O'Farrelly, who worked in the office, was told she was being paid off and laid off. Suppression of the paper had made it unfeasible, because, rather than the threat of prosecution, there was no income. Subscribers in America, unaware that the paper was being suppressed, were already looking for refunds and cancelling orders.

Ryan and Sheehy Skeffington had already drawn up plans for a replacement and within two weeks were producing another paper, named *Republican File* because "it had a twofold meaning – that of a newspaper file and the little instrument by which prisoners sometimes cut their way through iron bars to freedom".[25] Comprising a collection of articles culled from other papers "cleverly juxtaposed with suitable headings to make political statements", its first issue under Ryan came out on 28 November and its last a week later.[26] On 9 December, detectives shanghaied Ryan as he entered his office, then beat him for resisting arrest before charging him with seditious libel. Hoisted with his own petard indeed. He was taken to Arbour Hill where George Gilmore and other republicans, refusing to don prisoners' uniforms and wearing only towels when forced to do hard labour, were perished with the cold. There was no heat in the cells and the wretched men were beaten regularly by the guards.

When Ryan appeared before the Military Tribunal in early January 1932, he saw his opportunity to bring the barbaric conditions to public notice. He was charged with membership of the IRA and withholding information about his association "if any, with the IRA, Saor Éire, and the Workers' Revolutionary Party, all illegal organisations". Ryan replied *as Gaeilge* that he refused to make any plea as the court had no authority to try him. It couldn't shut him up either: "I will take the opportunity of demanding a public enquiry in to the conditions in Arbour Hill where the Gilmores are being slowly done to death, and where convicted prisoners are being treated like galley slaves and where unconvicted prisoners are being treated like criminals."

His contempt earned him three months imprisonment, at the end of which he would be returned to face the original charges. "That does not increase my respect for this court," he replied, before being taken away, still demanding an inquiry into the conditions he was heading for.[27] His protests continued once he was locked up, and he refused to wear the prison uniform or to do work. The governor greeted Ryan with the information that "I can now do what I damned well like with you." He alternated Ryan's diet of bread and water for three days with three days of total abstinence. The prisoner was placed in solitary with not even the chaplain allowed to visit, and given only two books to read, *Irish Fairy Tales* and *Elements of Botany*.[28]

As the witchhunt gathered momentum, the government collected more scalps, and Ryan's lot was shared by more of his comrades. The only public response thus far to coercion had been when the Armistice Day protest in 1931 had morphed into anti-coercion demonstrations. Mammoth crowds, ignoring attempts to proscribe their gathering, had arrived to voice disgust at the new legislation. That legislation did not prevent rioting and baton charges after the speeches, during which Ryan had hollered that if it weren't for the forces of repression, imperialism would be extinct in Dublin. The following day the League Against Imperialism, overlooked a month earlier, was proscribed.

The IRA knew it had to act. HQ had ruled out the sporadic and retaliatory attacks that had become a feature of Irish life, instead drawing up plans to reverse the "dump arms" order of 1923 and make a concerted effort to resist coercion with arms. However, the chances of transforming a rearguard action into a successful counter-attack were slight, and the leadership – what was left of it – were probably relieved when the compulsion on them to act positively was averted. The IRA's nemesis, William Cosgrave, provided them with an escape hatch when, in early January 1932, he called a general election.

That he did so came as a surprise – the country was still in economic tatters and reeling from the introduction of internment, but Cosgrave felt in a good position to fight the election on a law and order campaign. The core of subversion had been shattered, and he still basked in the endorsement of the elite of Irish society. Cumann na nGaedheal were eager to point to their new-born successes in maintaining law and order, because, apart from holding on to power, they had precious little else in their display cabinet. They constantly referred to the "Red Menace" and "murder gangs" so as to keep the blessing they had received from the Church at the fore of the electoral mind for fear that, whilst the Church's support of the government might be forgotten, the reality of recession would certainly not. That the government's maintenance of constitutional politics was quite an achievement was not particularly appreciated by an electorate more likely to associate it with the Great Depression, the ceding of the six counties to Orangemen and the jangling of jail keys.

Coercion was resented by a very high proportion of those citizens it purported to be shielding, most of whom knew well that the real target of the Red Scare had been republicanism, an ethos with which they had some sympathy. Cumann na nGaedheal's sanctimonious blunderbuss truly backfired with the electorate's suspicion that such conspiracy as existed was none other than a bastard son of the government's ineffectual policies. Even *The Irish Times* noted the paradox:

> The Roman Catholic Hierarchy has warned its flock very urgently against the menace of Communism, but the warning must be futile so long as 4,830 tenement houses shelter 25,320 families in the heart of Dublin. It is almost a miracle that hitherto Communism has not flourished aggressively in that hideous soil. What an irony it will be if the Free State, having throttled sedition, is killed by the cost of houses![29]

The smokescreen of Cosgrave's hysteria failed to shroud the government's desperation. It proceeded to smear Catholic and conservative Fianna Fáil with red in a clumsy campaign, the ugliness and incredulity of which did worse than gain the government no credit. On 29 January, the Dáil was dissolved and an election announced for 16 February.

Up in Arbour Hill, Frank Ryan was aware that an election had been called only because he overheard a guard mention it to one of his colleagues. He subsequently wrote: "Then one fine day my punishment was further increased. I concluded that the Cosgrave party had won the election."[30] The brutal livelihood of the inmates continued, despite objections in the Dáil and the press. The People's Rights Association had held protests and vigils outside various jails, led by Sheehy Skeffington (still editing *Republican File*), Maud Gonne and the octogenarian radical activist Charlotte Despard. Fitzgerald Kenny denounced Despard as a Communist agent and warned that the government was going to "put down people like these and put them in prison if they persist, and if it is necessary, we are going to shoot them".[31]

Ryan continued with his own protests in prison.

> The petty annoyances, persecutions and tyrannies
> were the worst. Punished for smiling, for looking
> glum (it was construed as "insolence") for having a
> stump of pencil, for nodding at a comrade. The blan-
> kets were a joke. They were specially selected, riddled
> with holes, old and thin as tissue paper. When I drew
> the Governor's attention to mine at inspection one
> day, he turned his back and walked out of my cell
> without answering me. The result of all this was that
> I started a hunger strike in protest. After some days
> of this I became so weak that my bed was restored to
> me, for a few days, when I had fainted. Then a pair
> of blankets came also. My brother's death was
> announced to me about this time.[32]

After numerous requests, the chaplain, accompanied by two
guards to prevent the passing of any news, was permitted to
deliver Father Paddy Brown's *The Life of Christ* to the prisoner. A few mornings later when, for the first time, he was not
flung from his bed, he suspected that something had happened
in the world outside. He was right. De Valera had led Fianna
Fáil to victory, but had no overall majority.[33] However, the support of Labour not only won de Valera the presidency of the
Executive Council but probably also facilitated a remarkably
tranquil and smooth transfer of power. The first act of the new
government, on the day it took power, was to send Minister of
Defence Frank Aiken and Minister for Justice James Geoghe-
gan, up to Arbour Hill to visit the prisoners. The two found
Ryan naked in his frozen cell. The next morning, all were
released unconditionally. Thirty thousand supporters thronged
College Green in welcome. The crowd carried aloft a jubilant
Frank Ryan following a parade led by the Dublin Brigade IRA
and Cumann na mBan. *The Irish Times* reported that

> Every inch of space in the wide roadway was occu-
> pied and hundreds climbed the railings around the
> Bank of Ireland and Trinity . . . as the released pris-
> oners were being conducted through the dense

crowds towards the platform, cheers burst out on all
sides . . . Mr Frank Ryan . . . was given a great ova-
tion as he was helped up onto the platform.[34]

Speaking first in Irish, he thanked the republicans of Dublin
and the country for their support and for expelling the previous
government of "little Britishers . . . there was just one thing more
they should do and that was to follow the example of Judas and
take a rope". He thanked Fianna Fáil for their alacrity in releasing himself and his comrades but reminded them that the injustice of partition had still to be rectified. A collective statement
from the erstwhile prisoners, comprising both a thank you and
a challenge to the new government, was read out:

> We were imprisoned because we want the freedom of
> our country achieved and a Republic established. We
> still hold the same opinion, and hope the people of
> Ireland will advance without further faults until a
> Republic is functioning freely. We intend to continue
> our work in the volunteer movement until the same
> has been achieved.[35]

After the speeches, Ryan went for a meal with friends and
on to a *céilí*, where he asked his sister Eilís to dance, only to
find himself too weak for any exertion. Within days he was
staying with his aunt in Kilfenora, recuperating. After ten days
of resting and being fattened up, he felt sufficiently well to
return to Dublin in time to write an "Easter Week message to
Republicans" for *An Phoblacht*. Two weeks after his release,
his work as editor resumed.

The conditional support of Fianna Fáil by the IRA was a
moot point much debated in the pages of *An Phoblacht*. Within the leadership, Moss Twomey, for example, was willing to
give de Valera relatively free rein at first so as to better evalu-
ate his republican worth. The left still hoped to shore up the
remnants of Saor Éire in order to fully distinguish the ambitions and strategy of the IRA from those of Fianna Fáil. Ryan
pressed the point at a meeting of the Army Council: "We are
in opposition to Fianna Fáil because we represent the aims of
1916 – because we are better men. If we do not stand by the
programme for which we have stood for years, we should
become a left wing of Fianna Fáil."[36]

De Valera put away the stick of coercion and instead dangled the carrot of removing the Oath of Allegiance and all the trappings of empire. He conceded that he could not yet guarantee the dismantling of partition. The IRA was amenable to de Valera's general intentions and thought it premature to push Saor Éire's social programme, callow and battered as it was. Invitations to be incorporated into Fianna Fáil were turned down by an IRA HQ that refused to be submerged into a governing apparatus still composed of pro-Treatyites. Further, de Valera would be under pressure from both Free State agencies and the London government to settle for a diluted republic, and, by 1932, it was understood that he was not the man of unyielding principle that he had appeared to be ten years earlier. From an IRA perspective, de Valera had proved willing to concede on his principles when it suited; the Chief needed a diehard watchdog snapping at his heels rather than a republican lapdog at his command.

To that end, editor Ryan had not only to scrutinise the machinations of Fianna Fáil policy – "our task must be to keep full light trained on their failure" – and be seen to loiter menacingly at the party's republican flank, but also to deter potential diehard defectors to parliamentarianism, which existed only to "enslave the many and serve the few".[37] De Valera, on the other hand, was making things most conducive to IRA men entering the mainstream. The Gardaí, already riven with anxiety by the turn of events, were informally told to put thier gloves back on when dealing with those formerly targeted as subversives. Republicanism was also much heartened when de Valera introduced, despite, and no doubt emboldened by, protests from London, a bill to unilaterally remove the Oath of Allegiance, which was subsequently passed with the support of Labour. Then in early July, the government defaulted on annuity payments to Britain – although it was still collecting monies owed by the farmers – thereby firing the first shots of an economic war.

Cumann an nGaedheal could do little but fluster and whimper. Both before the election and after, its meetings had been disrupted by republicans. Its slightly shadowy and more militant fraternity, the Army Comrades Association (ACA), responded by opening up membership to all who felt the country and democracy under threat from spectral communist hordes and the more corporeal republicans. Cumann na nGaedheal and the ACA frequently accused de Valera of a "Kerensky-like softness" in his dealings with reds and diehards, who they claimed were only waiting in the wings for him to step aside. Rather than denying what he knew was a misconception, Ryan gleefully poured petrol on the flames of their paranoia by referring to the dethroned Free Staters as the "White Army"! All the while, conservatives in the IRA delighted in watching de Valera's new republican flag unfurl.

Yet Ryan and radicals on the left were still unsettled after the electoral shake-up. They were fighting a rearguard action against the Church and Cumann na nGaedheal while trying to launch an offensive against Fianna Fáil. Saor Éire still had not taken hold of either the IRA or the masses it was to lead. De Valera's successes on the national issue overrode, in the public mind, the need for any radical alternatives on social issues. With the republican advances made in Dublin, the IRA turned its gaze northward, where de Valera's win had given a great boost to IRA membership and urban disquiet provided the left with an opportunity to validate itself. However, there were complications. On more than one occasion Ryan berated the Northern IRA for indulging in sectarianism and for its inability to evolve republicanism by imbuing it with cross-community appeal on the basis of class solidarity. So far as Ryan was concerned, the Northern IRA acted as little more than a Roman Catholic militia. In the summer of 1932, an anonymous article he published claimed "Belfast Republicans, on the whole, are possessed of a bigotry that is all the more dangerous to the cause they have at heart since they themselves are unconscious of its existence. They are too wary of making advances to non-Republicans."[38]

But he was equally frustrated by the sluggishness of Southern republicans on the issue of partition. Eighteen months after taking over at *An Phoblacht,* Seachránaidhe had written a series of articles entitled "The Ulster Question". His desire to write a historical account of the province, to better unravel its problems, had "occasioned surprise" among some of his colleagues, who revealed a mentality "directly due to the desertion of the North by the leaders of all Ireland, a mentality which regards the North and its problems as something beyond the knowledge – aye, and beyond the interest – of all who are not Ulster-born and Ulster-bred". To stress the need for an understanding of Ulster, he had even conceded of partition that "We seem to have no remedy for it".[39] Exercising the determination and optimism synonymous with his name, Ryan was among the most vigorous of those hoping to entice Northern Protestant workers into the republican brotherhood.

His work was cut out for him, despite apparently propitious circumstances. Belfast had been particularly afflicted by the Depression. Ryan thought the deprivation in the North must prompt unionists to reassess their position within the United Kingdom and perhaps consider that their salvation did, after all, lie with Irish Socialist republicanism. Therefore, in April 1932, Ryan could claim he saw on the horizon among "the progressive forces" in Belfast "a new consideration of the close British connection and of the whole economic and social system".[40] Yet sectarianism darkened that horizon when shots were fired at a Hibernian parade in March, pilgrims to the Eucharistic Congress were attacked in June and the Ulster Protestant League blossomed and prospered throughout. In July, Ryan published an address from the IRA Army Council to "The Men and Women of the Orange Order":

> Fellow Countrymen and Women. It is a long road from the ranks of the IRA to the marching throngs that hold the 12 July celebrations . . . You surely must see that your future is bound up with the mass of the people in the remainder of the island . . . Your stock were the founders and inspiration and North East Ulster the cradle of the modern revolutionary movement for National Independence and Economic Freedom.[41]

Citing the "strange alliance" at the Boyne of the pope and King Billy as evidence of common cause between the working classes of the North and South, unionist and nationalist, only highlighted the appeal's impracticability. Despite Ryan's predictions of new thinking and novel alliances, it was evident that the thinking of the IRA itself was bogged down in prejudice and historical grudges. The conservatism of its Northern leadership left a socialist vacuum for the Revolutionary Workers' Groups (RWG), which filled this space with remarkable

success during a general strike in late 1932. Related disturbances occasioned the worst violence for a decade in a city
well used to violence, but Catholics and Protestants, the IRA
and the United Protestant Association, did unite. They literally built and stood behind barricades together, as *An Phoblacht*
rhapsodised: "The blood of the working class flowing in the
streets of Belfast washes away the barriers that have kept our
people divided into two sectarian camps . . . Thus in Belfast
today does the Irish Revolution begin."[42]

This should have delighted Ryan as the culmination of his
efforts and the realisation of his prognosis. Instead, the IRA
had been largely eclipsed by the communists of the RWG.
Ryan watched in dismay from the wings, but as he was under
a barring order from the North, he could do little more than
write encouraging articles about revolution in the streets, articles that were hardly read by the revolutionaries themselves.[43]
Although he broke his exclusion order on at least one occasion to go with his friend Budge Mulcahy to visit her sister, he
was less likely to get away with inciting republican socialism
than taking tea.

The strike and its ramifications came and went, with a considerable victory for the strikers that strengthened the RWG,
temporarily at least. George Gilmore claimed that only in so
far as it "took on the appearance of a military situation, IRA
interest was roused. While the fight continued the columns of
An Phoblacht carried vivid accounts of it. . . . [But] no lesson
was learnt".[44]

The inability of the republican left wing to capitalise on the
turbulence in Belfast was an ill omen. With the prospect loom-
ing of de Valera stealing all the republican thunder, any
advance on partition by Saor Éire would have outflanked him.
Saor Éire had failed to win conservative socialists over to
republicanism or northern, Protestant republicans to socialism. Sectarianism and Northern IRA witlessness had presented formidable obstacles to bonding Catholic and Protestant
workers, but as an opportunity to surmount those barriers,
which the left would have to do sooner or later, and to promote Saor Éire nationally, the Belfast disturbances could not
have been bettered.

Its chance to impress on both counts was missed because
the movement was already impotent. Saor Éire had never

taken flight after the buffeting it had received while barely hatched. In truth, it was not merely the stupefying one-two blows of coercion and crozier that had maimed it irreparably, but the fact that it was ill-conceived and born a runt. The IRA had suffered damnation by the Church and by the governments in London and Dublin, yet it had survived. Indeed, recent increases in recruitment had been abated not a whit by the joint pastoral. However, the attraction of strident republicanism did not translate into enthusiasm for Saor Éire. Also, those who might be expected to favour the IRA's dabbling in politics rather than pure militarism were more often than not repelled by the nature of the politics.

The policies of Saor Éire were not anti-Christian, as its detractors claimed, but they were politically suicidal. Unbelievably Saor Éire overlooked the Irish obsession with land and the sanctity of private property that had been a driving force behind Irish nationalism for decades. Naivety was also evident in Saor Éire's assumption that Northern Protestants would flock to align themselves once it had been explained to them that hitherto they had been no more than the dupes of British capitalism, waving Union Jacks and making fortunes for English businessmen whilst themselves struggling in slum dwellings on meagre wages. Despite the efforts of Ryan and his ilk, the IRA left failed in its, admittedly mammoth, task of reassuring Northern Protestants that it could make a home for them in socialist republicanism by neutralising the Catholicism and conservatism of the IRA right. Evidently it couldn't.

More damning to Saor Éire was that many of its own ostensible followers were dismissive of it. It earned only indifference, even hostility, among political moderates within the IRA who, justifiably, thought Saor Éire was being foisted upon them by an influential socialist clique. The cool reception accorded to the project was evident even at its founding convention. One delegate recalled "to cap it all, Fionán Breathnach stood up and said we should adjourn the meeting as some wished to attend the All Ireland in Croke Park that afternoon. It shows you how seriously they were taking their socialism."[45] Support within the IRA file had been half-hearted at best, and within the ranks it was too often only tolerated as a front that might boost membership. As such it had served as little more than ideological window-dressing that, having proved offensive to the country's sensibilities, could easily and must quickly be discarded. For IRA right-wingers, therefore, the bishops' pastoral was indeed as much a God-send as it was for Cumann na nGaedheal, shooting down left-wing ideological flights of fancy. The experiment had cost the IRA dearly, but its lesson had been learned. At the autumn Army Convention, Saor Éire was shelved. Frank Ryan had capitulated to the concept of politics being as valid a means as pure force just as IRA socialism reached its high water mark before ebbing.

Notes to Chapter Four

1. Ernest Blythe papers, UCDAD, P24/477. In the report there is some confusion between Frank Ryan and the Clare IRA man T.J. Ryan, who is generally accepted as being O'Sullivan's murderer. The confusion is most surprising as the two were both so well known to police.
2. Department of Justice files, NAI, Jus 8/682.
3. Ernest Blythe papers, UCDAD, P24/169.
4. Shehy Skeffington reported in early August that twice since Ryan's arrest, his shadow, Superintendent Peter Ennis, "has, sheltering himself behind the pretext of a search warrant, subjected *An Phoblacht* to an illegal censorship while it was waiting to go on the machines. Twice within a month the accredited representatives of *An Phoblacht* have been debarred from reporting State trials of Republicans."*An Phoblacht*, 8 August 1931.
5. *Daily Express*, 24 August 1931, quoted in the *Irish Independent*, 15 October 1931.
6. *An Phoblacht*, 29 August 1931.
7. *Ibid.*, 5 September 1931.
8. *Ibid.*, 12 September 12 1931.
9. Department of the Taoiseach, NAI, 5864B.
10. *Irish Press*, 14 September 1931.
11. Department of the Taoiseach, NAI, 5864B.
12. *Ibid.*
13. *An Phoblacht*, 26 September 1931.
14. *Irish Independent*, 13 October 1931.
15. The article, subtitled "Why Ireland's Workers and Working Farmers Must Organize", was very likely not written by Ryan himself; instead of passionate rhetoric there is an economic-based and detailed analysis, bursting with statistics, of Ireland's agricultural and industrial misfortunes resultant from imperial and neo-imperial mismanagement. Its appeal to patriotism, being re-routed through

a fiscal discourse and the statistics of want, is too indirect for Ryan, and the article epitomises the distance of Saor Éire logic from the Limerick man's less refined republicanism. *An Phoblacht,* 3 October 1931.

16. Department of the Taoiseach, NAI, 5864B
17. The full text of Cosgrave's speech is quoted in the *Irish Independent,* 15 October 1931.
18. Quoted in Tim Pat Coogan, *De Valera: Long Fellow, Long Shadow* (London: Arrow Books, 1995), p. 409.
19. Seán MacEntee papers, UCDAD, P67/534.
20. *Irish Independent,* 19 October 1931.
21. The others were Friends of Soviet Russia, the Labour Defence League, the Workers' Defence Corps, the Women Prisoners' Defence League , the Workers' Revolutionary Party, the Irish Tribute League, the Irish Working Farmers' Committee, and the Workers' Research Board.
22. *An Phoblacht,* 17 October 1931.
23. Annie O'Farrelly papers, NLI, p. 7655.
24. *An Phoblacht,* 14 November 1931.
25. *Ibid.,* 22 October 1932.
26. Margaret Ward, *Hanna Sheehy Skeffington: A Life* (Cork: Attic Press, 1997), p. 297.
27. Quoted in Seán Cronin, *Frank Ryan: The Search for the Republic* (Dublin: Repsol, 1980), p. 40.
28. *An Phoblacht,* 19 March 1932.
29. Quoted in *An Phoblacht,* 24 October 1931.
30. *An Phoblacht,* 19 March 1932.
31. Quoted in Conor Foley, *Legion of the Rearguard* (London: Pluto Press, 1992), p. 99.
32. His brother John in New York. *An Phoblacht,* 19 March 1932.
33. For all the fluster of Cosgrave's red scare, the vote for two Communist candidates was predictably negligible.
34. *The Irish Times,* 14 March 1932.
35. *An Phoblacht,* 19 March 1932.
36. Moss Twomey papers, UCDAD, P69/187.
37. *An Phoblacht,* 12 March 1932.
38. *Ibid.,* 20 August 1932.
39. *Ibid.,* 8 November 1930.
40. *Ibid.,* 10 April 1932.
41. *Ibid.,* 16 July 1932.
42. *Ibid.,* 15 October 1932.
43. The organ of the RWG, the *Irish Workers' Voice,* enjoyed a wide circulation in Belfast compared to the few contraband copies of *An Phoblacht* passed from hand to hand.

44. George Gilmore, *The Republican Congress* (Dublin: Dochas Co-Op Society Ltd., n.d.), pp. 27–8.
45. Frank Edwards quoted in Uinseann Mac Eoin, *Survivors* (Dublin: Argenta, 1980), p. 6.

CHAPTER FIVE

IRA Renegade

Frank Ryan was by 1932 prominent in the IRA not just as a journalist and member of the Executive, but as a social-ist. "The failure of past revolts," he had decided, "was the lack of a social current in political thought."[1] He had been much frustrated by his inability to expedite the micro-revolution in Belfast and to prevent the effective demise of Saor Éire, but he still had battles to fight – despite the confusion as to against whom and how. The IRA had reverted to drilling in public, its membership was still growing, and as a slap in the face of the government that was trying to woo them, the few IRA men up before the courts were still refusing to recognise its authority. Conversely, recruitment into Cumann na nGaedheal's ACA was increasing vigorously, spurred by the scaremongers who predicted that de Valera was opening a gap for the "red" IRA. The two paramilitary groups did battle in locations as improbable as the sleepy, prosperous town of Trim, County Meath, no hotbed of revolution, on the occasion of a visit from Cosgrave. As conflicts between the two increased in regularity and intensity, de Valera the democrat urged his supporters to "set their face against action which would prevent our opponents from being heard".[2]

At the 1932 Armistice Day protest at College Green, Frank Ryan's reply was blunt and bellicose: "No matter what anyone says to the contrary, while we have fists, hands and boots to use, and guns if necessary, we will not allow free speech to trai-tors." The *Irish Independent* informed its readership that "amid cheering" Ryan declaimed Armistice Day as an exploitation of the dead and "told his hearers to tear down the flag of England and if they could not tear it down, they should shoot it down".[3] That same month at a Naas meeting of the Boycott British League, Ryan claimed that "the only free speech a traitor should be allowed is the right to say the Act of Contrition".[4]

Thereafter Ryan's phrase of "No Free Speech for Traitors" became a war cry of the IRA and featured regularly in bold letters in the pages of *An Phoblacht*. His definition of a traitor was taken to mean pretty much everybody who was not ardently republican. The Department of Justice saw his rejection of one of the basic tenets of democracy as proof of IRA intransigence, and the department's new-found tolerance for the IRA had its limits, as had de Valera's. An internal report claimed that the Armistice Day disturbances arose "directly from the inflammatory speeches delivered at College Green" and signalled that the summer of constitutional and extra-constitutional brotherhood was drawing to a close. The memo raised the bugbear of considering harsher laws not unlike those so recently rescinded.

> With reference to the language allegedly used by Ryan and O'Donnell . . . I am firmly of the opinion *that the ordinary law is not adequate* and any serious attempt to keep the Ryans and O'Donnells from carrying out their campaign must either fail or lead to legislation on the general lines of the 17th [coercion] Amendment . . . My advice is to give the Ryans and O'Donnells a last warning.[5]

Such a move plainly had potential to blight de Valera's premiership, inviting, as it would, the jeers of Cumann na nGaedheal and the furies of the IRA. The author of the memo despaired of the two out-and-outers' obstinacy: "Despite inducements they will not cooperate. Reason and clemency have failed to move them and the State is thrown back on the ultimate remedy of coercing them." Until it was time to take the drastic step, the government must be content to "bind these men to keep the peace".

The IRA was largely keeping the peace if only because it was too muddled to effectively disrupt it. Symptomatic of its frustration, HQ selected a boycotting campaign of Bass beer as an outlet for its membership's revolutionary vigour. Volunteer Paddy Byrne remembered it with shame: "While the revolution was being served up on a plate in Belfast, what was the IRA leadership doing? [It] sent armed units out to raid pubs, terrify the customers and smash perfectly good stocks of bottled Bass, an activity in which, I regret to say, I was involved."[6] Ryan and the left, in fact, saw the Boycott British campaign as counter to the IRA's interests. Protectionism of privately owned Irish industries and agriculture would only transfer the support of British capitalism to the development of Irish capitalism. Yet as part of his remit to relay orders from HQ, Ryan published notice of a Dublin Ale Party. On the night of the party, barrels were broken and huge quantities of Sassenach beer were dumped. The ACA took it upon themselves to guard future shipments, and 1932 "drew to a close to the sound of scuffles over ale kegs".[7] The campaign did little but further antagonise de Valera, even though he was never one for the high stool himself.

As had happened before, external events forced the IRA to take stock of itself. In this sense it was, in early 1933, truly reactionary, starting to find self-justification in the rise of the ACA just as Cumann na nGaedheal had propped itself up with the Red Scare. The IRA's hand was forced when de Valera called another general election in January, hoping to win a majority that would enable him to fight the trade war with Britain. After de Valera had refused to pass land annuity payments on to Westminster (although he continued to collect from farmers!), the London government imposed heavy duties on imports from Ireland to make good their losses. De Valera responded by taking the same line against British imports. A political war was being fought in the guise of an economic war. De Valera knew well that the main Irish victims of the trade war were not the small farmers who had fallen in behind Fianna Fáil, but the ranchers. Almost exclusively these were Cumann na nGaedheal supporters, and it was they and their arrested wealth that were filling the ranks and coffers of the ACA.

Senior IRA men met to plot their next move. They had helped de Valera to victory, but his failure to unilaterally declare a republic had disappointed those members with faith in him. Frank Ryan had never possessed such faith, particularly in de Valera's introducing any social reforms or alleviating the lot of the urban workers and small farmers. The IRA left had hoped de Valera would initiate such reforms while simultaneously aiming for the republican goals of an end to partition and any connection with Britain and the Commonwealth. The dead weight of Saor Éire may have been abandoned, but Ryan and the left hoped to rescue it as a socialist lobby on de Valera's flank. However, the Red Scare had cancelled any debts to the left that de Valera may have owed, and he was mightily pleased since he was not inclined to pay them anyway. The bishops had given the new premier, formerly excommunicated on at least one occasion though he was, an escape hatch from anything smacking remotely of socialism. Meanwhile, unfortunately for Ryan and his comrades, while the majority of the IRA was content to see its left wing gagged, awaiting an opportunity to smother it.

The average volunteer was more eager to resolve the immediate question of the upcoming election. As yet another example of the organisation's want of direction, it was ruled that while volunteers might actively ensure Cumann na nGaedheal's defeat, they should not work for Fianna Fáil's victory. If being positive meant brawling with the ACA, IRA men fulfilled that virtue, energetically denying free speech to traitors. Not that it was all one-sided; the public image of Cumann na nGaedheal's strong arm was of one complemented by a knuckle-duster. Yet knuckle-dusters did not prevent Fianna Fáil from gaining five seats and a majority of one in the Dáil which, with Labour support, gave the government security enough to lead the country "On to the Republic!", as its campaign motto had asserted it would. The implication that republicans were striding forward in unity was far from accurate, and the conservative/socialist fissure within IRA HQ was deepening.

Ominously for Ryan, the IRA leadership, weary of flirting with socialism, had decided that Ryan had been given too much leeway in *An Phoblacht*. It was time he was housetrained. *An Phoblacht* had become a mouthpiece for the republican left rather than the IRA leadership. In late 1932, Seán MacBride was appointed to work with Ryan on editorial policy, disseminating the views of the Army Council and moderating Ryan's socialist-leaning copy. Ryan threatened to

resign after fierce arguments with MacBride. He resented bit-
terly the loss of his control over editorial policy, taking it as a
demotion to the lowly status of a "working editor". He was
hardly fit for even that position, according to MacBride's
charges of gross inefficiency and mismanagement at the paper.
In the end a compromise was reached. Ryan stayed on at the
paper, and the Army Council set up a watchdog committee to
ensure that the paper toed the IRA line. Ryan took umbrage,
but his indignant outbursts were greeted with sighs and yawns;
he had had his own way too long and had been exploiting his
huge influence within the movement. The Army Council
reminded him that he was merely one of many "instruments at
the disposal of the organisation".[8]

In the pages of *An Phoblacht*, Ryan had earlier predicted a
republican "Retreat from Moscow" that would deflect
"Republicanism away from social agitation as part of a conscious effort to blunt the edge of the Irish revolution".[9] Now
he had to smuggle the word of the left into the pages of the
paper, but Moss Twomey soon got wise to Ryan's deceptive
use of his hearing problem: "Frank was deaf you know. I'd
explain carefully some point for *An Phoblacht* – and he would
write the opposite next week. I'd have to write out anything
important for him to make sure it was right."[10]

It was not solely in writing that Ryan was straitjacketed.
Jim Gralton, a republican returned from America to Leitrim,
joined the Revolutionary Workers' Groups and ran dances in
a local hall. The parish priest, Father Conefrey, decided that
these dances were a smokescreen for communist subversion.
In February 1933, the government ordered Gralton's deportation after pressure from the Church. Hanna Sheehy Skeffington organised a "Keep Gralton Here" pulpit-directed
campaign, which suffered an inauspicious start when Peadar
O'Donnell was the victim of an angry mob in Leitrim at a
campaign meeting. Ryan and Michael Price were to speak at a
similar meeting but were prevented from doing so; this time,
however, it was by the Army Council of the IRA, which was
trying to wash the red stain off its hands. Ryan was furious.
At a meeting of the Council, he "got into an angry mood . . .
and spoke very heatedly throughout", accusing the IRA of
"being run by a secret clique". On behalf of the "secret
clique", Moss Twomey told Ryan that his outbursts showed

"very bad spirit . . . I wish you could be more restrained".[11] Regarding Gralton's barring order, the Army Council told the organisers of the campaign that the Council was "taking steps, independently, to organise opinion against Gralton's expulsion, and so therefore considers it unnecessary to send representatives to your meeting".[12] Six months later, in August 1933, Gralton was deported.

At the IRA General Army Convention on the weekend of Saint Patrick's Day, 1933, the sparring between the left and right wings of the movement came to a head. However, while the latter were clear in what they wanted to do – bury the corpse of Saor Éire beyond hope of resurrection – the former had no fresh ideas to bring to the table. In his capacity as staff captain, Ryan was able to speak at length in opposition to proposals that the IRA estrange itself from any action that smacked of left-wing agitation. Ryan acknowledged that any IRA political movements would be open to attack as being no more than a disguised reincarnation of the vilified Saor Éire. He also understood those who objected to the very concept of "tacking on to ourselves a political organisation". Well he might, as he was only a recent convert to political props himself, after years of consummate diehardism. However, just as Saor Éire was being lowered into its grave, he revealed how much he had been won over to what he had once condemned as the "dirty business" of politics.

> The Army Council document that states we are not in a position to start a political organisation is a defeatist one. I thought of the IRA as a Citizen Army who knew what they wanted and were prepared to get it. It is strange that the programmes we decided on two years ago should meet with our indecision now . . . How do our military men think they can steer clear of politics? We accepted this programme and now we are looking to escape. Let us form our political organisation and get where we want.

As ever, Ryan was forthright in his appeal, but his political inflexibility is also evident. In wanting to press ahead with Saor Éire against such overwhelming opposition from both his comrades-in-arms and the public, Ryan proved that he was anything but an astute politician. At best it displayed the resolute nature of his personality in regard to the beliefs he held; at worst it only exposed his limited capacity for adaptation in accordance with a political world that was evolving faster than his ideological development.

The gradual distancing of the IRA from socialism was reflected in policy when a resolution was passed at the convention declaring that no volunteer might write or speak on social, economic or political issues without clearance from the leadership first.

Ryan went on to argue against a motion that called for the prohibition of members joining other political groups, claiming it was unjust, since the IRA refused to offer any alternative. Barring any association with communist groups only showed that "all the false propaganda is taking effect and we find ourselves on the defence. Sheer downright ignorance is the cause of this proposition".[13] Indeed, Ryan supported a contradictory motion that argued for an alliance with other separatist and radical groups that would forge a popular front among the small farmers and urban poor. It would be distinct from Saor Éire in that it would be built up from the bottom with a broad base rather than imposed from the higher echelons. Such details were too fine for the impatient delegates, who rejected the motion. Instead, a governmental programme was adopted which was indeed socially radical, but it was made clear that, until the Republic had been achieved, there would be no action towards implementing any of its plans. There was to be no political auxiliary to the army.

If the convention was disheartening for Ryan, it did not discourage him in his own views. Still not one to be swayed by the prevailing wind, Ryan sidestepped it by refusing to have his name put forward for re-election to the Army Council. His re-election, Ryan believed, would only place him in a token but muzzled minority to whom the leadership could point as proof of their allowing constructive opposition, although his impotence would be absolute. Gilmore remembered Ryan believing "that minority opposition within the Executive did more to protect the leadership than to influence its decisions".[14] The influence of the IRA left within the Executive had plummeted.

Violence in the streets further underlined the IRA's reluctance to be seen as fellow travellers of the radical left. After a particularly vehement denunciation of communist conspirators from the pulpit of the Pro-Cathedral, crowds marched to the headquarters of the RWG, Connolly House, and besieged those inside. It was not long before the notorious "Animal Gang", political thugs linked to the ACA, rendered their services. The singing of "Faith of Our Fathers" and "Hail Glorious Saint Patrick" gave way to stone-throwing and attempts to storm the building. The siege went on for three consecutive nights until the building was finally burned down and the occupants had to escape across the rooftops. The Workers' Educational College in Charlotte Despard's house, the headquarters of the Workers' Union, and the Kevin Barry Hall were all subsequently stormed and sacked. Only when the violence threatened the shopfronts of O'Connell Street did the gardaí intervene.

The IRA response was to debar all its members from the disturbances. Among the few insubordinates who went to their pariah comrades' defence were Ryan and Charlie Gilmore. Communist Eoghan Ó Duinnín was a witness: "*Nuair a thosaigh an ghramaisc ag ionsaí na gcumannach agus nuair a cuireadh Connolly House trí thine chuir sé sin déistin ar Phroinnsias. Sheas sé gan cúbadh nuair a dhírigh an Animal Gang a n-aire air féin; níor theip ar a mhisneach.*"[15] Gilmore was arrested for possession of a revolver, and, as a consequence of the ensuing publicity, had his actions publicly repudiated by IRA HQ. Ryan went to Gilmore's trial and "looked ferocious, leaning his chin on his hands and glaring at the court".[16] The rift between the leadership and the leftists grew ever deeper.

Never one to be placated by compromises, Ryan was still deliberating over his editorship of *An Phoblacht*. His position was tenuous, and he admitted to Twomey that his heart was no longer really in *An Phoblacht*, which he considered to have only lightweight significance since the defeat of Cosgrave. What he really wanted to do, he revealed, was to set up an Irish language paper, an ambition he had held for ten years. Uncharacteristically contrite, he expressed remorse for having "let minor points of difference arise with the result that there have been squabbles". He suggested Twomey find someone more "in" with HQ's thinking, conceding that "a man more amenable to discipline than me would not be so hard to find".[17] Few tears were shed on the Army Council, which let it be known that it had not cooled in its "resentment at the waste of time incurred in investigating the fictitious grievances you put forward".[18] Twomey, who thought Ryan "a bad man in a team", was more diplomatic: "Candidly, I do feel that many times Frank's attitude has not been too helpful . . . there is more than journalistic attainments necessary to the editor."[19] Two weeks after the General Army Convention, on 1 April 1933, there was a small notice in *An Phoblacht* underneath the editorial, informing the readership that "Proinnsias Ó Riain regrets to announce that he has resigned from the position of Editor of *An Phoblacht*."

The following month, Rosamond Jacob recorded in her diary what can only be described as a rather curious and mysterious episode. There are no other references to it. Ryan seemingly travelled to France with his brother Vincent to see an osteopath. Not only was it a "worthless visit" as regards curing his deafness, but, after a statue in Rennes was blown up, Ryan was arrested. He "had to resist search, having things he didn't want found". After some hours he was set free without charge and "otherwise, he seemed to have a good time".[20]

Having spare time on his hands, Ryan decided to travel down to the Kerry Gaeltacht, haven of boyhood summers and snatched weekends ever since. He and his friend Con Lehane decided to walk most of the way. First they went to Bodenstown for the Wolfe Tone commemoration. There they witnissed IRA harassment of members of the recently rejuvenated Communist Party of Ireland (CPI). Disgusted, and ashamed of his IRA colleagues, Ryan claimed of the unseemly scuffles at the shrine of revolutionary republicanism that "it would be a bad day for us when we cut ourselves off from the men who have been working for the breaking of the British connection".[21]

Setting off from Naas on foot and pitching their tent wherever they found a likely spot, they spent the summer days walking through the midlands to Tipperary and arrived for the Munster hurling final in Thurles. There they stayed for three days, "sleeping on a patch of ground near John Joe Callinan's pub". Moving on to Silvermines and to proper beds at the home of a college friend of Ryan's, they pressed on to the home comforts of the Ryan household in Knocklong.

"Frank was very much in awe of his father," recalled Con Lehane, despite their differences in politics.[22] Vere and Ann Ryan had often despaired of their wayward son, whom they considered the most gifted of their children. In the 1920s, when Ryan had just been released from prison and was without a job, and when his dedication to republicanism was mounting to a full-time preoccupation, he claimed that his parents had chided him about "a single ticket by the tube to perpetual bonfire terminus", but it seems there was never any serious fallout between them.[23] They were, all three, teachers with a love of books and literature, and although their son might have been for ever agin' the government, the devout couple must have been consoled that Frank had never turned his back on the Church, unlike many of his socialist colleagues. One can only wonder what the Ryans thought of the wisdom of their spiritual leaders who had condemned their son and indirectly informed them that they had reared an anti-Christ. Of Frank's politics, Eilís Ryan said later that "My father may not have approved but he always backed Frank up. Always."[24]

From Knocklong, Seachránaidhe and his errant companion travelled through Limerick into the Kingdom and down to the Dingle peninsula, where they stayed in Frank's brother's caravan.

After some weeks away, Ryan returned to Dublin, back to political activity and the centre of further turbulence within the IRA. When the IRA Adjutant General Donal O'Donoghue heard a rumour that Ryan had attended a meeting to launch the Communist Party of Ireland, the simmering tensions between Ryan and HQ, accompanied by the heightened sensitivities of both parties, bloated a trifle into a melodrama. In response to a memo from HQ, asking Ryan if he had attended the CPI launch, Ryan refused to verify or deny the report. He declared himself a victim of an "inquisition", comparable to "Mr Cosgrave's Military Tribunal", and accused HQ of trying to drum up a charge for something that he was within his rights to do. The questioning persisted. In tetchy exchanges by letter, Ryan pointed out that his attendance was not contrary to IRA regulations, and he added, for good measure, that "as an individual republican I would not regard membership of the Communist Party as a crime". An exasperated Moss Twomey retained his composure: "You are asked to answer a simple question, yes or no, and you will please do so." Ryan's resentment of a "lack of comradeship and frankness in GHQ" suggests the clash had gone beyond ideology and IRA policy. Finally, after Twomey had tried to reassure Ryan that it was "*not* a question of singling you out", Ryan let it be known that he had not been anywhere near the meeting. Atop the righteous high ground, he remained sullen: "It hurts to think that I could be even suspected of deceit towards the organisation."[25] Ryan's pouting indignation was sincere, but so was the "Big Brother" paranoia of the IRA's conservative leadership.

There was turbulence, too, at the far side of the political spectrum. The deposed Cumann na nGaedheal sought a new direction and an injection of dynamism that, paradoxically, de Valera seemed to provide them with by finally sacking Garda Commissioner Eoin O'Duffy. Almost immediately, O'Duffy took control of the ACA, initiating a militarist regime based on order and discipline and in July renamed it the National Guard. A uniform of blue shirts distinguished volunteers. The purported role of the Blueshirts was to protect free speech and private property, uphold law and order, deter communism and reunite Ireland; but Hitler had come to power only six months earlier, and O'Duffy's pretensions were clear. He encouraged the use of a raised arm salute accompanied by the acclamation "Hail O'Duffy" and expressed a severe distaste for the democratic party politics that now operated in Ireland. Jews and atheists were excluded from membership, and a planned display of strength outside the Dáil bore more than a passing resemblance to Mussolini's March on Rome. De Valera was alarmed enough to reintroduce military tribunals and proscribe the Blueshirts, albeit ineffectually, as it just underwent yet another of its name changes.

In September, Cumann na nGaedheal merged with the National Centre Party, a party of moderate nationalists. Formed only a year previously to represent the bigger farmers, they promised to end the trade war with Britain. The new party, called the United Ireland Party but known as Fine Gael, had Eoin O'Duffy as its leader but William Cosgrave as its leader in the Dáil. The Blueshirts, now officially the Young Ireland Association, were its militant auxiliary riding shotgun. They were supported by self-proclaimed but largely sincere defenders of Church and state who envisioned it as a Catholic militia, others whose Civil War hatred of republicans still festered and still others punished by the economic war with Britain. The autumn of 1933 was plagued with brawls, riots and shootings between republicans and the new militia, which to the optimistic were the final parting shots of the Civil War but to the pessimistic were warning shots that a second would soon commence. On the IRA Army Council, Tom Barry was unsuccessfully urging the assassination of leading Blueshirts, which had been resisted by Frank Ryan, presumably wary of creating martyrs. However, Ryan flared up at HQ again when volunteers were ordered "not to take part in any action against Fascist-imperialist organisations" for fear that profitless street brawls would only give de Valera justification for IRA suppression.[26]

Exactly how fascist the Blueshirts were under the borrowed continental trappings and paraphernalia is a moot point. The murmurings of Mussolini-style corporatism among the higher ranks reached few ears among the footsoldiers, but for Frank Ryan they were fascist enough to be a contagion of the Blackshirts and Brownshirts menacing Europe. Civil War animosities, which were far from extinct, were now given a new dimension. The republican left drew the assumption that it could now be of greater service to Ireland than ever, as the sole meaningful opposition to fascism in Ireland. It was invigorated in its appeals for the formation of a united front that was both separatist and leftist. Despite gaining some support among IRA men, still Twomey and MacBride resisted, seeming instead to be trying to curry favour with de Valera.

A complaint of Ryan's while he was at *An Phoblacht* was that the republican boy's movement, Fianna Éireann, only rarely sent him copy to fill the one or two columns earmarked for it in the paper. The organisation was wanting in leadership, vitality and appeal. Set up in 1909 by Countess Markievicz and assisted by Liam Mellows, the resuscitation of Fianna Éireann was placed in Ryan's hands. Among the more innocuous aspects of training were lessons in Irish history and language, which Ryan was well suited to oversee, as well as the more militant aspects such as drilling and small arms usage. He was by all accounts a popular chief scout: "We all loved Frank Ryan; everybody did," remembers one of his charges, Christy Quearney, while another, Michael O'Riordan, noted

that his charismatic mentor "had a particular attraction" for
him.[27] Among other members groomed by Ryan were two ten-
year-olds, future IRA Chief of Staff Cathal Goulding and his
boisterous friend Brendan Behan.

Ryan's considerable abilities as an organiser were tested
with the patriotic yet prosaic tasks of letter writing, adminis-
tration and ensuring that all members, most of whom came
from poor families, were provided with a uniform of deep-
green tunic, trousers and a slouch hat. Despite the amount he
managed to accomplish, Ryan was only at the task for a few
months: "Frank was a very terrible loss to the Fianna at that
time," recalled Diarmuid MacGiolla Phadraig, his successor.
"He was the one man who understood what Liam Mellows
meant when he spoke of what the Fianna could do."[28]

The 1934 IRA Convention was held near St Stephen's Green
in March to grapple with much the same problems as it had
twelve months previously. The pull of the membership towards
conventional republicanism had, if anything, increased. De
Valera had postponed the unilateral declaration of a republic
but instituted a Volunteer Reserve that attracted the triggerhappy with its advantages of being legal and lucrative. The
IRA left persisted in its demands for social agitation before
rather than after the republic had been achieved. Most of
Ryan's lobbying for a republican front had been somewhat discreet, but a month before the convention, Ryan revealed himself, writing that "The most pressing need is the creation of a
revolutionary party which will embrace the whole republican
party".[29]

At the convention, the leadership tried to forestall any
motions from the left by proposing that a "public auxiliary
body" be formed for the political education of volunteers and
"to mobilise the people behind the army". It was as vague and
unconvincing as earlier IRA rhetoric about social revolution,
and it appeased no one. Michael Price first threw down the
gauntlet for the left, merely by holding the leadership to its
word. He demanded confirmation that the IRA was committed
to a workers' republic and would not retire until that goal had
been achieved. In a flurry of semantics, the leadership virulent-
ly opposed the motion, it was defeated, and Michael Price
walked out of both the convention and the army. Next up were
Peadar O'Donnell and George Gilmore. They repeated the call

from the 1933 convention for a united front, "a Republican Congress which will restate the whole Republican standard and confront the imperialists with a solid form of nationalist masses pledged to the achievement of the Republic of Ireland and to the revolutionary struggle in association with the IRA".

Ryan then stood up to support the proposal, arguing that Seán MacBride wanted "a continuation of the present army policy – inactivity", because he was "afraid of leadership". The rest of Ryan's broadside was more indiscriminate and undoubtedly expressed the feelings of the majority of frustrated IRA men: "What is wrong is a lack of decision. To prevent ourselves doing wrong, we are prepared to do nothing . . . We in the IRA today, by gagging ourselves, are gagging the whole revolutionary movement in the country. I do not see another year's life for the army if it continues this inactivity." Ryan concluded with a claim that must have exasperated the traditional physical force men, declaring that he supported the motion for a political dimension to the IRA "because it prevents the wrecking of the organisation".[30]

The debate over the establishment of Republican Congress led into the following day when the motion was put to the vote. It was carried by a small majority of the delegates but defeated by a single deciding vote from the Army Council. Thereupon, O'Donnell, Gilmore and Ryan took the example of Price, quitting both the convention and the Irish Republican Army. The sundering of the IRA that had been threatening for at least a year seemed to have finally come to pass. Both leadership and dissidents thought the other would see the error of their ways and renege. The dissenters thought HQ would do so rather than risk a split that could cripple the army. However, when IRA HQ showed no sign of bowing to the demands of the Congress proponents, they effectively detached themselves from the army. A handful of socialist republicans, around the nucleus of Ryan, O'Donnell and Gilmore, went on a frantic tour of IRA units to announce the holding of a Republican Congress in Athlone only three weeks after the Army Convention, Twomey was incensed by their insubordination. *An Phoblacht* reported that the dissidents had "theatrically" left the convention, tried to induce others to do the same, attacked the policy of the IRA and had sought the disruption of the army.

If leaving the organisation to which he had dedicated so much for sixteen of his thirty-two years appears to show inconstancy or a rare defeatism on Ryan's part, he did not consider it to be so; rather, he felt he had merely "continued to oppose the reactionary tendencies and withdrew from the Army".[31] Whereas there were undoubtedly many IRA men pleased to see the back of O'Donnell and his fanciful notions and theorising, Con Lehane keenly felt the departure of his good friend Ryan for both his own and the army's sake: "His defection in 1934 with O'Donnell, Gilmore and Price on the Republican Congress issue was the biggest threat to the leadership. He was greatly admired by the younger men."[32] One of them was Walter Mitchell from Offaly, "a spare buckshee officer at the time that Congress was founded. I was present at the Athlone meeting, mainly because I was acquainted with Frank Ryan and had a very high opinion of him".[33]

Yet Ryan's undoubted magnetism was insufficient to seduce others to dabble in class politics. Packy Early remembers that among the IRA in Leitrim, Ryan was the favourite from HQ staff, being so "personable and full of energy and boldness"; yet his proselytising for radical socialist policies placed a barrier between himself and the men.[34] When Ryan asked Dublin Fianna Éireann graduates Christy Quearney and Arthur O'Leary about joining Congress, "We had to say no; that Congress was no longer giving allegiance to the Republic and we could not give allegiance to an organisation that would not recognise the Republic. 'It is only a matter of convenience,' Frank laughed, but I could see he was disappointed."[35] Quearney had obviously followed the Army Council line that stated Republican Congress would siphon off energy dedicated to nothing more or less than national sovereignty. Indeed, it claimed that the offshoot was not inherently republican at all and existed as nothing more than a "new political party" that would "contest elections and enter the Free State Parliament".[36]

Athlone was picked as a location partly for the practical reasons of accessibility but also symbolically to show that Republican Congress would be nationwide, urban and rural, aiming for much the same audience as Saor Éire: small farmers and impoverished agricultural labourers, the urban poor and the lower middle class. Within that movement, Ryan's cherished

Pearse was far from being the icon he was in the IRA. Most of its ideology derived from the mouth and pen of Connolly, but also, to a far greater extent than was acknowledged, from Liam Mellows.[37] The conference sought to distinguish the new organisation from the IRA, stagnant and living in the shadow of Fianna Fáil, while attracting the politically minded of the former and the left-leaning among the latter and the Labour Party, as well as members of trade unions, tenant leagues and land agitators. Some 200 delegates arrived in the midlands town for the speeches of Ryan – on the misrepresentations of true republicanism – O'Donnell, Síghle Uí Dhonnchadha and Brian Corrigan representing the Achill peasantry. The conference also marked the unveiling of the Athlone Manifesto, signed by Ryan and twenty-two others:

> We believe that a Republic of Ireland will never be achieved except through a struggle which uproots capitalism on its way. We cannot conceive of a free Ireland with a subject working class; we cannot conceive of a subject Ireland with a free working class. This teaching of Connolly represents the deepest instinct of the oppressed nation . . . As the Republic when established will be a Republic of the workers and small farmers the forces that will achieve it must be drawn from these sections of our life. In order that these forces may be drawn to our task, we, on their behalf, call for a Republican Congress, and pledge ourselves to take up the work necessary to build it.[38]

The manifesto was an unremarkable document containing few surprises in its ebullient claims of whom it represented and how the honour of republicanism was being sullied by others purporting to adhere to it. There only remained the tasks of setting up an Organising Bureau, on which Ryan sat as secretary, electing officers to prepare for the great Congress itself, intended to be a public forum for socialism and republicanism, and putting everyone to work to enlist future members. A military wing was established in the form of a reincarnated Irish Citizen Army (ICA). "We 'dug up' some ICA veterans (Connolly's men) to give it some legitimacy and colour," says one volunteer.[39] Many IRA units, mostly from Dublin, simply transferred to work for Congress, keeping their military formation intact. Very soon, the army numbered little short of 300 men and women and commenced drilling and exercises in the hills outside the capital. Among the operations planned were the assassination of a particularly detested landlord and a raid on a Free State army arsenal, with inside help, to secure arms. Kit Conway, a builder's labourer and communist much respected in Congress, concocted the latter plot, but neither project was realised.

A newssheet was a necessity for propagating the word, and Ryan was the obvious choice as editor. The first issue of *Republican Congress* appeared on 5 May, four weeks after Athlone, comprising four full size pages. Significantly, the masthead this time displayed no quote from Pearse but only from Connolly, that used in the Athlone Manifesto: "We cannot conceive of a Free Ireland with a subject working class." Ryan was also keen to impress upon the readership the difference between the new paper and *An Phoblacht* in editorial policy, when he pointedly informed them that "If the *Republican Congress* is to be the organ of the plain people, their day-to-day struggles must be recorded in it. We call now for those chronicles. Write us your views; tell us your suggestions and criticisms. This is your paper. Avail of it."

The inside pages carried an analysis of the split with the IRA, a copy of the Athlone Manifesto and an account of a Congress rally in Rathfarnham. At the rally Proinnsias Ó Riain gave his reasons for leaving the IRA as being that the organisation was no longer carrying out the tasks for which he had joined it. He claimed that it was detrimental to progress. Ryan explained that "the IRA leadership had brought the revolutionary movement to a standstill. The Republican Congress would again open the road for an advance."[40]

Encouraging messages were received at Republican Congress offices in Marlborough Street from some trades councils and influential unions, while others left it up to their members to affiliate to Congress as either branches or individuals. George Gilmore was dispatched to America to explain the aims of Congress to the likes of the indifferent Joe McGarrity, who was pleased that the left arm of the IRA had been amputated, and Gerald O'Reilly, who had established a Republican Congress support group in New York. Congress welcomed the "wholehearted support" from the Communist Party of Ireland somewhat brazenly, while independent candidates in some local council elections allied themselves with the fledgling collective. Significantly, there was support from workers in Belfast, many of them Protestant, who formed themselves into Connolly Clubs, drew up lists of grievances and possible solutions and placed themselves under the Congress umbrella.

Tenant leagues in the cities did the same, and it was probably in the slums of Dublin, nicknamed the "Calcutta of Europe" since its infant mortality rate had been higher than that of the Indian city, that Congress had most impact. The notoriety of the Dublin slums, as Gilmore pointed out, "have been a byword for so long that we are maybe a bit inclined to take their frightfulness for granted". They were acknowledged as being the worst in Europe. In June, Ryan spoke at a meeting chaired by Charlie Donnelly, for tenants in Dublin's York Street area, where 429 people lived in just twelve tenements. Throughout the city, roughly 18,000 families were living in one-room tenements, some 8,000 of these condemned, while a further 1,440 families were living in condemned basements. "In the year of Republican Congress," Gilmore remembered later, "it was not uncommon to find two families occupying one room, a screen of newspapers pasted together being strung across from wall to wall to separate one home from the other."[41] Conditions in parts of Waterford, Limerick and Cork, though on a smaller scale, were not much better.

With Congress branches establishing themselves around the country almost immediately (there were six in Dublin alone), by late June it was ready for its first show of strength at the Bodenstown Wolfe Tone commemoration. The week beforehand, *Republican Congress'* editorial warned that the IRA might not afford Congress the warmest welcome but that hostility should be ignored and all parade regulations observed. About 300 Congress members travelled down from Belfast and laid wreaths at Connolly's grave in Arbour Hill before joining the 2,000 strong Congress contingent in Bodenstown. Frank Ryan was leading the marchers out of the assembly field, taking up the tail end of the huge procession to the cemetery, when Connolly scouts ran up to inform him that the Northerners were being prevented from marching. Immediately he halted the parade and ran back to the commotion. A picket of Tipperary IRA men had been ordered to seize inappropriate banners from the Belfast contingent ("Break the Connection with Capitalism", "James Connolly Club, Belfast") and the inevitable fighting broke out before the Northerners were able to break through, reform and march again, holding aloft torn and damaged banners. Ryan resumed the head to lead his followers through the village of Sallins, the band defiantly playing "The Red Flag", to the cemetery where more Tipperary men greeted them. Paddy Byrne remembered that

> We were in strength too, with several thousand members, men and women, ready to meet the challenge, but to avoid unseemly scenes, Frank gave the order to retire. So having left our wreaths on the roadside we withdrew to Sallins. The *Irish Times* commented next day on the irony of Ulster Protestants being prevented by Tipperary Catholics from honouring Wolfe Tone.[42]

Indeed the clash made headlines in all the major papers, most of which saw it as evidence that republicanism would surely destroy itself. *Republican Congress* claimed the fracas was symbolic of the relationship between Congress and the IRA: the Tipperary men were not blamed but commiserated with for having to carry out the orders of the IRA leadership, and the paper claimed that some had even fallen in and marched under the Congress banners. It was true that while the leaderships of both organisations would increasingly denounce each other, their followers remained on good terms, fraternised and not infrequently, if discreetly, helped each other. The Bodenstown clash tarnished the IRA leadership, and Volunteer Peter O'Connor remembered it caused "me and several of my comrades to leave the IRA for good".[43]

There were of course differences between *Republican Congress* and Ryan's *An Phoblacht*. While there had earlier been expressions of hope, if not from the editor, that de Valera might yet declare a republic, the new paper was void of faith in "the Long Fellow", who was peddling softcore republicanism in league with capitalism. Column space was also given over to sniping at the IRA and bombarding the Blueshirts.

Gone were the socialist and republican theorising, replaced by columns dedicated to the bread-and-butter issues that lay at the core of the Congress groups. Congress' focus on tenant leagues was plain from the pages carrying accounts of rent strikes, reporting specific cases of outstandingly squalid homes and often naming slum landlords with tales of their negligence and parsimony. Ryan provided far more coverage of labour news, of Congress members picketing industry and the building trade and being arrested or injured in so doing. Wherever there was a strike or employers were deemed to be exploiting their workers, Congress members were outside with banners and posters, urged on by *Republican Congress*, which revelled in bold type exclamations such as "Keogh Workers Win – All the Scabs have been Dismissed".[43]

Ryan likewise took glee in reporting the exchange in court between Charlie Donnelly and a Sergeant Byrne, who had arrested him for picketing outside the Somax Clothing factory and preventing scabs from entering. Donnelly cross-examined the sergeant, asking him "what he considered a reasonable size for a picket and, after a hesitating reply, asked, 'Would it be true to say that a picket becomes too large as soon as it becomes large enough to be effective?' The Sergeant said that he did not understand the question."[45] An impatient judge told Byrne he was not obliged to answer and remanded Donnelly and two others for refusing to be bound to the peace.[46]

Two aspects of republicanism that enjoyed generous column inches were troubles in the North and the decline of the Gaeltacht. Both happened to be particularly important to Ryan, but they also received increased attention from Congress. Thus half of the first front page was given over to revolutionary organisations in Belfast, and the paper largely remained overly optimistic at the prospect of Northern Protestants' Pauline conversions to republicanism. Typically filled with zeal, Ryan claimed that

> Congress committees in Belfast will play such a role
> as no movement attempted in Ulster since McCrack-
> en and Tone . . . Republican organisations have been
> not only weak but bad on working class struggles.
> Among the most reactionary factors in the IRA has
> been, for years past, the leadership of the Belfast units

... Once the question of sending a delegation to the
Republican Congress has been settled, the troubles of
these Republican leaders will begin.[47]

Unlike *An Phoblacht*, the paper went on to occasionally
publish fairly even-handed accounts of Protestant objections
to Irish nationalism, although it shied away from acknowl-
edging any legitimacy in the loyalist position. Moreover, it
increased focus on the disease of sectarianism over the defence
of Catholic ghettos. Even so, *Republican Congress* was immediately banned in the North and thereafter went under the title
Northern Worker, a move that did not prevent its distributors
from finding themselves before the judge for its sale.

Oddly enough, it was Ryan who appeared to be more con-
cerned about the Gaeltacht and the poverty of the western
seaboard than O'Donnell, who was from the Donegal
Gaeltacht and often spent time in Achill. It was in Achill that
Congress was the strongest among Gaeltacht areas, and there
had been a specific appeal to the Gaeltacht in the Athlone
Manifesto. Disparaging articles concerning attempts on the
part of the government to instil cottage industries in the
Gaeltacht were commonplace, and readers were told that
"Congress Groups must not give any quarter to play-acting at
saving the Gaeltacht. The Gaeltacht is inseparable from the
struggle of the Irish working class."[48] Ryan's journalism, in
both Irish and English, was as incisive as ever, according to
Lehane, who claimed he "was the master of the sharp, clear,
Anglo-Saxon sentence. He was very definite. His Irish writing
was even clearer."[49]

Despite his organisational, speaking and editorial commitments to Congress and the Citizen Army, Ryan was still very
much an active member of the Gaelic League, where his abilities were recognised, as were his subversive tendencies.
Amongst the conservative and apolitical membership of that
body, whose love of the language was coloured by a retro-
spective cultural nationalism, he was outstandingly progressive and political. Síghle Uí Dhonnchadha went so far as to
declare that Proinnsias Ó Riain was "almost unique among
Irish patriots of the last hundred years in that he was entirely
devoted to the restoration of the language and at the same time
a firm believer in equal rights and opportunities for all."[50]

119

Predictably, not all *Gaeilgeoirí* were as impressed as Ryan's radical sidekicks, particularly when Ryan founded Craobh Cathal Brugha. In explicit contradiction of the League's ethos of remaining aloof from politics and the tribalism it engendered, the club commemorated a diehard icon. Ryan's blatant objective, echoing his UCD days in the Gaelic League, was to twin language revival with extremist republicanism. If his mutinous behaviour elicited little surprise within the Coiste Gnotha,[51] it certainly antagonised them. But worse was to come. In 1934, Ryan, Lehane and Fionán Breathnach decided to "stage a putsch" at the League's Ard Fheis by putting up sixteen candidates for the Coiste Gnothe, republicans all, who would then have a majority. All sixteen won. However, in the long run, the three conspirators' plot backfired, and Lehane admitted that "it was probably the worst thing we ever did . . . In retrospect I'd say that I don't think we did any good for the Gaelic League or the Republican Movement".[52]

Meanwhile, invitations issued from Marlborough Street for delegates to the first Republican Congress, to be held at Rathmines Town Hall over the last weekend of September. There promised to be a wide spectrum of political views represented, but the most apparent divergence was among members of the Organising Bureau, who had proposed two conflicting resolutions. Mick Price and James Connolly's daughter, Nora Connolly O'Brien, had been publicly predicting the emergence of a party to establish a workers' republic from Congress rather than the consolidation of a united front. At a meeting at which Ryan himself spoke, Price had promised that Congress would give birth to "A Workers' Revolutionary Party". Speaking in Irish and English, however, Ryan told listeners that "Congress would be in effect, the parliament of the plain people and would plan their campaign and direct it towards its goal – a Workers' Republic".[53] Although they agreed on their ultimate aims, both sides wanted a clarification of tactics by which to work to achieve those aims.

One hundred and eighty-six delegates arrived at Rathmines Town Hall, from organised labour groups north and south (although often, significantly, in a personal capacity), anti-fascist groups, tenant leagues, the Gaeltacht, the Northern Ireland Socialist Party, the Communist Party, miners from Kilkenny and Leitrim, the unemployed movement and

Congress branches nationwide. There was even another Frank Ryan, representing Irish workers' clubs in America. The clarion call to Congress was such that it was even attended by thirty-six Blueshirts, who neglected to enter but paraded outside waving Papal and Eucharistic Congress flags in the company of a score of policemen. Although he later scoffed at the protest in print, Ryan, no doubt mindful of mob-swelling and its consequences at the siege of Connolly House, dispatched Paddy Byrne to the house of quartermaster Christy "Sniper" Clarke for twelve revolvers. In the event, the protesters drifted away harmlessly.

Communist historian Mike Milotte has suggested that the meeting in Rathmines was the "most representative gathering of working-class and militants seen in Ireland. It was, moreover, the first time in public that serious consideration was given to the relationship between the struggles for national reunification, independence and socialism."[54]

Notes to Chapter Five

1. *The Irish Times*, 8 April 1975.
2. Quoted in Tim Pat Coogan, *De Valera: Long Fellow, Tall Shadow* (London: Arrow Books), p. 466.
3. *Irish Independent*, 11 November 1932.
4. *An Phoblacht*, 5 November 1932.
5. Department of Justice, NAI, Jus 8/684.
6. Paddy Byrne, *Irish Republican Congress Revisited* (London: Connolly Publications Ltd, 1994), p. 10.
7. Bowyer Bell, *The Secret Army: The IRA* (Dublin: Poolbeg, 1998), p. 102.
8. Moss Twomey papers, UCDAD, P 69/190.
9. Jonathan Hammill, "Saor Éire and the IRA: An Exercise in Deception", *Saothar* 20.
10. Quoted in Seán Cronin, *Frank Ryan: The Search for the Republic* (Dublin: Repsol, 1980) p. 46.
11. Moss Twomey papers, UCDAD, P 69/53.
12. Quoted in Pat Feeley, *The Gralton Affair* (Dublin: Coolock Free Press, n.d.), p. 44.
13. Moss Twomey papers, UCDAD, P 69/187.
14. George Gilmore, *The Republican Congress* (Dublin: Dochas Co-op Society Ltd., n.d.), p. 30.
15. "When the mob starting attacking our comrades and Connolly House was set on fire, Frank was infuriated. He stood without bending when the Animal Gang directed their attention toward

him; his courage did not fail him." Eoghan Ó Duinnín, *La Niña Bonita agus An Róisín Dubh* (Baile Átha Cliath: An Clóchomhar Tta, 1986), p. 85.

16. Rosmond Jacob Diaries, NLI, 32/582, 6 April 1933, p. 69.
17. Moss Twomey papers, UCDAD, P 69/179.
18. *Ibid.*, P 69/178.
19. *Ibid.*, P 69/170.
20. Rosamond Jacob Diaries, NLI, 32/582, 20 May 1933, p. 72.
21. Moss Twomey papers, UCDAD, P 69/187.
22. Quoted in Cronin, *Frank Ryan*, p. 47.
23. Rosamond Jacob papers, NLI, MS 33/130.
24. Aodh Ó Canainn, "Eilís Ryan in Her Own Words" *Saothar* 21, 1996.
25. Síghle Uí Dhonnchadha papers, UCDAD, P 106/2038.
26. Byrne, *Irish Republican Congress Revisited*, p. 12.
27. Quoted in Uinseann Mac Eoin, *The IRA in the Twilight Years* (Dublin: Argenta, 1997), pp. 753, 769.
28. Quoted in Cronin, *Frank Ryan*, p. 49.
29. *An Phoblacht,* 3 February 1934.
30. Seán MacEntee papers, UCDAD, P 67/525.
31. *Republican Congress*, 5 May 1934.
32. Quoted in Cronin, *Frank Ryan*, p. 50.
33. Quoted in Uinseann Mac Eoin, *Survivors* (Dublin: Angenta, 1997), p. 390.
34. Interview with the author.
35. Quoted in Mac Eoin, *The IRA in the Twilight Years*, p. 769.
36. *An Phoblacht,* 14 April 1934.
37. Ryan seems to have attached no significance to it, but as a young soldier he had had the privilege of meeting the republican figurehead. The extent of his admiration for him as a class war strategist rather than a diehard martyr is unknown. See Mac Eoin, *Survivors,* p. 328.
38. *Republican Congress*, 5 May 1934.
39. Byrne, *Irish Republican Congress Revisited*, p. 15.
40. *Republican Congress*, 5 May 1934.
41. Gilmore, *The Republican Congress*, p. 40.
42. Byrne, *Irish Republican Congress Revisited*, p. 24.
43. Peter O'Connor, *A Soldier of Liberty*, (Dublin: MSF, 1997), p. 9.
44. *Republican Congress,* 16 June 1934.
45. *Ibid.,* 28 July 1934.
46. The two other men were Dinny Coady and Jack Nalty. The three men later followed Ryan to take part in the Spanish Civil War, where they were all killed.
47. *Republican Congress,* 1 September 1934.

48.   *Ibid.,* 28 July 1934.
49.   Quoted in Cronin, *Frank Ryan*, p. 48.
50.   *Ibid.*, p. 17
51.   The governing body of the Gaelic League.
52.   Quoted in Cronin, *Frank Ryan*, p. 47.
53.   *Republican Congress,* 16 June 1934.
54.   Mike Milotte, *Communism in Modern Ireland* (Dublin: Gill &
      Macmillan, 1984), p. 154.

CHAPTER SIX

Republican Congress

O ne wonders if Brendan Behan had in mind Rathmines
Town Hall and the first Republican Congress when he
quipped that the first item on the agenda of every new
Irish organisation is the split.[1] Unfortunately, it had never
clearly been established what Republican Congress was actually going to be; some thought a series of "public parlia-
ments", others expected it to act as a socialist and republican
pressure group, or united front, and others still wanted it to
take the form of a political party in its own right. Advocates
of the formation of a new political party, the "majority" resolution, locked horns with united front "minority" resolution
proponents, including Ryan, in a lengthy debate about revolutionary strategy, the definition and overt use of the words
"Workers' Republic" and what Connolly would have done.

Whilst it may seem to be an obscure wrestle in semantics,
the issue was crucially important; Republican Congress could
not develop without first deciding on the vehicle for progress.
"Feelings were strong and speeches heated," recalled Paddy
Byrne. "The whole atmosphere was charged with emotion."[2]
Bobbie Walsh remembered James Connolly's son Roddy
"whipping off his pullover in the excitement of addressing the
delegates. His name, the Connolly name, swayed many of
them. Nora was there too, throwing her full weight in with
Roddy." Up from Waterford, Frank Edwards was bewildered
by it all; contemplating the "majority" resolution, he thought,
"You would have to be de Valera to understand it. I found it
hard to make up my mind. Frank Ryan was rushing us to come
on his side. He did not bother to explain his to us either."[3]

In fact, Ryan spoke at some length arguing for the united front. He denied Michael Price's contention that he supported a capitalist republic as opposed to a workers' republic and declared the issue was how best to rally the republican forces under working class leadership. Like most of the others, he too claimed heirdom to the vision of Connolly. Ryan alleged that while the "majority" resolution was valid as a "profession of revolutionary faith", the other, "minority" resolution enjoyed more credibility as "a programme of revolutionary work". Ryan concluded that Price's resolution

> would mean the breaking up of the United Front and the betrayal of the working class to middle-class politicians. If Congress thus refused to maintain and extend the United Front, the opposition to Fascism would collapse. By adopting the minority resolution they would initiate a movement that would put the working class at the head of the national struggle, and thus make the Workers' Republic a reality.[4]

Finally put to the vote on Sunday evening, the united front resolution was won by 99 votes to 84. Victory by such a small margin was thereby pyrrhic and effectively split the movement. Everyone, both the defeated and the victorious, were downcast.

Disappointed as they were, Ryan and his colleagues, hardened by a history of setbacks, were too resilient to be deterred from their cause. The week following the Rathmines hosting, *Republican Congress* claimed that "the first Republican Congress has been an achievement that will find a place in the history of revolutionary strivings in our day".[5] Despite the bragging, the loss of Michael Price, the Connolly siblings, Nora and Roddy, and Séamus MacGowan of the ICA, subtracted from Congress some of its most inspiring and dedicated members.

Additionally, braggadocio could not disguise the fact that only two weeks later there was already something seriously amiss with the paper when a front page appeal was launched to raise £300 "in order to put this paper on a firm footing".[6] Its circulation had never been high, and it had had to weather the storm of a newsagents' boycott, the price to pay for its politics.

125

Its fostering of industrial *jacquerie* ensured that only a minuscule income derived from business advertisers. Indeed the paper paradoxically supported a printer's strike that muted the press in Dublin, but, perhaps because of its stance, Ryan found a sympathetic printer in the midlands to run off copies. Ryan's optimism was apparent when in November, on the strength of loans the provenance of which can only be guessed at, he doubled the size of the paper and launched a circulation drive to substantiate the increased sales that he claimed.

One victory that prompted confusion rather than celebration was O'Duffy's resignation from Fine Gael and the decline of the Blueshirts. Republican Congress' most conspicuous target was fast evaporating. Ryan was vague about where it should level its sights: "Fascism must find another method of expression. It will seek that method. Blueshirtism is dead. Fascism is still the menace."[7] There were precious few signs of that menace in Ireland to excite anti-fascists. In early November, Ryan spoke at and led a protest march against a meeting held in the Mansion House by O'Duffy and his ally, Fine Gael TD Patrick Belton. Despite the claims of *Republican Congress,* it is hard to imagine the protest really "marked not only the opposition of the Dublin working class to fascism but the capturing of the streets by the working class".[8] Lashing rain dampened the protest, and in any case, O'Duffy's "fascist rally" was negligibly attended.

The following week, the usual spectacle of Armistice Day celebrations and its limpet demonstrations were marked by an unusual twist. Congress had, at the instigation of Paddy Byrne, formed a branch of ex-servicemen from the Great War, led by Captain Jack White (formerly of the British army, then the ICA under James Connolly), who in turn had organised the protest march for 1934. Two thousand veterans marched in protest against war and poverty, wearing medals, carrying tricolours and waving banners with exhortations to "Honour the Dead by Fighting for the Living". It was a novel and imaginative form of protest for republican socialists and adds to the evidence that Ryan was becoming more open-minded as his politicisation developed. He seemed hardly able to credit it himself.

Did you ever believe you would see me, on an Armistice Day in Dublin, marching beside an ex-

British soldier who wore his Great War medals? For ten years or so, I have shoved my way into the front of the anti-Imperial demonstration. I've taken and given blows in clashes with ex-Servicemen and police. I claim the record for capturing Union Jacks. Armistice Day was our day for demonstrating against Imperialism, and Imperialism to us was typified by Union Jacks and be-medalled ex-soldiers. And last Sunday I walked with be-medalled ex-soldiers.[9]

Unprecedented as this was, a story from Paddy Byrne is even more revealing of Ryan's growing ideological accommodation. The two had made their way somehow to a socialist meeting in Belfast at which a Northern speaker declared

that the working class should learn to trample on both the Union Jack and the Tricolour. Trampling on the Union Jack presented no problems to Frank; he had been doing it all his life, but to subject the sacred Tricolour to such treatment was another kettle of fish. But, he said, the Belfast comrade was right. I concurred.[10]

As was clear enough by this stage of his life, Ryan was far from given to hasty conversions, nor was he in any way inclined to accommodate his hosts out of politeness or pusillanimity. Although there is certainly no record of Ryan's actually besmearing the Irish flag, the story signifies a monumental shift in his concept of patriotism and his designs for his country. The transformation that Ryan exhibited in Belfast revealed the mechanics of his ideological evolution as he weighed and discarded or nurtured political wheat and chaff. Some concepts were novel while others had hitherto been anathema to him. Yet he was no political butterfly, and once he found a home in a notion, he dug in. Although Ryan's development over the years could be measured in inches, his eyes were continually opening to a wider choice of options. Interwar Europe was a hothouse of ideas and socio-political experiments, in which the politically charged, like Ryan, thrived.

Furthermore, although Congress' call from Rathmines had hardly set the heather blazing, Ryan, unwearied by his Sisyphian

127

struggles for republican socialism, still had plenty of fight left in him, as he proved once again to Byrne. Despite clerical, public and political witch hunting, he placed a large red flag over the words of Jim Connell's song on the front page of a May Day *Republican Congress* issue. His less forthright colleagues protested that such a brazen display would only beg more thunderbolts from the influential. "I too felt that it was coming on a bit strong," remembered Byrne, but Ryan in explanation told him the story of having pulled down a red flag from the Knocklong creamery in 1921: "This had since weighed heavily on his conscience and he was now making atonement!"[11]

That Ryan was not buckling under the strains that weighed upon Congress was confirmed during a controversy in Waterford in January 1935. Ryan and the movement were gratefully thrust back into the public eye after Frank Edwards had initiated a campaign to rouse slum-dwellers against their landlords the previous year. He had subsequently been fired from his post at the Christian Brothers' school, Mount Sion, and was the recipient of a public condemnation from the Bishop of Waterford and Lismore, Dr Kinnane. The local Monsignor Byrne, who had vigorously warned his flock off Congress membership, was, it transpired, a trustee of some of the slum property that Edwards had railed against. In anticipation of the condemnation, Ryan had interviewed the bishop, during which ensued a heated exchange revolving around canon law, the clergy's attitude toward republicanism, the moral legitimacy of the Blueshirts and the Edwards case itself. Published in *Republican Congress,* the interview and Edwards's case became the subject of public debate when the national press took them up. Ryan was delighted at the attention given to the very public row between himself and Dr Kinnane and Monsignor Byrne, whose statement in *The Irish Times* he immediately challenged in the same paper.

> If Frank Edwards were a Blueshirt, he would not be the subject of a Pastoral. That is admitted. The Pastoral and subsequent pronouncements have achieved a purpose that was not intended by their respective authors. The widespread publicity they have given to that case makes certain the ultimate undoing of the wrong done to Edwards.[12]

Ryan and a few friends wished to travel to Waterford to a meeting in support of Edwards. Not having the wherewithal to do so, he called a taxi to pick him up from a nursing home in Dublin, disguised as a patient. The friends travelled down to the meeting in a manner Ryan, wrapped in the blankets of a sick man, described as "revolution *de luxe*". He claimed that the Mayor of Waterford told him that "ninety per cent of the people of Waterford are behind Frank Edwards".[13] All to no avail, it transpired.

The issue of *Republican Congress* in which Ryan reported his interview with Dr Kinnane was the first in three weeks. It would also be the last for nearly three months. The issue contained an appeal for donations and claimed it would be up and running again within weeks, citing the reason for the "temporary cessation" as being that "we have exhausted not merely our finances but our credit".[14] As Seán Cronin has pointed out, the paper's production, particularly in the face of the prevailing political wind, "would require a full-time staff, which did not exist . . . The financial burden on an organisation that was supposed to be a co-ordinating bureau for a United Front could not be borne indefinitely."[15]

By the spring of 1935 it was clear that the umbrella movement had not surmounted the problems ensuing from the disastrous fissure at Rathmines. There had been precious few converts to Congress to fill the vacuum left by the dissidents, while the squabbling with former allies showed no sign of relenting. In a letter to Caitlín Brugha, republican stalwart Mary MacSwiney claimed that it "would be a good thing if PO'D and FR had their heads knocked together until they learned sense . . . We agree with much of their programme but their fundamental principles are wrong." Despite having sympathy for the plight of Frank Edwards, MacSwiney discouraged any support for his cause as it might only rejuvenate Congress and "the sooner that dies, the better".[16] A private ICA memo claimed that Ryan was "spreading falsehoods about the Irish Citizen Army" in a desperate yet unsuccessful attempt to win its members back to Congress.[17] Only months after its foundation, a prominent and enthusiastic member, Eithne Coyle, had been pressured into leaving it by the Cumann na mBan leadership due to its animosity towards the IRA. Síghle Uí Dhonnchadha's initial attraction to Congress had already been soured at a meeting during which Ryan allegedly stated "that his chief aim as editor of *Republican Congress* was to expose the hypocrisy and dishonesty of *An Phoblacht* to such purpose that the latter would be forced out of existence . . . This attitude of divisiveness chased away many members and potential members."[18]

In January 1935, Congress lost Charlie Donnelly, whom Ryan had taken under his wing as a UCD activist some years earlier. Beset by personal frustrations, Donnelly had left for London, where he nonetheless set to work organising a London chapter of Congress with its own newssheet, the *Irish Front*, but neither enjoyed much success. Republican fratricide and disillusion within the Congress ranks aside, there were still old reliables working against Congress: the spring pastorals of 1935 were particularly barbed. That same year, James Hogan of Cork University, formerly chief theoretician of the Blueshirts, published his *Could Ireland Become Communist?*, a warning, tardy as it was alarmist, of the communist threat.

Ryan continued to struggle against the stigma of socialist republicanism, to speak at meetings and demonstrations while trying to raise funds to get the paper started up again. Police reports recorded him telling crowds of demonstrators that Fianna Fáil, "who had got into power by the votes of Republicans and workers, had turned out to be a Capitalist and Fascist government, and that if the police prevented their marches again by force, they would be met by force".[19] In January, he was barred from chairing an An Cumann Gaedhealach debate "That a Socialist Republic is the Only Solution for Ireland's Ills" in UCD by President Coffey. The motion "was of a propagandist nature", claimed Coffey, that would be at odds with the Catholic membership of the college, and "the part played by Mr Frank Ryan in the controversy with the Bishop of Waterford made it inadvisable to have him as chairman".[20] Ryan's objections that he was a graduate of the college and had been instrumental in setting up the Cumann were brushed aside.[21]

Additionally, Congress scored own goals as regards projecting itself as a force to be taken seriously. In December 1934, members stormed the Savoy Cinema during the showing of newsreels about the British royal family, intimidating the audience and destroying property in the name of anti-imperialism. Still, the organist, a resolute Mr Philip Dore, remained unperturbed, according to the *Irish Independent*, and kicking off with "My Dark Rosaleen", "His programme, just after the excitement had died down, was much enjoyed."[22] Republican socialism's finest hour it was not.

Still Congress limped on. Paddy Byrne soldiered on in the tenements where he "visited families that lived in semi-darkness in tubercular eighteenth century cellars: 'They survived on bread and rice, unwashed because they couldn't afford soap . . . Jesus, the smell was brutal. It would knock you down.'"[23] He was assisted by Cora Hughes, a beautiful and determined Joan of Arc figure in the slums, who, within a few years, would be dead from tuberculosis contracted in the hovels where she exercised her vocation. A Dublin tram workers' strike in March of 1935 occasioned a brief alliance of Congress, the CPI and the IRA, leading an elated Ryan to claim that "Congress was formed for this alignment of Republicans behind the workers' battles".[24] Following sporadic IRA sniping at police and army trucks moving in strike-breakers to the scenes of disturbance, the government swooped; Ryan and dozens of other republicans were detained with the prospect of a Military Tribunal hearing, but most of the Congress members, Ryan among them, were released by the next day.

Ryan reported the arrests under the title "De Valera Travels Cosgrave Road" in the first issue of a revived *Republican Congress*, which now had its offices at Middle Abbey Street. The new paper still suffered an absence of advertisers, a boycott from news dealers and intimidation from the authorities. Ryan realised that what was needed was a printing works that would run off his and other ostracised papers such as the communist *Irish Workers' Voice*. Too many printers had been cowed by the prospect of losing government, Church and business contracts if they dealt with Ryan. He therefore registered a limited liability company, the Liberty Press Ltd., and hawked shares at five shillings each to enable the "founding of a printing works in Dublin which will serve the needs of the Republican and working class masses".[25]

Ryan implied that those masses were united behind Republican Congress, but events at Bodenstown in the summer of 1935 underlined the distressed state of the movement and the consistently fragmented nature of republicanism. Rather than the 2,000 supporters who had marched under Congress

banners twelve months previously, the umbrella organisation
of the socialist and separatist masses mustered only a paltry
forty-something marchers. Depressingly consistent with 1934's
march, Congress members were halted, and a tussle ensued for
possession of their banners, which were tattered and torn by
the time the contingent was able to resume marching. Ryan
wielded one flagpole to great effect during the scuffles to rescue Frank Edwards.

According to Eoghan Ó Duinnín, the fault lay with Ryan,
the stewards having made clear, in light of the previous year's
brawl, that no banners were to be allowed. The CPI had taken
down their banners and held their own commemoration,
whereas Ryan flaunted the standard for Republican Congress.
If he had been trying to provoke the IRA into shameful heavyhandedness, he failed. He even resented the communists for
their compliance: "*Níor cháin Proinnsias Ó Riain an Páirtí go
poiblí faoin eachtra seo ach, go príobháideach, deireadh sé
'theip an Páirtí Cumannach orainn'.*"[26] That same week
George Gilmore finally returned from America, where his
fund-raising and organising tour for Congress had met with
only limited success.

Perhaps the biggest disappointment for Ryan that summer
was when his prophecy of impending unity amongst Northern
workers went up in the flames of urban rioting and loyalist
pogroms of the Catholic poor. Violence following the Twelfth
of July celebrations left thirteen dead and hundreds of nationalists homeless. Ryan's analysis of the rioting was remarkably
non-partisan. He berated Northern nationalism almost as
much as loyalism, while simultaneously deflecting criticism
that he was not supportive enough of murdered, hounded and
harried Catholics. Calling relentlessly for unity and drawing
on the alliances in 1932, Ryan chided the combatants and
foretold their futures, declaring that the government

> are holding the ring with a view to fostering sectari-
> anism rather than to squelching the pogromists . . .
> When you have slaughtered enough of one another,
> back you will be driven to your reeking slums, back
> to work at decreased wages, or back to the Exchange
> for lesser relief. And neither King William nor the
> Pope will avail you.[27]

By the autumn of 1935, despite the success of some rent strikes in Dublin and occasional victories in Congress-supported labour disputes, it seemed that no matter how hard Ryan and his companions solicited the adherence of the masses, Congress dwindled. Such interest as had been shown by the trade unions had evaporated quickly after the Rathmines split. Calls for increased vigilance against the rise of fascism (prompted by Mussolini's escapades in Abyssinia) left most Irishmen unmoved, and the apathy that greeted rallies against unemployment reflected their impotence. In the countryside, Congress barely existed. In November Ryan, ever optimistic, wrote to Gerald O'Reilly: "I am getting more relief now from financial worries so I am able to give my attention more to making the *Congress* a better paper and to improving its sales . . . After Christmas I will try to get a typist and then I could look after the Congress paper better. I live in hopes."[28] The 14 December issue of *Republican Congress* announced that the paper would return to the street corners in the new year, but it never did.

Ryan was seemingly beset by obstacles in his working and political life but always managed to put on a brave face. He had no real personal or social life except for the odd *céilí* or the occasional pint or two, and his relationship with Rosamond Jacob had finally ground to a halt by 1935. It was a relationship that he had never acknowledged publicly, much to her irritation, despite its lasting for several years. Ryan, with his fine stature, boundless energy and lively sense of humour, had always been attractive to women, and Jacob remained enthralled by him, but he seems never to have had the inclination for long-term relationships. He was wary that they would demand of him too much time and commitment which could be better utilised in politics. After a full five years of secret trysts with him, Jacob had recorded that he was as introverted emotionally as he was extrovert politically: "If only his soul was more friendly," she complained. A year later, she wrote that she still hadn't "yet succeeded in getting through the wall of reserve that encompasses him. He has given me a good deal of confidence and a little love, but so little of his company." Yet Ryan was known for being both gregarious and garrulous.

By the mid-thirties, however, Ryan considered himself to have enough on his hands with journalism and political meetings. He regularly slept where he worked and only met those who called to him on Congress business. When not actually working, Ryan's mind was nonetheless occupied plotting how best to further his political causes.

It is hardly surprising therefore that, after the collapse of *Republican* Congress, the indefatigable Ryan launched a successor of sorts on 29 February 1936, named the *Irish People,* its title on the masthead in English and Irish. Predictably, it had political content very similar to its predecessor, only the new paper had a decidedly artistic bent. It was an eclectic and eminently readable fusion of politics, history, the arts in all their forms, and social comment. Comprising only eight pages, almost a whole page of the first issue was given over to the debilitating effect on Irish literature of the Irish patronage of English authors. An article by renowned painter Seán Keating explaining why "Art Does Not Get a Chance in Ireland" filled another page. Further pieces were forthcoming from fellow artists Maurice MacGonigle and Harry Kernoff, along with other writers and activists such as Rosamond Jacob and Erskine Childers. Hanna Sheehy Skeffington also contributed. Out of solidarity, she had left *An Phoblacht* a week after Ryan, who confessed, only half in jest, to be "terrified out of his life of her, because of her brains – one of the best politicians in Ireland".[29]

The editor had, however, perhaps still too much propagandist blood flowing through his veins. Despite stating in the first editorial that the paper's columns were open to debate amongst all forward-thinkers, Ryan refused to publish an article by Frank O'Connor that he thought denigrated the Irish language. O'Donnell unsuccessfully tried to persuade him that it might foster the debate Ryan claimed to be providing a forum for, before further enraging him with the suggestion that he give over a column to soccer news.[30] Ryan was extremely, and justifiably, proud of the *Irish People,* but such sentiments did not pay the bills. The seventh issue was the last, although, in typical Ryan fashion, readers were informed that the paper was being suspended "temporarily to organise its team of contributors more fully".[31]

The one success Ryan did have at this time was the establishment of a printing works, named the Co-Op Press Ltd, having been able to raise £1,000 by selling shares at £1 each.

However, even after the demise of *Republican Congress*, Ryan found himself overworked, printing publications for others. Regardless, the press was heavily in debt, and to cut down on costs, Ryan did almost everything himself, which may not have been so intolerable had not the machinery been so old and the poster type so limited that each job took hours longer than it should have. Ryan was regularly putting in sixteen or even twenty-four hour shifts, all of which, done in haste and exhaustion, led to further trouble when Ryan found himself the subject of a writ for "atrocious libel". As printer, he was being sued by a priest who had been named in an article in the communist *Irish Workers' Voice* as having refused sacraments to a dying man. Ryan had been too busy to read and check the article before printing it.

The exhaustive work and constant strain punished more than accuracy in reportage. In April, just as the *Irish People* was folding up, Ryan went to Liverpool to stay with a cousin for a weekend, due to return to chair a meeting of Congress members and the visiting Scottish Communist MP, Willie Gallacher.[32] His cousin, a doctor, had given the weary visitor a check-up upon his arrival and immediately dispatched him to his brother Vincent, the TB specialist in a sanatorium in Dewsbury in Yorkshire. Ordered to rest temporarily and then return to a more regular life comprising less stressful work, fewer cigarettes and no whiskey, Ryan was told that while his lungs were fine, his heart was swollen and his blood pressure too high.

Even so, he took time off from taking time off and went to Manchester to order printing machinery to be sent to Dublin, and he never took time off from worrying about the dissolution of Congress. Whilst he had been in England, Easter commemorations at Glasnevin had been disrupted by violence against the left wing of republicanism, as represented by Congress members and communists, on an even greater scale than was now the norm. George Gilmore and Cora Hughes, in particular, were badly hurt.[33] When he returned to Ireland, at meetings and in letters to the papers protesting the outrages, Ryan claimed enemies of republicanism, rather than socialism, had perpetrated them. The man who had demanded there be "No Free Speech for Traitors" castigated the heirs of the Murder Gang of 1922 "for not allowing free speech, a fascist-imperialist trait"![34]

In January 1936 there was an attempt to organise four active service units (ASUs) to work in four areas of the movement's concern. Ryan later had little to say of the plan except that "the ASU idea went wallop. Party loyalties are still too strong", intimating that what there was of a united front was not even very united. The only outside interest in Congress seemed to come from the Department of Justice, which noted of the ASU plan that "despite this effort to infuse new life into Republican Congress, the movement languished through lack of funds". The authorities were not, however, cheered into complacency by the failure of the *Irish People,* conscious that, despite it, Ryan, O'Donnell and Gilmore "did not relax their personal efforts to propagate their doctrine of national communism, and they were backed up by a handful of faithful supporters".[35]

Although Ryan knew the umbrella organisation was incapacitated, he still had great faith in the concept behind it, and, thus armed, the opinions of others or developments in the world around him could do little to shake his fidelity. Whereas Chairman O'Donnell was fast losing interest and returning his mind to postponed literary projects, Ryan was desperately racking his mind for a political vehicle that could carry forward the notion of a united, leftist, separatist front, even if the hulk of Republican Congress was abandoned. The fervour still possessed by Ryan for such a movement while his comrades were led away by disillusion and apathy is evident from a letter he wrote in the spring of 1936, in which he gives, for Ryan, a surprisingly temperate appraisal of the situation:

> The Congress – from an organisational point of view – is only a name. It exists only in Dublin . . . Yet the Congress idea has not failed, and if we did nothing else but propaganda and the holding of meetings, representative (even to a limited extent) of Republican and Labour elements, we would be doing good work. Eventually there must be a United Front; at our worst, we make it easier of achievement . . . The Congress is stagnant, as I say. It consists merely of the original pioneers.

While his assessment of the non-party front was legitimate, he went on to be more specific as regards his own position within the political rainbow. In so doing he once again displayed the durability of his own beliefs, impervious to the recriminations heaped upon his and other red heads since the days of Saor Éire.

> The future lies in working-class rule. In my opinion,
> not in the Communism advocated today, but certainly in that direction. That explains, at once, why I
> associate on a platform with the CP and at the same
> time why I would not join the CP. And eventually the
> gap between the CP policy on the one hand and the
> Fianna Fáil IRA policies on the other hand will be
> filled by a new movement. We will just have to slog
> along for that.[36]

Ryan's constant expectation that he would win a significant number of others to his position raises questions about his judgment. Yet within two months, he took up the challenge to do just that and paraded his apparent conversion to democratic politics by putting himself forward as a candidate for Dublin North-East in the city's corporation elections at the end of June. George Gilmore also put himself forward, as a candidate for Dublin North-West. The two did so in an attempt to bring what they considered to be true republicanism on to the political agenda. It was a considerable turnaround for Ryan, and not one that he ever fully accounted for. Yet it implies that his appreciation of politics was still deepening, even if his core beliefs remained largely unchanged. He had earlier promised that Congress would not be a step toward constitutionalism but toward revolution, and perhaps desperation at the plight of Congress was as much a motive for his running as his softening toward constitutional politics. Ryan's and Gilmore's decision at the time to throw their revolutionary caps into the democratic ring is probably summed up accurately in a garda report of the time. It surmised that now the members of Republican Congress ". . . claim to be wholehearted democrats . . . They do not exclude armed insurrection; but they regard it as being the last and not the first step, and as being feasible (as well as justifiable) only when power is being withheld from a majority of the people by the 'forces of reaction'."[37]

Ryan himself tried to explain to the electorate why their votes should go to himself and Gilmore, members of the Republican Congress but running as independents.

> The election of Republican candidates not affiliated to a party would give a voice to the real aims and genuine grievances of the mass of the people of Dublin. The various party members would vote en bloc. The unaffiliated Republican member could fight for the right of the hardworking Dublin citizen and the poor of Dublin generally.

Theoretically sound perhaps, but, unfortunately for Ryan, being an independent also meant he had no party machine to carry him. Rather, he had neither "the price of paper on which to print posters" nor time enough away from his printing press to run a campaign of any worth. It was woefully close to election day by the time he started holding rallies, principally on his old stomping grounds at College Green. There he issued a Challenge to Government, a government that had "turned its back on Republicanism" to the extent that in banning Bodenstown commemorations, suppressing *An Phoblacht* and imprisoning Moss Twomey, it was trying to "rid the country of Republicanism".[38] Only two weeks previously, the de Valera government had proscribed the IRA. By referring to its persecution, Ryan was clearly appealing for traditional republican as well as leftist republican votes, and he stressed that his platform was based firmly and sincerely on a drive for republican unity.

In Marino, Ryan turned his guns on the Labour Party for not pursuing the republican ambitions outlined in its Constitution, as exemplified by its support for the Treaty fifteen years earlier. His insistence on the country's need for unified, true republicanism was further hammered home at last minute speeches at Five Lamps and the North Strand.

In lashing rain, 418 people went out to vote for Ryan out of a total of 32,117 voters. He came fifteenth in a field of twenty-two candidates, with the highest number of votes going to Alfie Byrne, Lord Mayor of Dublin and independent TD with Blueshirt sympathies.[39] So far as Ryan was concerned, there were various reasons why he had done so badly.

Alfie Byrne was in my area and the whole fight centred around him and Fianna Fáil. Then my organisation was bad. I could give no personal attention to it,
being at work all day and often at night . . . I didn't
get even ONE second preference from Fianna Fáil. The
lesson of the elections is that Republican disunity
resulted in Republican apathy – abstentionists all on
anti-Cosgrave side. The people didn't rally to IRA or
to us. We'll do better next time, though.

Ryan's only consolation was that, compared to his 1.3 per
cent of the poll, Gilmore won 2.2 per cent, or 730 votes, which
led him to deduce that "George made a good show. Had he
got 200 more first preferences, he'd probably be elected."[40]
However, as with most of the setbacks Ryan suffered, he considered he had learned something from the elections; ground
had been given away by republicans rather than won by their
opponents. "It was not a rainstorm that won the campaign for
the Lord Mayor's nominees," he concluded, "it was Republican apathy," which he considered to be the inevitable result of
the "senseless jealousies and friction between various sections
of the Republican movement". In a letter to the papers, referring to the followers that he was for ever looking expectantly
over his shoulders for, Ryan claimed that they

> . . . could be roused to enthusiasm if there were a real
> drive for the re-establishment of the Republic . . .
> Surely we ought to have learned from recent events
> that it is not one Republican faction merely that suf-
> fers from the disunion of the various factions, but the
> whole Republican movement . . . I believe there are
> sufficient numbers of conscious and determined
> Republicans in the different – and differing – sections
> to put a stop to the disintegration of the Republican
> movement.

Yet Ryan then poured grapeshot into the ranks of those
republicans who differed from him: Fianna Fáil, who "reserve
to themselves the right to dictate to the people", and the IRA
"which, and which alone, is to be allowed – by them – to
achieve the Republic".[41] Was it gall or delusion that so filled

Ryan? Republicans blamed none other than him and his comrades for the factionalism caused by Saor Éire before cleaving the nation's republican army with the foundation of Congress; he, with his confreres, was an IRA wrecker. Ryan airbrushed the discrepancies out of his sketch of recent republican history. He neglected to mention that he had spent five years infusing republicanism with a brand of politics that most in the movement considered offensive. More importantly, Ryan does not even hint at what compromises he and the republican left were willing to concede so as to achieve the unity he professed to so yearn for. Those who knew Ryan appreciated many of his personal traits but knew also that ideological immolation was not among them.

As ever, Ryan had more practical than ideological worries, centring around the beleaguered Co-Op Press, but he was relieved of these when it closed down shortly after the elections. The *Irish Workers' Voice* had ceased publication in June, and what income there was was insufficient to cover costs. At least Ryan did not have to worry any more about libel cases.

It seemed that all that was left to do was to put Republican Congress out of its misery. The fact that there was, by the summer of 1936, nobody to administer the *coup de grâce* highlights the want of leadership, a central focus, in Congress whenever it was most needed. O'Donnell, Gilmore and Ryan viewed the organisational and administrative work that was essential to holding a purportedly national movement together with distaste, particularly as the results of such donkey work were no more than mediocre.

Of the three pioneers who formed the nucleus of Republican Congress, it was Ryan who held out the most hope for a rejuvenated front. Since Congress' foundation, he had been kept overly busy at his printing press and fretting over finances. His personality and bearing may otherwise have made him an ideal figurehead around whom to centre a mass movement of the country's disaffected, even though he was not its chief architect. Gilmore, on the other hand, disliked public speaking and was probably too reserved a man for the job. Widely respected as a man of action in the 1920s, he had since become more of a theoretician and expounder of Connolly's writings. Then there was Chairman O'Donnell. An outstanding agitator with a sharp mind and sense of humour, he was, however, not known for his humility or his willingness to dirty his hands doing the spadework that the less cerebral could be put to. Paddy Byrne and Ryan, over a pint or two, would refer to their ascetic and somewhat imperious chairman as "Sitting Bull". More crucially, he was, according to Byrne, "hard to discipline . . . always likely to go off on one of his own ploys . . . he preferred to pass on his ideas and let others implement them."[42]

A couple of weeks after the Dublin elections, O'Donnell took himself and his wife off to Spain for some political sightseeing. Shortly after his arrival, a revolt led by General Francisco Franco against the democratically elected government had spread from Morocco to the Spanish mainland. The ensuing Civil War was to make Spain the battlefield for European ideology and would demand of Frank Ryan perhaps his greatest commitment to republicanism, socialism and, uncharacteristically, democracy.

Notes to Chapter Six

1.   MacDara Doyle, *The Republican Congress: A Study in Irish Radicalism* (Unpublished MA thesis, UCD, 1988), p. 51.
2.   Paddy Byrne, *Irish Republican Congress Revisited* (London: Connolly, 1994), p. 30.
3.   Both quoted in Uinseann Mac Eoin, *Survivors* (Dublin: Angenta, 1980), p. 9.
4.   *Republican Congress,* 13 October 1934.
5.   *Ibid.,* 6 October 1934.
6.   *Ibid.,* 20 October 1934.
7.   *Ibid.,* 6 October 1934.
8.   *Ibid.,* 10 November 1934.
9.   *Ibid.,* 17 November 1934.
10.   Byrne retrospectively regretted his acquiescence. Byrne, *Irish Republican Congress Revisited,* p. 20.
11.   *Ibid.*
12.   *The Irish Times,* 16 January 1935.
13.   Frank Edwards himself remembered that Ryan's optimism was misguided: "Despite the tremendous support I received from every quarter . . . I was bested. I had to leave Waterford. They would not leave my mother alone. She had a post as a public health nurse. They boycotted her and she had to resign, dying shortly afterwards."
14.   *Republican Congress,* 12 January 1935.
15.   Seán Cronin, *Frank Ryan: The Search for the Republic* (Dublin: Repsol, 1980), p. 61.

16. Caitlín Brugha papers, UCDAD, P 15/8.
17. Department of Justice files, NAI, Jus 8/320.
18. Síghle Uí Dhonnchadha papers, UCDAD, P 106/1490.
19. Department of Justice files, NAI, Jus 8/339.
20. *Ibid.*, NAI, Jus 8/392.
21. As were those of The O'Rahilly, a member of the UCD governing body who wrote to the *Irish Press* that the ban was "most unjust . . . Furthermore, the puerile reasons given will have no effect other than to make the National University the laughing stock of educated Europe." *Irish Press,* 24 January 1935.
22. *Irish Independent,* 4 December 1934.
23. Quoted in Peter Hegarty, *Peadar O'Donnell* (Cork: Mercier Press, 1999), p. 222.
24. *Republican Congress,* 30 March 1935.
25. Department of Justice files, NAI, Jus 8/407.
26. "Frank Ryan did not disparage the party publicly about the incident, but privately he said 'the Communist Party failed us'." Eoghan Ó Duinnín, *La Niña Bonita agus An Roisín Dubh* (Baile Atha Cliath: An Clóchomhán, 1986), p. 85.
27. *Republican Congress,* 20 July 1935.
28. Quoted in Cronin, *Frank Ryan,* p. 61.
29. Rosamond Jacob Diaries, December 1929, NLI, 32/582, p. 42.
30. *Ibid.,* January 1931, p. 17.
31. *Ibid.,* September 1927, p. 29.
32. As Seán Cronin points out, this was a reasonable suggestion as "soccer was the sport of the urban working class in Ireland". *Frank Ryan* p. 69.
33. *Irish People,* 11 April 1936.
34. The meeting degenerated into a riot thanks to the attendance of over 4,000 onlookers, of whom a policeman present surmised with accurate understatement "it was very obvious that they were not there for the purpose of supporting the communists". Seán MacEntee papers, UCDAD, P 67/532.
35. One friend of Ryan's, Dick Whittington, claimed to have been by Ryan's side during the disturbances at Glasnevin: "He shielded me from being beaten up because of the red ribbon I wore with the Easter lily. Poor Cora Hughes was terribly mauled that day. Frank got us all out of the cemetery across the railway – at gunpoint." As Ryan was in England at the time, Whittington clearly had the identity of his protector mistaken or, more likely, the date and location of the incident he recalled. Rosamond Jacob papers, NLI, 33/130.
36. *Irish Press,* 1 May 1935.
37. Government Notes on Republican Congress, Seán MacEntee papers, UCDAD, P 67/527.

38. Quoted in Cronin, *Frank Ryan*, p. 65.
39. Seán MacEntee papers, UCDAD, P 67/527.
40. *Irish Press,* 27 June 1936.
41. Other seats within the same constituency went to O'Duffy's lieutenant, Paddy Belton of Fine Gael, but also to Jim Larkin.
42. Quoted in Cronin, *Frank Ryan*, p. 68.
43. *Irish Freedom,* Mí Lughnasa 1936. The IRA had recently founded a political party, Cumann Poblachta na h-Éireann, led by Seán MacBride.
44. Quoted in Hegarty, *Peadar O'Donnell*, p. 223.

Frank Ryan as an IRA volunteer, ca. 1920.

As a leading member of An Cumann Gaelach in UCD, 1924. Douglas Hyde
and Eamon de Valera are in the front row.

On his graduation from UCD with Celtic Studies BA. (*National Library of Ireland*)

Ryan carried aloft by crowds on his release from Arbour Hill, March 1932
(*National Library of Ireland*)

Speaking to a crowd of thousands in College Green on the day of his release
(*National Library of Ireland*)

t a celebratory *ceilidh* on the night of his release. (*National Library of Ire-
nd*)

'ith fellow international brigaders, flanked by Peter Daly of Wexford and
ddy O'Daire of Donegal; Frank Edwards is at the extreme right; Dublin's
mmy Prendergast is seated centre with beret.

In a long-awaited officer's uniform, Spain.

With drinking buddy Ernest Hemingway in Spain, 1937.

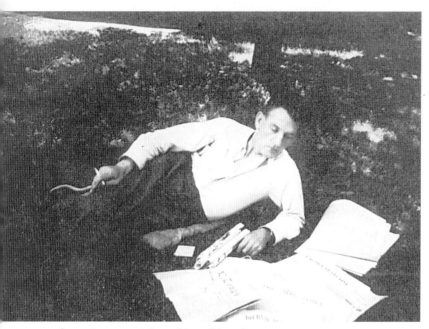

Just sprung from Burgos: sick and bewildered in Paris, summer 1940.

A few weeks before his death, May 1944.

PART TWO

CHAPTER SEVEN

Spain

Frank Ryan had been an assiduous observer of Spanish affairs during the turbulent years since 1931 when the monarchy was replaced by a Republican-socialist coalition. The Spanish social order, crippled by retarded development, was almost feudal by the standards of western Europe. Alarming rates of illiteracy existed among a peasantry whose living and working conditions were mercilessly primitive. In the shadows cast by Spain's overlords of the Church and landed classes, the urban and, particularly, the rural poor endured lives of unrelieved hardship. Before the momentum for change could gather pace, in 1933 a centre-right government had been returned, one unabashed in its use of force to crush Asturian miners and regional nationalists who rose against it. Articles in Ryan's publications had directed attention to the strikes, revolts and transfers of leadership that the country had suffered until the establishment of a Popular Front Coalition government in February 1936. In mid-July, insurgent General Franco quickly took control of what were to be known as the Nationalists, a heterogenous composition of monarchists, democratic conservatives, fascists, landowners and businessmen, with the backing, for the most part, of the army, police and Roman Catholic hierarchy. Arrayed on the side of democracy, the Republican force was an even more motley confederacy comprising liberals, socialists, communists of various hues, regional Basque and Catalan nationalists, and the world's largest anarchist party.

Appreciation of the war's complexities did not travel well to Ireland, where it was soon diminished to the good forces of religion and the right to private property bucking the evil forces of communism and murderous sacrilege. Of course, the Irish were more than familiar with the tenets and vocabulary that such a conflict induced, having recently witnessed related skirmishes in their own country. Such apathy towards the war as existed in Ireland was soon swept away by reports of Republican atrocities. Churches were burned and Nationalist prisoners shot out of hand before Franco's forces gained control of large swathes of the north and west and gave free rein to the retributive nature of their governance.

Unsurprisingly, the standard-bearer of Franco's crusade in Ireland was the *Irish Independent,* which on 11 August 1936, only three weeks into the revolt, was demanding to know why the Red government in Madrid was still being recognised by the Irish government. The paper unceasingly outlined the reasoning behind its stance.

> On the one side is a so-called government which has abandoned all the functions of government to a Communist junta bent on the destruction of personal liberty, the eradication of religion, the burning of churches and the wholesale slaughter of the clergy. On the other side are the Patriot army, gladly risking liberty, property and life in the defence of their Faith – fighting the same fight that our ancestors fought for centuries for the same cause.[1]

Spain provided a mirror to Ireland's fate should it desist in its resistance to communism, and Ireland was awash with stories of churches desecrated, nuns raped and honest landowners murdered or being driven off their property at the point of (red) pitchforks. Returned from Spain, Peadar O'Donnell conceded that the stories were not devoid of truth, yet he remained enthusiastic for the Republican government.

Ryan too was, for once, enthusiastically on the side of a democratically elected government rather than the rebels, but more pressing was the advancement of Irish republican unity. Consequently, he remained passive in his sympathy for Republican Spain while his adversaries were mobilising. In August, Paddy Belton[2] had set up the Irish Christian Front, with Church blessing, to help support Franco's Nationalists. Cardinal MacRory, meanwhile, had been contacted by agents of Franco in London, impressing upon him the glory that Ireland would reflect should she help Catholic Spain in the most direct way possible. The Cardinal replied that he knew who "seems to be the man who would be of most help . . . a chivalrous, courageous, upright man and a good Catholic and above all, a fine organiser".[3] Eoin O'Duffy was the man, and the primate met the paramilitary to discuss the options of Spanish aid open to him. By the end of August, O'Duffy claimed that over 6,000 men had volunteered to travel to Spain with him.

Still Ryan was preoccupied. IRA man Sean Russell, devoted and old school, was on a fundraising tour of America that only further disheartened Ryan, as Russell's "bombastic speeches are not conducive to republican unity". Ryan's closest friends in America, Gerald O'Reilly and Mike Quill, had been threatened with expulsion from Clan na Gael because of their work for Republican Congress; on advice from Dublin, they closed up the Congress shop in New York and remained in the Clan. Ryan had tried to persuade O'Donnell to go to New York to explain Congress' position, but he obserned that the movement's chairman "was too full of Spain and could think of nothing else. I wouldn't go to Spain, or to USA, just now, because I feel I have to stand my ground here and rally our own. The frontline trenches of Spain are right here."[4]

Ryan spoke truer than he knew. While he was fruitlessly pacing the floor about Congress' demise, a letter from Charlie Donnelly, who was running the Congress office in London, dragged Ryan into the battle lines being drawn up for a new conflict as he was still mourning the losses in the last. Donnelly declared that it was imperative that Republican Congress make an assertive stand on the war in Spain, to which Ryan replied that the movement was in no position to do so, withered as it was. It had no newspaper, few members and less money. Donnelly returned to Dublin to see friends before leaving for Spain but also to exert weightier pressure on Ryan to be more proactive.

When the two friends met, a furious row broke out, during which Donnelly accused Ryan, the self-professed internationalist, of "betraying the legacy of Connolly unless Congress publicly supported the Republican government" in Spain.[5] Ryan retorted that while Donnelly had been sitting in London firing off letters of accusation, he himself had been working tirelessly to hold together the disintegrating movement that Donnelly was now calling on. The argument was finally settled by wiring a cablegram of support to the beleaguered Republican government in Madrid. A press release, giving notice of the cablegram, claimed that a triumvirate of the Christian Front, O'Duffy's National Corporate Party and the *Irish Independent* was "shamelessly and recklessly trying to use the name of religion to further the rise of the discredited Fascist groups in Ireland".[6] Furthermore, George Gilmore was soon dispatched to the Basque country to find a Basque priest, Father Ramon La Borda, to invite him on a lecture tour of Ireland to inform the public about the truth of the Republican government and Franco's designs on Spain.

In Ireland, to even question the extravagance of the stories about Republican atrocities was to sprout horns. Within days of the press release, Cardinal MacRory, addressing pilgrims to the shrine of Blessed Oliver Plunkett in Drogheda, devoted a speech to "Irish Republican Congress – a body of young Catholic Irishmen" supporting a "campaign that was being carried on to destroy belief in God and Jesus Christ, the Catholic Church and . . . every Catholic state in the world. I hope that these young men did not realise what they were doing." The primate thought it "a scandal and an outrage . . . a serious matter that the government should take note of". Still, he did remind the congregation that "you and I have a duty . . . to pray for those poor misguided sons of Ireland". He called for prayers for Spain (though presumably not for its legitimate government) and went on to say that "we should all help from our purses, help her to obtain war supplies – what I should say is medical supplies for her sick and wounded. I do not want to say anything about any other kind of help."[7]

The response from Ryan, well used to fending off blows from the crozier, was sufficiently speedy, lengthy and well-argued that one cannot help but wonder if he had the bulk of it composed before MacRory had uttered a word in Drogheda. He first defended the Congress' cablegram as being a message of support and sympathy to the Spanish, Catalan and Basque peoples in their fight against fascism. "That there have been outrages is unfortunately true," Ryan wrote. However, support for the Republicans did not translate into advocating the murder of priests and the burning of churches, just as MacRory's support of the Nationalists did not mean that he applauded the Nationalist "massacre of two thousand Catholics at Badajos, that you believe the Mohommedan Moors are fighting for Christianity, or that you approve the Godless scum of the Foreign Legion". Ryan deeply resented the representation of "the Almighty as God become Fascist" and presented parallels in Irish history wherein the Church elbowed its way to the centre stage of politics with the spurious justification that religion was at stake. "Finally, may I assure your Eminence that, as a Catholic, I will 'take my religion from Rome', but that as an Irish Republican, I will take my politics from neither Moscow nor Maynooth."[8]

The address was classic Ryan disputation, informed, articulate and unambiguous, and it received much attention in the press. Charlie Donnelly could not have been more amply rewarded for his persistence. An Irish voice in support of Republican Spain had finally surfaced after being submerged by the deluge of clerical, press and popular supposition that not to support Franco was to not have any concern for God or His creation.[9] "The Republican Congress alone upheld the cause of the Spanish Republic and became the rallying ground for all who supported it," recalled Paddy Byrne.[10] The Spanish cause gave Congress "a new infusion of life",[11] even if its activities barely extended beyond it.[12]

The hushed and relatively few doubters of Franco's divine right to power were at least now willing to declare themselves as such. Soon offers were coming in from men around the country volunteering for active service, wanting to enlist in an Irish brigade to serve in Spain with the International Brigades of volunteers from around the world in the army of the Spanish Republic. Ryan took charge of the venture.

Why did Ryan change his mind about going to Spain? Certainly neither Gilmore (on crutches after his plane crash-landed in Spain) nor O'Donnell were won over to the idea that anything more than material aid, much less Congress' precious few members, should be sent to Spain. Ryan himself said little on the subject, and even that was contradictory. Frequently he claimed that the brigade was formed to counter O'Duffy's fascist volunteers, tarnishing the name of Ireland abroad, yet on other occasions he dismissed this notion. Perhaps he was provoked into leading the mobilisation of volunteers by the unlikely combination of communist Donnelly and Cardinal MacRory. The two men certainly seemed to snap him out of his grievance for a Congress that was all but lost. Eoin O'Duffy, too, must deserve some credit in his capacity as recruiting sargeant. Ryan's friend Annie O'Farrelly had the vague "impression that he left the country more because he was sore with everyone here than on account of his leanings towards Communism".[13] If her explanation is negative, the incipient momentum of support for the government in Spain provided Congress with its life-blood, and Ryan, rather than O'Donnell or Gilmore, was bound to be the one to step forward for the mission's captaincy. He was the youngest and boldest of the three. "He was intelligent and a good soldier, but always willing to take a risk," his IRA friend Packy Early remembers. Furthermore, Ryan "always had plenty of energy, especially if it was for a fight".[14] Perhaps, in spite of himself, the prospect of battling for Republican democracy in Spain and, by extension, the world, also appealed to the romantic in him.

Ryan's assumption of the Spanish Republican torch in Ireland was welcomed by the Communist Party of Ireland, tardy though it was. The communists had already started to enlist from their tiny membership volunteers for the International Brigades but were concerned that potential republican, socialist and liberal volunteers might be deterred by the stigma of communism. Therefore, as communist Mick O'Riordan remembers, the mobilisation campaign was delighted to have as a leader a man who "personified as no one else did the best militant and revolutionary characteristics of the Irish people".[15]

Who were the men who volunteered for such an unpopular and dangerous cause? Paradoxically, it was revolutionary socialist republicans and communists who, in Ireland, stepped into the firing line for a liberal democracy. For the most part, they were members of Republican Congress or the CPI, well used to swimming against the current of popular opinion, and were veterans of opposition to fascism in Ireland. A young Dublin communist, Bob Doyle, calculated that

> O'Duffy and his Blueshirts intended following in the footsteps of the Nazis . . . I thought there was a danger that Ireland would go Fascist and that was one of

the motivating factors in making up my mind to go. I didn't know much about Spain, but my thoughts on the way to Spain were that every bullet I fired would be a bullet against a Dublin landlord and capitalist.[16]

Others were less parochial. In London, Waterford emigrés Peter O'Connor, brothers Johnny and Paddy Power and Jackie Hunt "saw it as our internationalist duty to support Spain. In our view, taking a stand against Fascism in Spain was the most important issue of the time."[17] Probably most of the volunteers had at one time been members of the IRA, and some still serving signed up despite an order from Chief of Staff Tom Barry forbidding IRA men to enlist under Ryan. Two volunteers, whose enthusiasm was not wanting and whose republican credentials were well-known to Ryan, presented themselves for enlistment, but Ryan curtly dismissed them; Brendan Behan and Cathal Goulding were barely fourteen years old.[18] Some undoubtedly were inspired by the hope that Spain would enable them to take a few legitimate potshots at O'Duffy and his followers, and it can be safely assumed that the ranks of the politically motivated were complemented by the triggerhappy and the restless, adventurers and down-at-heel romantics.

Meanwhile, travel arrangements had to be made, passports obtained and a propaganda war fought. The Spanish Republic was castigated regularly from the pulpit and Fine Gael platforms, and a special Church collection in October raised the extraordinary sum of over £43,000.[19] Gilmore and O'Donnell wrote to papers and told anyone who would listen about their experiences in Spain. Barely conceivable during the summer, public meetings were held in November and December to collate Irish support for Spanish Republicans. The Department of Justice noted in early December that Ryan, in a meeting in Cathal Brugha Street, called on his audience "to let the world know that Ireland repudiated O'Duffy and the Christian Front".[20]

De Valera meanwhile had gladly fallen in line with Britain and France to declare his country neutral and non-interventionist, despite pressure from the Fine Gael opposition and sections of the press to recognise Franco as the head of a new Spanish government. It was common knowledge that non-intervention was aiding Franco by default so long as the Germans and Italians were supporting the general with men, arms and aeroplanes. Ryan conceded that a Non-Intervention Pact, to which Germany and Italy were cynical signatories, was "a well intentioned effort to end German and Italian interference", but as he ruefully noted, "the immediate result of the Pact was that the Spanish government could not receive even those arms it had ordered and paid for before the outbreak of the revolt".[21] Russian assistance to the Republican government was only slightly more discreet but less substantial.

Still, de Valera felt compelled to uphold the facade of non-intervention and was happy to perpetuate the diplomatic farce that surrounded it so long as it suited politics at home. The government refused to offer protection to its citizens who wished to travel to Spain, and passports were not granted lightly. Frank Edwards claimed to need one for a teaching post in France, and communist and republican Civil War hero Kit Conway received his only after insisting that he wanted urgently to visit the Marian shrine in Lourdes. It is hard to imagine that de Valera was not privately delighted by the supposedly discreet machinations that were to spirit away radicals, militant republicans and the hardline remnants of Blueshirtism to the battlefields of Spain, where, if they could not actually dispose of each other, their disruptive energies might at least be dissipated. De Valera did not interfere with any pending departures.

Ryan told eighty volunteers for Spain to head for the night boat to Liverpool on 11 December 1936. Either because of the venture's supposed secrecy or, more likely, for personal reasons, he had not even told his sister Eilís that he was leaving, although she had heard rumours to that effect. That evening she met a journalist friend who told her what was afoot, and she made her way to Westland Row Station and the train bound for the docks. Her brother was there with Frank Edwards, being seen off by O'Donnell and his wife, Lile. "Frank got out of the carriage when he saw me and he walked away down the platform. He put his rosary beads into my hands and said, 'Tell mother and father that I'm not a red. I am going to fight for democracy in Spain.'"[22]

At the quayside, Ryan digressed from slipping away anonymously to read out a statement to the press:

The Republican contingent, besides being a very effi-
cient fighting force – every member of it having been
in action – is also a demonstration of the sympathy of
revolutionary Ireland with the Spanish people in their
fight against international Fascism. It is also a reply
to the intervention of Irish Fascism in the war against
the Spanish Republic which, if unchallenged, would
remain a disgrace on our own people. We want to
show that there is a close bond between the democracies of Ireland and Spain. Our fight is the fight of
the Spanish people, as it is of all peoples who are the
victims of tyranny.[23]

That same day, thirty men left Belfast to reconnoitre with
Ryan in London, and the following day a further ten left Ross-
lare. On the Sunday of that same weekend, 500 or so men left
the quayside of Galway with Eoin O'Duffy to board a German
ship in Galway Bay flying a swastika, to fight for Nationalist
Spain. They were seen off by hundreds reciting prayers and
singing hymns and by the blessings of clerics.

Passing through London and picking up more Irish volunteers, Ryan's party made its way to Paris where it was vetted
and processed by communist officials. There was by now a
sense among the men of no going back, and Frank Edwards
jibed Ryan about the military appearance he had acquired. In
London he had kitted himself out in khaki dress with top
boots and a leather coat, and Edwards claimed that Ryan
looked for all the world like a Boer commander: "Having told
the boys to keep a low profile, he looked the real guerrilla
leader."[24] Yet Ryan was not the sole Irishman making manifest
his ambitions; an Englishman bound for Spain viewed with
distaste a few dozen of Ryan's followers taking up residence in
the bar on the French ferry and regaling their fellow travellers
with rebel songs and vocal denunciations of Franco.

From Paris, Ryan wrote to his parents to assure them that
he would be in little danger in Spain since he was to work
mostly in the government's publicity department, writing and
broadcasting. His deafness, he claimed, precluded military
activity on the front line; "Besides, when I die, I want it to be
in Ireland – my life is of more value to Ireland than any other

place." Presumably because he was concerned that his sister might not have passed on his message with sufficient conviction, he also let them know that he "was at confession last Saturday – and I'll have more opportunities here".[25] From Perpignan he wrote to both Eilís and Gerald O'Reilly full of optimism and buoyed by the spirit of his fellow volunteers.

In the early hours of 15 December, Ryan and a much reduced following of a dozen men (to facilitate crossing the border), passed into Spain and were brought to a Republican base at Figueras. That night's sleep was disturbed when a gunshot sounded in the sleeping quarters as two Catalan guards arrested a drunken member of the Irish party and trained their guns on the others. Thanks to what French Ryan remembered from his school days, the situation was soon under his control, but the problems thrown up by the International Brigades' amalgamation of different nationalities using different languages were apparent; particularly so in the morning when it transpired that the errant Irishman was suspected of being a fascist infiltrator and risked facing a firing squad. After a slanging match conducted through interpreters, the fortress commandant, who had raised much mirth amongst the Irish because of his resemblance to Eoin O'Duffy, released the prisoner and the men moved on to Barcelona.

Travelling on a train ornamented by the initials of the various Republican factions and festooned with red flags, the Irish contingent arrived in Barcelona to the cheers of the largely anarchist crowds. Holding aloft a red flag with which he had been presented as a gift of welcome, Ryan led the men in parade through the city. They were then entrained for Valencia, then on to a training camp at Albacete and billets at the laughably named Gran Hotel. Such were the hotel's sanitary conditions that the men used the public toilet, despite being embarrassed by its female attendant who collected tips in exchange for strips of newspaper. This sense of shame, for some reason, afflicted the Dubliners in particular.

It was in Albacete that they first met André Marty, base commander and leader of a French naval mutiny in the Black Sea some fifteen years earlier when France had supported the White Army in Russia. Veteran Peter O'Connor thought Albacete "a haven for deserters, saboteurs, black marketeers, spies, fifth columnists and rumour mongers. It was the most demoralising place in Spain."²⁶ There were other aspects of war-torn Spain that the Irish objected to before they even came under fire. The sight of desecrated churches in Barcelona had distressed these supposed heretics, and, more practically, they were alarmed at the scarcity and poor quality of rifles.

Further, the attempted application of principles of equality caused confusion among soldiers who all addressed each other as "comrade" while at the same time having to obey orders and observe the hierarchy that made up the necessary chain of command. The International Brigades were essentially in the shadow of the Comintern. Just as the Comintern was not known for its toleration of dissenting voices within the ranks, Ryan was hardly an avatar of discretion. Yet, despite some very trying times in Spain, he seems to have restrained himself sufficiently to avoid censure. A South African volunteer by way of London, Jason Gurney, was in Albecete in December alongside the Irish. As an example of the "'comrade' hypocrisy", he cites the occasion when "two dishevelled figures arrived at Battalion H.Q. They had obviously been engaged in a fight and the less severely damaged of the pair was dragging along his badly-battered opponent shouting 'This comrade has stolen my watch!'"²⁷

In a letter to his parents, Ryan wrote that the locals were friendly, and "so are the peasants who, for the first time in their history have land to till. This war is 85 per cent of the Spanish people against Franco and his Moors, and Germans and Italians. And you should see how they welcomed us. The International Column is representative of every country . . . and there is great camaraderie among them all." The days were hot and dry, the nights were cold, and the cigarettes were terrible. He let them know that he was writing the letter on the steps of a church, still standing despite the presence of the sacrilegious militias.²⁸

The Irish were sent next to Madrigueras for minimal training. As Ryan himself appreciated, "all our years in the IRA were to good purpose; these lads are well trained, and they'll never let us down. What comes home from this scrap will be of good use in Ireland, too. Quite a lot of our crowd were in the IRA right up to their departure; this will be the making of them."²⁹ They were joined by new arrivals from Ireland, Irishmen from America and Britain and a number of Dutchmen.

With one eye always on politics at home, Ryan was insisting on the establishment of a distinct Irish force and was trying desperately to collect enough Irishmen to make it feasible. Until such a time, a section was organised comprising forty-three Irishmen and placed in the Saklatvala Battalion[30] of the XIV Brigade under the command of Captain George Nathan, who had risen to the rank of captain in the British army during the First World War. Speaking to the men, Ryan thanked Nathan for his being amenable to the development of a section to represent the Irish, before Nathan in turn thanked and praised Ryan for his help in organising the company.

However, Ryan also announced, to the "amazement" of the Irish unit, that Kit Conway had been named as Section Commander rather than himself. Conway's communist credentials probably favoured him for the post, and Ryan, as he had foretold, was more likely to be deployed as a propagandist. Furthermore, he told his astonished men that he would not be at the front with them until he had been able to organise the Irish into a separate entity: "Sorry boys that I am not going with you. You will obey orders and uphold the honour of Ireland. But do not be needlessly careless with your lives because Spain needs you. And above all, Ireland needs you."[31]

It is beyond question that Ryan was taken aback by his superiors' appointing him a staff, rather than field, officer. When, on 24 December, the first contingent of Irish was sent to the front, Ryan remained behind, mostly in Albacete, but his exact role is unclear. Anticipating their censorship, Ryan furnished his letters with few details. He apparently moved around to different sections along the Republican line defending Madrid (the former capital, the government having decamped to Valencia) in between settling in new candidates for his Irish brigade. The XIV Brigade command evidently desired to keep the esteemed Ryan safe for more important work than common soldiering. A pen portrait of Ryan written thirty years later by Jason Gurney, who knew him more by reputation than acquaintance, reveals the popular estimation of the Irishman and the uncertainty of his duties.

> Frank Ryan – one of our prestige figures – had apparently been a prominent member of the IRA since the days of the First World War, and a hero of the Easter

Rising and all the subsequent battles for Irish independence. He had acquired a great reputation as a fighting man, and whilst still a Republican, had become an ardent Socialist . . . He seemed to have very little in common with the command of the Irish platoon: he remained with the British Battalion when the Irish left us, but appeared to have no particular function . . . No one really seems to know what happened to him.[32]

Ryan's men's destination was the village of Lopera, on the Córdoba front some 200 miles south of Madrid and west of Albacete. The Republicans, only six months into the war, were already being boxed into a corner, confined to central and eastern parts of the country, with a pocket of fierce Basque resistance holding out on the northern coast. Nationalist success in Lopera would open the way for a drive against the Republican flank in the south that would cut off the Republicans from the sea and encircle Madrid. Leaving Madrigueras for the front on Christmas Eve was touched with poignancy for Dubliner Joe Monks: "The people turned out to wish us *bon voyage;* the little girls kissed us. Their mothers cried for us because in their eyes, most of us were but boys."[33] By the twenty-eighth of the month, the Irishmen, already having been strafed by German and Italian aircraft, were in action. The ground was hilly and rocky, offering little cover except among the few scattered olive groves. Donal O'Reilly described the confused emotions of excitement and trepidation as the *brigadistas* passed over the threshold into the furnace of battle:

A forced march to the front lines is broken half-way by the arrival of lorries. The whirr of planes come from overhead, the lorries halt and we scatter. The planes move away and we are off singing . . . The lorries stop at an olive grove; we're out and down among the trees. The company forms and moves to the attack. Kit Conway is fair bursting to get to grips . . . We move through the olive grove with the zing-zung of the bullets playing a tune. Occasionally the snick as a bullet clips off a cluster of leaves. Out from the friendly trees, down a short valley crossing a stream, then up, up among the hills . . . We move to the crest. The fire is terrific. The language is terrific. Prendergast's and Dinny Coady's guns are shot to pieces. Bits of guns fly and we think we're all hit.[34]

Frank Edwards was beside O'Reilly in the advance:

It was pretty grim. Their firepower was far greater than ours and their equipment much better. The first shot I fired as I advanced, the rifle broke up in my hands. I did not know what to do. I had no gun. At that moment a comrade fell so I grabbed his rifle. In that attack it was just run, run against the enemy.[35]

Courage could not compensate for the hopelessness of their cause. The attack was repulsed, and in the morning the Republicans found themselves fighting off a counter-attack.

Kit spreads us out. Duff, Nalty and myself are on the edge of the road . . . We realise we are now fighting a rearguard action. Cummins and Gough are wounded and move back. Jack Nalty is hit. I won't look. I glance and see both sides of his chest are hit. I must cry or else act the pig, so I go back to the gun for relief. It's clear Jack is badly hit. I think he is finished."[36]

With enemy aircraft overhead and its troops advancing, the *brigadistas* were forced to withdraw. However, the Nationalist advance halted, and opposing forces were content to disengage and concentrate their efforts on battlefields less barren. Kit Conway's courageous and inspiring command had been exemplary. During the battle for Lopera, of the twelve men who had crossed into Spain with Ryan, six were dead and four wounded. Two further Irishmen who had left Dublin with Ryan were also killed.[37]

In Albacete, Ryan was still organising the new arrivals from Ireland, and apart from a present of cigarettes, his Christmas was spent without reward in his attempts to establish an Irish company. Despite the increasing numbers of volunteers and all his backroom work, Ryan was driven to explain to the various groupings of his men "why all Irish comrades are not just now together", sending a circular to all Irish volunteers dated New Year's Day 1937, expressing both his impatience and optimism.

> The fact is that the military situation does not allow the war to be held up so that all Irishmen can be collected and formed into a unit. At the earliest possible opportunity that will be done. The unit now at the front, the unit now in training, and the other comrades now on their way to us will be united as one unit . . . It must also be made clear that in the International Brigades in which we serve, there are no national differences. We are all comrades. We have come out here as soldiers of liberty to demonstrate Republican Ireland's solidarity with the gallant Spanish workers and peasants in their fight against Fascism. If we stress the fact that we are Irish, it is mainly to show the world that the majority of Irish people repudiate Fascist O'Duffy and his mercenaries who are helping Franco and his Moors . . . I will visit every Irish group in this country and at the first available opportunity I will reunite all groups in a distinctive Irish unit. Until then, I ask every man to play his part as a disciplined and eager soldier – just as if we were all together in a single unit.[38]

Ryan's activities and movements during the first month of 1937 are obscured not only by the fog of censorship that curbed his letters but also by the fact that Kit Conway, for some reason, adopted the *nom de guerre* of Ryan. It seems the real Ryan was travelling between different Irish units between being given out, "on loan" as he said, to the XII Brigade of Italian and German volunteers for liaison duties. They were fending off their Nationalist compatriots' hard-fought drive for Madrid. On 10 January, after a forty-eight-hour journey, the remnants of the XIV Brigade holding the line in Lopera arrived in the same north-west outskirts of the city as Ryan, near the village of Las Rozas. Only about a third of the 150 or so men of the No. 1 Company, which included the Irish section, remained. They trudged their weary way to Las Rozas in the foothills of the Guadarrama mountains.

Swirling mists hampered a Republican attack that was to pre-empt a Nationalist offensive, and the Brigaders were told to snatch what sleep they could before going into action the next morning. Alongside the Irishmen of No. 1 Company were the Italians and Germans of the Garibaldi and Thaelmann Battalions, to which Ryan had been seconded. The Nationalist artillery opened up at dawn, and moving into forward positions, Dubliner Paddy Smith thought it a "great sight to see our Brigade, Irish, English and French, moving into action in deployed formation across a flat plain". Machine-gun and particularly effective sniper fire from the church tower in Las Rozas ripped into the columns of Brigaders below.

> A shell burst nearby and I saw three English comrades fall. It was getting very hot, but Frank Ryan managed to guide us to our allotted positions. All that day our activity was confined to exchanges of rifle and machine gun fire and that night we got orders to dig ourselves in. We were instructed to be constantly on the alert for the Fascists were expected to attack.[39]

The attack materialised the following morning, directed in the main at Ryan's Italians holding the Irish right flank. "The cheering and singing of the Garibaldis as they went into action against the oncoming Fascists gave new courage and inspiration to the other battalions along the line." So rousing was the success of the Italians that their fellow Brigaders were ordered to prepare themselves for an immediate counter-attack.

> The receipt of this news was greeted with the singing of the *Internationale*. The inspired singing of this great song coming from thousands of throats in many different languages, gave the Fascists warning that something was amiss, for they sprayed our lines with machine gun fire and trench mortars exploded all around us. The surprise burst of fire took a terrible toll of life among us . . .[40]

Frank Edwards was lying on a ridge with Pat Murphy and Dubliner Dinny Coady when a shell landed near by, wounding him and killing Coady, the twelfth Irishman dead in little over three weeks. Once more, Kit Conway distinguished himself, leading the defence of his position during a counter-attack by the Moors. The battle went on for five more days, culminating in a stalemate when the two sides dug in to keep hold of what they held. Franco's advance had been halted again, but at great cost.

Meanwhile Ryan was darting between diverse battlefields and staff HQ. Accounting for his first six weeks in Spain, he told Gerald O'Reilly that he had been in the contested Madrid outskirts of Casa de Campo, University City and Guadarrama, and "I have been in the firing line continuously from four days after my arrival in Spain."[41] This is clearly an exaggeration, presumably for propaganda purposes on behalf of the Irish contingent. Conversely, other claims can be dismissed as being to ameliorate his parents' anxieties: "I fear you worry too much about me. Don't. I've run more risks in a day during the war at home than I do here in weeks."[42]

Juggling his time at the front between various battalions and the Irish unit, between working for battalion staff doing liaison and publicity and spending time with the newly arrived Irish who had followed him to the war, Ryan found himself being pulled in different directions simultaneously. He was frustrated by having to give radio broadcasts and write articles for newspapers that limited the amount of time he spent with his men.

> The censorship here is sensible: you go up the line as
> a soldier or you stay behind as a correspondent. And
> if you stay behind, what can you write of? . . . . I'd
> have to omit mention of places, dates and units, so it
> wouldn't be worth the trouble. And anyway, what
> did I come out here for? To be another O'Duffy,
> directing his men from the rear?[43]

On at least one occasion, the frustrated soldier in Ryan got the better of the publicist, and the duties of a common soldier overwhelmed those of a staff officer: "In the line, the first day, I was so annoyed with the number of brass hats on the

Battalion Staff, that I took a rifle off a dead man and stayed on the line."[44]

Wherever Ryan was being deployed, he certainly was not spending sufficient time back at the base camp in Albacete, where dozens of Irishmen were being put through a training course severely limited by the scarcity of rifles. In his absence, depending on which version of events is believed, the Irish were chafing under their British commanders or else were feuding with British volunteers in a neighbouring billet.[45] Certainly, battalion commander Wilfred McCartney was little respected by the Irishmen. According to one account, a platoon antagonistic to the Irish took advantage of being put on a police detail by arresting nearly all the Irishmen, which in turn led to threats of mutiny if the Irish were not transferred to the newly formed Abraham Lincoln Battalion of American volunteers. An English volunteer, Bill Alexander, claimed that the source of the tension was that many of Ryan's men "tended to be hostile to anything British".[46] Yet another claimed that "the Irishmen drank like fish . . . They wouldn't take orders from McCartney. Finally, they and the English got drunk and had a punch-up."[47] Either way, in the absence of Ryan, Assistant Commissar Dave Springhall called a meeting of the Irish to let them decide for themselves which battalion they wanted to be with.

The scene was depressingly familiar. Much the same kind of argument that had fractured Irish republicanism at home was again being fought out in Spain, those with traditional republican grievances clashing head on with the left-wingers. Charlie Donnelly led the Waterford men, Peter O'Connor and the Power brothers, in trying to persuade the less class-conscious that fighting alongside British working men symbolised their political maturity. It was an opportunity to demonstrate that the enemy of all those present was British imperialism. A majority of five voted them down, and on 20 January the unit moved off to the American training base at Villanueva de Jara, eight miles distant, to join the Abraham Lincoln Battalion.

When Ryan returned to Albacete, ahead of the Irish unit at the front, and learned what had happened, he was furious. All his plans for consolidating his compatriots had been shot to pieces. Further, the man he had left in charge in his absence, Dublin IRA man Terry Flanagan, had been declared "suspect" by McCartney and was undergoing deportation proceedings. Ryan managed to recall Flanagan from Barcelona and expulsion. He also obtained the release of one of his "most important men", whom McCartney had summarily sentenced to two months' imprisonment for disobeying an order.

Ryan was still seething when a party to celebrate Burns Night was held a day or two later. He interrupted proceedings to give a speech protesting the treatment of the Irish and their partition, demanding they be reunited as a single entity. André Marty was understandably outraged and remonstrated with Ryan to no effect: "He went solidly on with his speech. Marty lost his temper and literally screamed for him to sit down. This produced no result at all. Frank continued in better spirit than before, with the lusty help of some of the Irish, American, Canadian and British delegations." Marty called men near by to fall in and ordered Ryan's arrest, whereupon he was taken away to detention. "This caused an uproar, and that night, deputations armed to the teeth appeared, demanding his release."[48] He had in fact been set free already after the intervention of his fellow officers.

In Ryan's mind, since "Ireland's nearest enemy is British Imperialism", her greatest potential ally was the British working class and "therefore the Irish and the British must be side by side in the International brigades". The fault for the whole debacle lay not with Irish insubordination, but with McCartney, who had told him a "pack of lies", and British communist officials. Writing weeks later, free from censorship, Ryan could still hardly contain his fury: "The representatives of the British CP [Communist Party] wrecked the Irish Unit . . . Some day I'll tell you the whole sordid story of the political density of some so-called British revolutionaries. The tragedy is that the English send out the worst officer-type." Rather than capable leaders or solid working-class communists, "we got the in-between crowd of the swell-headed adventurer type . . . What a fool I was that I didn't just bring one or two hundred lads with IRA training out with me."[49]

The Irish were now split; one unit made up the Connolly Unit of the Lincoln Brigade, while those who had been at the front remained with their original battalion, joined by fresh-faced arrivals. Yet, after the return of the veterans from the front in late January, an incident not unrelated served as a bizarre sequel to the split. That Captain Nathan had served in the British army was common knowledge, and he had informed the Irish during his first speech to them that he had served in Ireland. In the spirit of solidarity that the Brigades were supposedly founded on, no more questions were asked, particularly since Nathan had since proven himself to be a courageous soldier and an excellent leader of men. However, while at the front, Kit Conway had gathered his men together to tell them, "Comrades, we are being blackguarded. They've put the Black and Tans to command us."[50] Either acting from a tip-off from somebody none too fond of the captain, or else because he had been recognised by one of the Irishmen, Nathan was identified as having been a member of a Dublin Castle "Murder Gang" responsible for the murders in 1921 of the mayor and ex-mayor of Limerick, Michael O'Callaghan and George Clancy. Ryan himself was fighting with the Limerick IRA at the time.

How it came to pass is unclear, but Nathan found himself in the chillingly absurd position of being tried by his own men on a fantastic charge. Irish communist and witness Jimmy Prendergast told a colleague:

> At Madrigueras, Ryan and the other Irishmen put Nathan on trial for his life, charging him with being a spy for the Franco forces. It was a secret trial . . . Nathan denied the charge and said he had come to Spain because he was anti-Fascist. "I'm a Jew, though I've never bothered with the Jewish community, and I'm against Hitler. If you want to shoot me for what happened in Ireland, all right. But I was under orders. I was a member of the British Crown forces and I had to do what I was told. What you said I did was true." [The Irish "court"] eventually accepted his explanation and deleted all references to the past.[51]

Exactly how Nathan was supposed to have spied for the Nationalists, the relevance of his murderous times in Limerick and the details of Nathan's execution if he had been found guilty, Prendergast did not reveal. Neither does he elaborate on Ryan's role in the affair, which seems at odds with his own character. Ryan held Nathan in esteem and affection and had even made him a gift of the distinctive military boots from London. Although Ryan had far from cooled down over the arrests and division of his men while he had been at the front, the blameless Nathan had himself been at the front, and it was an amenable Nathan who had given Ryan the nod for an independent Irish unit in the first place. Ryan perhaps let the "trial" go ahead, calculating that Nathan could never be found guilty of treachery in Spain but that it would serve as a sop to restless IRA men still smarting after the earlier run-in with English officers.[52]

Whatever the persecution of Nathan and the defection of the Irish says about discipline and solidarity in No. 1 Company, it is evident that although the Irish had left Ireland, they had not left Ireland's affairs behind. Marching to the battle of Lopera had been done to renditions of "The Merry Ploughboy", and veteran Tom Murphy remembered that in response to frequent rumours that O'Duffy's men were in the line opposite, "Frank Ryan used to speak on the speaker, he says: 'Irishmen go home! Your fathers would turn in their graves if they knew you'd come to fight for imperialism. This is the real Republican Army, the real men of Ireland.'"[53] Ryan saw much of the volunteers' activity in the green light of home, despite resenting

> . . . this talk of a "bloodfeud" between O'Duffy and
> I. We would be out here if there never was an
> O'Duffy. We smashed his attempts to set up his dic-
> tatorship in Ireland – he came here to find the career
> he could not get in Ireland. We came here to fight Fas-
> cism; it's just an accident for us that O'Duffy happens
> to be here fighting for it.[54]

What Ryan witnessed in Spain – the atrocities, the camaraderie and the political machinations – all had a great impact on him, and little wonder: "The bodies of babies cluttered in a schoolyard after an air raid, breadlines of women blown to bits, working-class houses razed." It is unquestionable that he was a dedicated and dauntless soldier of the Spanish Republic, yet he never gave of himself absolutely, never committed himself to the extent that his vision for Ireland was eclipsed by the crisis for democracy in Spain. Ryan was not, in truth, the internationalist that Connolly was or that he aspired to be; his studies of global struggles customarily dovetailed to their relevance to his home country. Ultimately, all his reflections on, and reactions to, the tragedies in Spain were placed in an Irish context.

> I have been in wrecked churches and I have seen the hiding places in them where Fascist arms were stored, and the bulletmarks on the houses opposite that were made when the churches were used as Fascist barracks. And I have been in other churches that were not wrecked because they were used only as churches.
>
> I wish some of those who talk of "fighting for the Faith" with O'Duffy could come over here to see how O'Duffy's masters do it. Today I visited a hospital, the most of whose occupants were children and women wounded in air raids. Franco's forces bomb and shell the civilian population in order to smash the morale of the people. But he bombs and shells in vain. The hospitals filled with wounded and the cemeteries filled with dead make the people all the more determined to fight on. "Madrid will be the tomb of Fascism" is a general slogan. And they mean it. If the worst comes to the worst, they'll fight to the last house and the last man and woman.
>
> I feel sad when I think of how the Irish people – or a lot of them anyhow – are being misled by lying propaganda. But I'm glad I'm not on the side of the baby-killers. There's more Christianity in any one worker than there is in the whole of the miscalled "Irish Christian Front".
>
> So, I'll come back in a couple of months, for I have a strong prejudice against dying anywhere else except Ireland. The people here would not give me the wake I'd expect![55]

Ryan's frustration and anger would soon find a channel. The Nationalists, having been held up in their advance on Madrid at Las Rozas to the north-west of the city, now

concentrated their forces on the south east in the valley of
Jarama. Their objective: to cut the main road between Madrid
and Valencia on the coast. It was about the battle of Jarama
that veterans would later sing, to the tune of the "Red River
Valley",

> There's a valley in Spain called Jarama
> It's a place that we all know too well,
> For 'tis there that we wasted our manhood
> And most of our old age as well.

Notes to Chapter Seven

1. *Irish Independent*, 11 August 1936.
2. Dáil deputy and a victor over Ryan in Dublin North-East.
3. Quoted in Dermot Keogh, *Ireland and Europe 1919–1948* (Dublin: Gill & Macmillan, 1988), p. 70.
4. Quoted in Seán Cronin, *Frank Ryan: The Search for the Republic* (Dublin: Repsol, 1980), p. 72.
5. Joseph Donnelly, *Charlie Donnelly: The Life and Poems* (Dublin: Dedalus Press, 1987), p. 29.
6. *Irish Press*, 16 September 1936.
7. *Ibid.*, 21 September 1936. MacRory obviously had digressed from his script more than he ought, but his inadvertent reference to money for Franco or volunteers for O'Duffy's more sanguine form of assistance was overlooked. Indeed, readers of the *Irish Independent* would have remained ignorant of the gaffe, as it was the victim of an ellipsis in the paper's lengthy quote of MacRory's speech.
8. *Irish Press*, 23 September 1936.
9. The Labour Party and trade unions had been woefully reticent on the issues raised by the war in Spain, subservient to populist pro-Franco leanings. The party machine tactically hushed pro-Republicans within Fianna Fáil and *The Irish Times* remained detached and impartial.
10. Paddy Byrne, *Irish Republican Congress Revisited* (London: Connolly, 1994), p. 37.
11. *Ibid.*, p. 32.
12. Years later, Gilmore claimed of Congress that "chief amongst its achievements was the leadership of its campaign against Fascism in Spain". Joseph O'Connor, *Even the Olives are Bleeding: The Life and Times of Charles Donnelly* (Dublin: New Island, 1992), p. 92.
13. Annie O'Farrelly papers, NLI, p. 7655.
14. Interview with the author.

15. Michael O'Riordan, *Connolly Column* (Dublin: New Books, 1979), p. 56. In fact, two communists had already made their way to Spain independently; Achill man Tommy Patton's death in the defence of Madrid brought the war closer to Ireland, whereas the letters from Bill Scott to his comrades at home both encouraged and informed the enlistment drive. Dubliner Bill Barry had fallen in the defence of Madrid before Ryan even left the dead man's home city.

16. Bob Doyle transcript, International Brigades Collection, 000806/04, London: Imperial War Museum.

17. Peter O'Connor, *Soldier of Liberty* (Dublin: MSF, 1997), p. 13.

18. Ryan's refusal did not dampen their ardour. They planned to cycle up to Belfast where they would sell their bikes and, proffering both money and undeniable enthusiasm, board a ship for Spain. However, their venture came to an end when Behan's bike got a puncture in north County Dublin, and the two foiled heroes had to return home.

19. Although it was implied that the money was to be used to rebuild destroyed churches, the sum went via the Church hierarchies in Ireland and Spain to Franco's coffers.

20. Department of Justice, NAI, Jus 8, 254.

21. Frank Ryan, ed., *The Book of the XV Brigade, (*Newcastle upon Tyne: Frank Graham, n.d.), p. 82.

22. Aodh Ó Canainn, "Eilís Ryan in Her Own Words" *Saothar* 21, 1996.

23. *Irish Press,* 14 December 1936.

24. Quoted in Joseph Donnelly, *Charlie Donnelly: The Life and Poems* (Dublin: Dedalus Press, 1987), p. 44.

25. Quoted in Cronin, *Frank Ryan*, p. 84.

26. Peter O'Connor, *Soldier of Liberty*, p. 14.

27. Jason Gurney, *Crusade in Spain* (Newton Abbot: Readers Union, 1976), p. 65.

28. Quoted in Cronin, *Frank Ryan*, p. 85.

29. Donal O'Reilly, for example, had, as a thirteen year old, got caught up in the GPO fighting in 1916, where his father and three brothers were, and graduated to fight in the Tan War, then the Civil War. He remembered his time in Madrigueras as a "few days of restless training, checking the impatience of those 'old soldiers' who had worn the by roads of Ireland forming fours and taking cover". *Irish Democrat*, 2 October 1937.

30. Named after the Indian-born politician in Britain who served as the first Communist MP in Westminster.

31. Joe Monks, *With the Reds in Andalusia* (London: John Cornford Poetry Group, 1988), p. 6.

32. Gurney, *Crusade in Spain*, pp. 71–2.
33. Monks, *With the Reds*, pp. 7–8.
34. *Irish Democrat,* 2 October 1937.
35. Quoted in Uinseann Mac Eoin, *Survivors* (Dublin: Angenta, 1980), pp. 11–12.
36. *Irish Democrat*, 2 October 1937. Jack Nalty staggered three miles back to a dressing station and recovered from his wounds, only to be killed on the Ebro front over eighteen months later.
37. As were the well-known socialist writer Ralph Fox, who had written a treatise detailing Marx's views on Ireland, and the poet John Cornford, shot the day after he celebrated his twenty-first birthday.
38. Quoted in Peter O'Connor, *Soldier of Liberty*, p. 16.
39. *Irish Democrat,* 9 October 1937.
40. *Ibid.*
41. Marcel Acier, ed., *From Spanish Trenches* (London: Cresset Press, n.d.), p. 116.
42. Quoted in Cronin, *Frank Ryan*, p. 89.
43. Acier, *From Spanish Trenches*, p. 115.
44. Quoted in Cronin, *Frank Ryan*, p. 91.
45. See Peter O'Connor, *Soldier of Liberty*, pp. 14–15; Gurney, *Crusade in Spain*, p. 77; Bill Alexander, *British Volunteers for Liberty* (London: Lawrence & Wishart, 1982), pp. 68–9.
46. Alexander, *British Volunteers*, p. 68.
47. Fred Copeman, quoted in Robert Stradling, *The Irish and the Spanish Civil War* (Manchester: Mandolin, 1999), p. 157.
48. *Ibid.*, pp. 83–4.
49. Quoted in Cronin, *Frank Ryan*, p. 91.
50. Quoted in Stradling, *The Irish and the Spanish Civil War*, p. 242.
51. Maurice Levine, *From Cheetham to Cordoba* (Manchester: Neil Richardson, 1984), p. 39.
52. It is also possible that the Ryan spoken of was Kit "Ryan" Conway. Perhaps, and possibly with the collusion of others in authority, Conway had it in for his superior, Nathan, but there is nothing on record to counter the high praise accorded Nathan by his troops and fellow officers alike.
53. Tom Murphy transcript, International Brigades Collection, 805/2, London: Imperial War Museum.
54. Acier, *From Spanish Trenches*, p. 115.
55. Quoted in Cronin, *Frank Ryan*, p. 89.

CHAPTER EIGHT
The Battle of Jarama

In early February, Frank Ryan was preparing to lead those members of the Irish contingent still in the British Battalion to the Jarama Valley where Republicans and Nationalists were simultaneously planning offensives to break the deadlock around Madrid. Both sides had been hindered by problems of logistics and weather. The British and Lincoln Battalions were part of a newly formed XV Brigade, alongside the Dimitrov (Balkans) and Franco-Belge Battalions. Nathan had been replaced by Kit Conway, and McCartney had been invalided home after a shooting accident in his hotel room. According to Ryan: "The bastard wounded himself in the left arm with his own revolver on the day of departure and got the London *Daily Worker* to say he 'was wounded by Fascist rifle-fire near Madrid'!!!"[1]

The Nationalist offensive in Jarama commenced on 6 February, and 40,000 troops, German machine-gunners, tanks and artillery capitalised on their initial success by crossing the Jarama River five days later. In their bid to isolate Madrid and drive a wedge into Republican territory, all the might the Nationalists could spare thundered towards the prized Madrid to Valencia highway. To Republicans it was clear what was at stake. Ryan was waiting with his men to go up to the line, having arrived in the nearby village of Chinchón, "where the sound of artillery fire gave an ominous warning of the Fascist advance. The Brigaders were given a warm welcome and the villagers rounded up every egg to supplement the evening meal."[2] The fascist advance was more effective than they knew, and there were gaps in the Republican defensive line that would have to be plugged by the XV Brigade. The majority of the men were as yet inexperienced in battle, and although new guns had been issued, as often as not the ammunition supplied with them was of the wrong sort, yet it was upon such men and munitions that the Republic depended.

The Irishmen of No. 1 Company were preparing to move to its forward position when Ryan returned from the front line. It was the first time Jim Prendergast had seen Ryan in a steel helmet that actually fitted him.

> Frank explained. By the simple process of sitting hard on it, he had managed a tight fit. "We'll need 'em boys," he said. "It's hell up there and we are in for a tough fight." He told us of the position in the line and that the Fascists were expected to launch a powerful attack under cover of nightfall to finally capture the road. Our Brigade would move in to smash this attempt at all costs . . . Dan Boyle gave me an English cigarette. Dan was in fine form although he just read his obituary in a misinformed paper. We could not read the future and we did not care overmuch anyway. But Dan, handing the last of his cigarettes around, did say his generosity was based on the possibility of not finishing them later.
>
> After receiving final instructions, we moved off . . . The sound of the "International" smote the air and swelled into a mighty roar.[3]

The Brigaders moved forward, barely aware that their whole left flank was exposed following Nationalist advances the night before; the low hills that constituted the Pingarron Heights where they were to entrench were now in the sights of Nationalist machine-gun nests. In the intense heat they reached a plateau and pressed on, heartened by an overhead dogfight that treated them to their first sight of a Republican victory over fascist aircraft. They crossed a sunken road and welcomed the shade and cover of an olive grove as a barrage of enemy artillery hit, tearing up the trees and ground around them. Conway led the men as Ryan worked to bring up reserves and machine-gun crews. The Irish came down the side of a valley, climbed its opposite ridge and moved forward across a plain to be deployed between a knoll and what would soon be known as "Suicide Hill". In the distance ahead they saw the Nationalist reinforcements being rushed by lorries toward their forward positions to press their advantage and break through the lines at Pingarron. And there was little doubt that the ill-armed and ill-trained citizen army were up against professionals: "In one machine-gun nest a group of us wiped out," wrote Ryan, "I picked four German passports out of the pockets of the crew. I saw letters and papers in Italian taken from dead fascist infantry."[4] Already, 500 yards to the Irish left, the Nationalists were advancing under cover of the direct fire that the Irish now came under.

> The Fascist fire was growing pretty heavy and they were directing it uncannily well. Men were being hit pretty fast. A young English chap fell close by. A yell for stretcher bearers. John Goff tumbled over, his hand to his head . . . Kit danced furiously from position to position. "Don't waste your fire, boys," he kept shouting . . . The fire had grown so heavy now, nobody could tell what would happen, and fear was not felt any more, because it was no use feeling afraid now.
>
> The forces of the Fascists seemed overwhelming. Moans of our wounded filled the air on all sides. It was no use . . . We moved back under an ever-increasing hail of lead . . . Paddy Duff moving back, hit in the leg. Shells were exploding on our left. Holy God! If they shell us in these, we would be blown to eternity. Low flying planes screamed towards us.
>
> Kit was standing on top of the hill. He was using a rifle now, and after every shot turned towards the men issuing instructions. I got closer to him. Suddenly he shouted, his rifle spun out of his hand and he fell back. My God, Kit was hit . . . Tears glistened in the eyes of the lads as they watched Kit. Many were from other companies, but Kit was known and loved by them all. And his gallant leadership that day had won them completely . . . I was stunned.[5]

The wounded Conway was carried back to a dressing station. His replacement was soon dead, succeeded by the commander of No. 3 Company, who was killed later that day. "After a heroic four hours' stand, all that were alive of his men were falling back, disputing with red-hot rifles every yard of the way," recalled a member of battalion staff.[6] Under the cover fire of machine-guns that had finally been equipped with the right ammunition, the wounded, the weary and the lost groped their way back over terrain they had tramped that morning. Ahead of the sunken road where Battalion Commander Tom Wintringham had brought up his HQ, new positions were taken up. Less than half the battalion remained. Those that made it back were able to snatch some rest, but "sleep was brief, deep and troubled. Everyone knew that the attack would begin again at dawn."[7]

At the rising of the sun, the Moors were seen to have moved up to the left of Suicide Hill and the Republican forward positions, while the Franco-Belge to the right had been forced back. The outposts on the Republican salient and exposed flanks were thus open to artillery, rifle and machine-gun fire. More worrying was the blood-chilling threat of infiltration by Moor troops who seemed possessed of the infernal ability to slither forward undetected to spring from the ground to the throats of their enemy. Ryan and his men had come under fire at dawn, when "machine-gun fire drove us back, so I let the men retreat a mile. They were decided on another attack and went forward again, and, meeting desperate fire, we reoccupied our positions."[8]

However, while the enemy, held at bay by heavy machine-gun fire above and behind the Irish, were preparing for a further attack, the commander of a forward company in the British Battalion lost his nerve and unexpectedly ordered his men to withdraw to the sunken road. The catastrophe was compounded shortly thereafter; the vacant position enabled a party of Nationalists to infiltrate the British machine-gun position that had held off their advance, take forty men prisoner and turn the prized guns toward the battalion's defensive line. This was soon untenable, particularly after the arrival of Nationalist tanks, and the astounded Brigaders retreated in dust and chaos to re-form along the sunken road.

That night, along the road, there remained only about 160

of the battalion's original 600 fighting men. Dawn of 14 February rose to a fresh fascist offensive. The Nationalist onslaught seemed incessant; fresh Legionnaires had joined the Moors and the fascist superiority in equipment and firepower was insurmountable. Tanks and infantry were hurled at the ill-prepared and exhausted Republican line and soon enfiladed it.

> A tank shell burst a few yards away. Across to the left a big tank, bigger than any of ours, loomed up. Behind it swarmed Moors. Their main fire was on the Spanish company on the left. Simultaneously, the din on the right became terrific. Nothing could live in the face of such fire. The Spaniards stood up to it for a full ten minutes, until the tanks were enfilading them from the road itself. We had no anti-tank guns, no grenades, no anti-tank material. The left flank broke and the rout spread to the whole line. The slaughter was terrible. One would see five men running abreast and four of them suddenly crumple up.[9]

The defences disintegrated. The men scattered as best they could. Scrambling towards the slopes and down to the Chinchón road and the battalion cookhouse, they mingled with their fellow vanquished from other battalions, Spanish, French, Belgians, men from the Balkans. Ragged groups of dispirited men, many wounded, were all that now stood between a relentless fascist advance and the vital road linking Madrid to Valencia.

Ryan had been pushed back with his men; "the tanks walked through us, and we were driven back nearly a mile". He was obviously taken aback by the events of the past three days, and considered that "Jarama was the toughest fighting I ever saw. The machine gun fire was terrific and then there were the mortars, tanks and aeroplanes . . . those Fascists were good fighters and well-officered." Wintringham had since been wounded, and Ryan was one of the few officers left: "I was (unofficially) in command."[10] But it was at exactly such a time as this that Ryan's diehard spirit possessed its premium worth. He described the general dismay in the rout's aftermath and subsequent events:

The Battle of Jarama

On the road from Chinchón to Madrid, the road along which we had marched to the attack three days before, were now scattered all who survived – a few hundred Britons, Irish and Spaniards. Dispirited by heavy casualties, by defeat, by lack of food, worn out by three days of grueling fighting, our men appeared to have reached the end of their resistance.

Some were still straggling down the slopes from what had been, up to an hour ago, the front line. And now there was no line, nothing between the Madrid road and the Fascists but disorganised groups of weary, war-wrecked men. After three days of terrific struggle, the superior numbers, the superior armament of the Fascists had routed them. All, as they came back, had similar stories to tell: of comrades dead, of conditions that were more than flesh and blood could stand, of weariness they found hard to resist.

I recognised the young Commissar of the Spanish Company. His hand bloody where a bullet had grazed the palm, he was fumbling nevertheless with his automatic, in turn threatening and pleading with his men . . . Groups were lying about on the roadside, hungrily eating oranges that had been thrown to them by a passing lorry. This was no time to sort them into units. I noted with satisfaction that some had brought down spare rifles. I found my eyes straying always to the hills we had vacated. I hitched a rifle on my shoulder.

They stumbled to their feet. No time for barrack-square drill. One line of four. "Fall in behind us." A few were still on the grass bank beside the road, adjusting helmets and rifles. "Hurry up!" came the cry from the ranks. Up the road toward the Cook-House I saw Jock Cunningham assembling another crowd. We hurried up, joined forces. Together we two marched at the head. Whatever popular writers may say, neither your Briton nor your Irishman is an exuberant type. Demonstrativeness is not his dominating trait. The crowd behind us was marching silently. The thoughts in their minds could not be inspiring ones. I remembered a trick of the old days when we were holding banned demonstrations. I jerked my head back: "Sing up ye sons o' guns!"

> "Then comrades, come rally
> And the last fight let us face;
> The Internationale
> Unites the human race."

On we marched back up the road, nearer and nearer to the front. Stragglers still in retreat down the slopes stopped in amazement, changed direction and ran to join us; men lying exhausted on the roadside jumped up, cheered, and joined the ranks. I looked back. Beneath the forest of upraised fists, what a strange band! Unshaven, unkempt; bloodstained, grimey. But, full of fight again, and marching on the road back.

Beside the road stood our Brigade Commander, General Gall. We had quitted; he had stood his ground. Was it that, or fear of his reprimands, that made us give three cheers for him? Briefly, tersely, he spoke to us. We had one and a half hours of daylight in which to recapture our lost positions.

Again the "International" arose. It was being sung in French too. Our column had swelled in size during the halt; a group of Franco-Belge had joined us. We passed the Spanish Battalion. They caught the infection; they were singing too as they deployed to the right. Jock Cunningham seemed to be the only man who was not singing. Hands thrust into his great-coat pockets, he trudged along at the head of his men . . . We were singing; he was planning.

*

The Battle of Jarama

As the olive groves loom in sight, we deploy to the left. At last, we are on the ridge, the ridge which we must never again desert. For, while we hold that ridge the Madrid-Valencia road is free.

Bullets whistle through the air, or smack into the ground, or find a human target. Cries. Shouts. But, always the louder, interminable singing. Flat on the ground, we fire into the groves. There are no sections, no companies even. But individuals jump ahead and set an example that is readily followed – too readily, for sometimes they block our fire. In the thick of the battle we organise ourselves with a certain amount of success into sections.

The Spanish problem is quickly solved: "Mañuel! What's the Spanish for 'Forward'?" "Adelante!" yells Mañuel, and waves the Spanish lads on. "Abajo!" And down they flop to give covering fire. A burly French Lieutenant runs over to ask me for grenades. We have none. Waving a ridiculously tiny automatic, he advances, shouting "En Avant!" Ahead of us are little cones of blue-red flame. Now we know where the Moorish and German machine-gunners are. Oh, for grenades! As we hug the earth, we call to one another to direct group fire on those cones.

Flat on our bellies we push forward. Inch by inch. Darkness falls like a blanket, still the fight goes on. Advancing! All the time advancing. As I crawl forward, I suddenly realise, with savage joy, that it is we who are advancing, they who are being pushed back. And then, in actual disappointment: "The bastards won't wait for our bayonets!"

We are in the olive groves. Firing ceases. We are on our feet, feeling for one another in the inky blackness. I stumble against a soft bundle. I bend down. His spiked bayonet scrapes my hand. He is one of ours. His face is cold. He has been dead for hours . . . So we are back where we were at midday.

Mañuel, André and I dig in. Our rifle-pit completed, Manual reaches back for the blanket he had so carefully laid down. It is missing. Mañuel rattles his bayonet and shouts lurid threats to the "bloody bastard who stole my blanket!" From the trees all around, he is answered by roars of laughter.

*

And thus the men who had been broken and routed a few hours before settled down for the night on the ground they had reconquered. They had dashed Fascist hopes, smashed Fascist plans. Thenceforward, they were to fight and many of them to die, in these olive groves. But never again were the Fascists to rout them . . . fighting in the dauntless spirit of the great rally of that afternoon, fighting too in the spirit of those reckless roars of laughter that night in the Wood of Death. [11]

The Nationalists had been caught off guard by the great rally of the Brigaders, and, with the fall of darkness, fell back from the ridge they had just taken to their original positions. The Nationalist forces were spent. During the night, reinforcements joined the Republican survivors, taking up positions to the left and right and bolstering the line of defence. The gap in the line had been plugged. The Madrid to Valencia road had been retained, and its line of defence was now steadfast. The initiative and example of Ryan and Cunningham, a Scotsman who had left hospital to command the battalion, had finally halted three days of steamrolling fascist advance and prevented the encirclement of Madrid. [12]

The following day, the positions seemingly consolidated, Ryan was given no reason to be complacent. "I got a flesh wound in the left arm from a bullet that went through the head of a man beside me. It made me – even gentle me! – fighting mad. Curious how reckless I got." Whether because of his lack of caution or not, he remained in the enemy's sights. Half an hour after the wound, "a tank shell burst beside me and I got a wallop in the left leg that knocked me down. My pantaloons weren't cut, there was no blood. It must have been a stone thrown up by the shell." Ryan picked himself up, the bruising to his leg enabling him to only limp forward, but otherwise, after a few minutes, "I felt okay. I then decided we'd dash ahead of the barrage to better positions. Shortly after we'd done so, I got a bullet through the left arm."[13]

Ryan retired from the front to get his arm seen to. The wound was clean, near his shoulder, and although no bones were broken, he was told he would be out of action for some weeks. Just as he was retiring, the Irishmen in the Lincoln Battalion were taking up positions at Jarama. Although the Nationalist advance had ground to a halt, the Republican command was drawing up plans for an offensive, rather than defensive, victory. The Irish in the Connolly Unit, led by Bostonian Paul Burns, were approaching the front, among them Group Leader Peter O'Connor, the Power brothers and Charlie Donnelly: "We were in a valley just behind the lines when we came under heavy artillery bombardment. It was a nerve shattering experience . . . Aerial attacks followed the artillery fire as we moved closer to the line."[14] Ahead of them, other Brigaders were already contesting Pingarron at great cost to their manpower. The fighting was fierce, and in one day alone, the high ground of Suicide Hill changed hands four times. During the afternoon of that day, 23 February, the Irish were moved up to that same ground, contested so terrifically by their compatriots ten days earlier.

Morale among the men was high, remembered Burns, as they led the Republican advance, moving forward against well-entrenched opposition with neither air nor artillery support: "Donnelly joined me under an olive tree and we fired until our rifles burned in our hands, with scarcely a word beyond the 'Hi, Charlie, how's it going?' and the reply, 'Pretty good, how's the rest of the boys?' The infantry continued the advance. Explosive bullets split the air and the machine-gun bursts raked the field."[15] With the Company Commander dead after three bullets hit him, Belfast man Bill Henry took command. Killed the following day, Henry was succeeded by Irish-American Ed Flaherty, and the following couple of days witnessed sporadic fighting and sniping before the Irish were shifted to take part in a fresh offensive against heavily defended hills adjacent to the Jarama River.

Planned for 7.00 a.m. on the morning of the 27 February, the attack was delayed when a supporting Spanish column to the left failed to materialise. Of the twenty planes promised for air support, only three were available; the purported tank support transpired to be two ineffective armoured cars, and the artillery cover was to be provided by guns lightweight in calibre and limited in number. The commander of the Lincolns, Robert Merriman, argued fiercely against the assault with Vladimir Copic, his superior and now in command of the XV Brigade, but to no effect. At noon, the men went over the top and into an inferno that cut down over a hundred of their number within moments. Merriman barely made it out of the trench before he was hit.

> Whole groups of men would barely reach the top of the parapets before being smashed back into the trenches by the withering fire . . . Each time the pitiful line rose to continue the advance, the deadly cross and direct fire of whole batteries of guns cut into them, thinning their ranks so that entire squads and sections were melting away in death and agony.[16]

In a torrential downpour the men struggled forward, seeking cover, which they finally found in the olive groves. A Canadian volunteer found himself mixed in with the Irish.

> We ran for cover. Charlie Donnelly, Commander of the Irish company, is crouched behind an olive tree. He has picked up a bunch of olives from the ground and is squeezing them. I hear him say something quietly between a lull in the machine gun fire: "Even the olives are bleeding."[17]

The attack was repulsed, and the men started to retreat. Donnelly's fire covered them until he was hit three times, in the right arm and side and the head, in a burst from a fascist machine-gun. His comrades were unable to retrieve the young poet's body.

With the failure of the offensive, the battle of Jarama effectively drew to a close. Although both sides claimed that victory had been theirs, the result was a stalemate similar to Las Rozas and other struggles for Madrid. Along the Jarama front, the Republicans lost well over 10,000 men to death, sickness and wounds, and the Nationalists about 6,000. The two sides, severely depleted, dug in as their commanders turned their attentions elsewhere, to Guadalajara, north-east of Madrid.

Of the Irishmen in the two battalions, twenty were lost as well as Donnelly, whose body could not be recovered for over two weeks. Peter O'Connor found his remains and, with the help of the Power brothers, carried him down the hillside and buried him. Kit Conway had died of wounds after two days. Veteran of the Four Courts and adjutant of No. 1 Company Paddy McDaid had been killed. Reverend Robert Hilliard, a Church of Ireland minister, known as the "Boxing Parson" having won medals for pugilism, was killed resisting a tank attack with only a rifle. Also dead was Derryman Eamon McGrotty, who in previous lives had been a member of the IRA, active in the Gaelic League and an Irish Christian Brother. Danny Boyle, he of the generosity with English cigarettes, had smoked his last at Jarama.

Sent to a hospital in Alicante near the Mediterranean coast to recuperate on his way home, Ryan was expecting to return in about two months. Still limping from his leg injury and with his arm in a sling, he yet remained busy. The government paid for a flight for "El Commandante Ryan" to Toulouse from Valencia. While in the capital, he had an interview with Foreign Minister Del Vayo to press for a Spanish consul in Dublin. He was writing to Gerald O'Reilly about his plans for a speaking tour of America, and he did his best to catch up with his followers from home who had been wounded.

And he kept up a steady stream of letters back to Ireland. Ryan objected to Irish papers referring to O'Duffy's Irish Brigade as the Wild Geese: "The Wild Geese were honest-minded men who went out to fight against their country's enemy. To compare O'Duffy's dupes with them is to insult a national tradition." He also resented Irish Nationalists who distanced the fight in Spain from domestic politics: "'We serve Ireland only' they cry, but they would have us wait until it would be too late to make effective use of our services. Catalonia recognises that it must not wait until Franco reaches its borders. Is Ireland to commit the error Catalonia avoids?" Ryan's major concern, though, was that he persuade Irish men and women that the lives of their countrymen who fell in Spain

> . . . have not been wasted, that their deaths are not
> tragedies that need not have happened. Honour to

those who died for the freedom of the Irish people; honour even greater to those who die here for the freedom of ALL HUMANITY . . . They chose to come here asking for neither pay nor preferment, coming because they believed it was their duty to participate in this decisive fight against Fascism. And, for my part, while it would be wrong to accuse me of bringing them here, I would never regret having done so. Our 50,000 who died in the Great War were sacrificed uselessly; no life here is given in vain.

And look at it from the purely selfish viewpoint. Which is better; that some of us should die here or that thousands should die at home? For if Fascism triumphs here, Ireland's trial will soon be at hand.

Ryan was genuinely sorry to be leaving Spain and sincerely believed that "if it so happened that my corpse was now rotting with those others whose stench nearly drove me insane in University City, my life would not have been wasted". Whereas he had initially thought that his work was more valuable in Ireland than in Spain, he now alleged to believe that "If I died in Spain I would die for human liberty as certainly – perhaps more certainly – than I would in Ireland today."[18]

Taking leave of his comrades induced feelings of grief and guilt in Ryan, though neither his courage nor his commitment to the cause in Spain were ever questioned by his men. Just before he left the Jarama battlefield, Bill Scott had approached him to ask if Kit Conway had succumbed to his wounds.

Frank's spirit is unbreakable. When I asked: "Is it true, Frank?" he did not speak, but the look on his face said "yes, it is true". When Frank broke the silence, he said, "Bill, we must never let Kit down; we must fight it to a finish." We know Frank Ryan well enough to know he will not break his promise. He has been at the head of his men in the thick of the fight. He would be with the rest of the glorious Irish column today, were his arm not in a sling. He has lost his best lieutenant, he has seen his column getting smaller every day, he has seen the grim determination of his small but gallant band of heroes, to carry on to the end. They know Frank will never let them down; they would follow him to hell with rifles on their shoulders. He is determined to carry the flag of the Irish column to victory or death.[19]

Notes to Chapter Eight

1. Quoted in Seán Cronin, *Frank Ryan: The Search for the Republic* (Dublin: Repsol, 1980), p. 91.
2. Bill Alexander, *British Volunteers for Liberty* (London: Lawrence and Wishart, 1982), p. 94.
3. *Irish Democrat,* 13 November 1937.
4. Marcel Acier, *From Spanish Trenches* (London: Cresset Press, n.d.), p. 117.
5. *Irish Democrat,* 20 November 1937.
6. Frank Graham, quoted in Frank Ryan, ed., *The Book of the XV Brigade* (Newcastle upon Tyne: Frank Graham, n.d.), p. 51.
7. Alexander, *British Volunteers,* p. 98.
8. *Irish Democrat,* 24 July 1937.
9. Quoted in Ryan, *The Book of the XV Brigade,* p. 57.
10. Acier, *From Spanish Trenches,* p. 117.
11. *Ibid.,* pp. 59–61.
12. Ryan's version of events is corroborated by Bill Alexander: "Cunningham and Ryan began to collect the small groups along the road . . . Ryan started singing. All joined in, marching together to the ridge where they had been routed . . . the British had filled the gap: the Madrid-Valencia road was not cut." Alexander, *British Volunteers,* p. 100. Joe Monks says much the same: "Ryan and Cunningham actually led the march back to the line. Each time that Ryan shouted to the marching ranks 'Are we downhearted?' a forest of clenched fists was raised as, unafraid, the men answered with a resounding 'No!'" Joe Monks, *With the Reds in Andalusia* (London: John Cornford Poetry Group, 1985), p. 22.
13. Acier, *From Spanish Trenches,* pp. 117–18.
14. Peter O'Connor, *A Soldier of Liberty* (Dublin: MSF, 1997) , p. 17.
15. Quoted in Joseph O'Connor, *Even the Olives are Bleeding: The Life and Times of Charles Donnelly* (Dublin: New Island, 1992), p. 104.
16. Quoted in Victor Hoar, *The Mackenzie-Papineau Battalion* (Copp Clark Publishing, 1969), pp. 75–6.

17. Quoted in O'Connor, *Even the Olives are Bleeding*, p. 105.
18. Acier, *From Spanish Trenches*, pp. 118–20.
19. *The Worker*, 6 March 1937.

CHAPTER NINE

Battles on the Home Front

By early March 1937, Ryan was in Paris making his way home, full of enthusiasm for republican causes in both Spain and Ireland: "I go home full of faith in our people – and more an Irishman than I ever was."[1] By the time he got to London, his leg injury, a twisted tendon, was sufficiently bad for him to procure a walking stick. Since medical attention in Spain had been negligible, a friend arranged for a doctor to treat the wound in Ryan's arm. Out of funds, he stayed with a friend, Peter O'Flinn, who advised him to go to the Communist Party offices to get the wherewithal for his return fare home. But Ryan would not. Not wanting to be beholden to the communists, claiming he would rather walk home, Ryan finally applied to the Spanish Embassy for assistance; it was forthcoming, and Ryan was soon back in Dublin.

Upon his arrival, Ryan found that passions for the war in Spain had become more muted, even if the balance in favour of Franco had remained consistent. Sheehy Skeffington and others were sending parcels to the men in Spain containing blankets, chocolate and the greatest luxury, decent cigarettes. In January, the Basque priest, Ramon La Borda, had arrived for a Congress-organised lecture tour during which he wished to "declare myself a follower of the army of Justice and Truth in the Spanish conflict . . . I do not see the Saviour approve of the enterprise which aims at deciding unlawfully by force of arms differences pronounced on peacefully by the ballot box." Fourteen friends of La Borda, priests all, had been executed by the Nationalists. "It is not a religious war; it is a political war," the Spanish cleric declared. "It is a social war

187

inspired by the rich to enslave the poor striving to free themselves through the polls." La Borda went so far as to claim that no Irish priests had asked him about the war because "they know of the atrocities committed by Franco's side against our bishops and priests and children and women and the poor of Spain generally. That is why they do not ask . . . they are partisans of fascism."[2]

The pronouncements of La Borda had a decidedly limited audience in Ireland. His lectures were often disrupted or cancelled, and he was prohibited from saying mass in Dublin. Neither the Labour Party nor the trade unions had removed their Francoist Sacred Hearts from their sleeves, and newspapers refused to print appeals on behalf of Sheehy Skeffington's Aid Committee. From London, the Irish writer Desmond Ryan had tried to organise a petition amongst Irish writers and intellectuals in support of the Spanish government, but, notwithstanding contributions from Sean O'Casey and Samuel Beckett, the response was sufficiently apathetic to condemn the project. Next to the bellowing for Franco in Ireland, the cheers for the Spanish government rose barely above a whimper.

When La Borda left in April, Ryan claimed that he had been "virtually deported . . . We must fight in this country the same enemy as opposes the enemy of Spain. The only difference is that here, at the moment, it hasn't come to a question of arms."[3] Nourishment for the Spanish enemy was ubiquitous, pervading the press, clerical obtusity and governmental disavowal of democracy in Spain. Ryan was appalled by the misinformation about the war being propounded in Ireland, much of it concerning himself. Particularly galling were the claims that in Spain he was a communist leader, whereas, in truth "I don't even happen to be a member. But on the other hand, no one is going to get me to join an anti-Communist ramp. Hence my persistent refusal to answer on my party affiliations."[4] One evening Paddy Byrne accompanied Ryan to the launch of an edition of the works of Connolly.

> Some troglodyte sitting behind us kept interrupting the speakers with shouts of "What about the works of Jesus?" and "What about the works of Saint Patrick?" Frank stuck it for a while before turning round, grabbing the offender and, shaking a massive fist under his

nose, advised him "to keep his bloody mouth shut or he'd give him the works of Frank Ryan".[5]

Fortunately, efforts to confront the propaganda of "the enemy" in less physical ways had been set in motion before Ryan's return. The *Irish Democrat* newspaper was founded jointly by Republican Congress, the Communist Party of Ireland and the Northern Ireland Socialist Party, the three colluding to set up the Progressive Publications Society, based in Belfast.[6] Ryan returned from Spain just as the first issue of the weekly paper was being prepared for issue on 20 March, and he assumed the editor's chair. The paper, in its first editorial, claimed itself to be "a product of the growing unity of the Workers, Socialist, Republican, Communist, and men and women of no party. We will proclaim that, regardless of present differences of opinion, all workers and freedom-loving citizens should unite their forces against the common foe of all."[7] Ryan was hardly on alien ground.

Frank Ryan was a busy man, reuniting with his friends and family (his parents came up to Dublin from Elton for a while), speaking on political platforms and running the new paper, all with one arm in a sling and a leg dragging behind him. The trip to America was off for Ryan as it could not take place until September, by which time he would be back in Iberia.[8] Predictably, Ryan's life was complicated by the obstacle of finding printers who would work with him. Even the Church of Ireland Printing Co., approached by a clearly desperate Ryan, had been asked by Dublin's Catholic archbishop, in writing, to do no work for "Ryan the Red". Ryan became reacquainted with all the other familiar saboteurs of the mellifluous running of a radical paper: newsagent boycotts, lack of advertisers, proscription in the North and hard-pressed volunteer contributors.

Inevitably, the *Irish Democrat* scrutinised developments in Spain and regularly printed letters from Irish combatants. The paper also flew colours for the next bout of domestic political jousting; the upcoming general election – by which de Valera's staying power and his gratification of the electorate's republican instincts would be tested – and a simultaneous referendum on the new Constitution that the taoiseach claimed sealed a republic for the twenty-six counties. More advanced republicans pointed out that the new Constitution brought about changes that were largely symbolic while the Free State remained in the Commonwealth. The dismantling of the Northern border by words and in principle only left them unimpressed. Further, the new departure prohibited divorce, consigned women to a role dubiously close to Hitler's ideal of "kinder, kirche, kuche" and conferred upon the Catholic Church a "special position" within the state. Ryan and O'Donnell drew up a Republican Congress manifesto that contested the notion of a semi-state Church, claimed that "private property is raised here to almost the dignity of a sacrament" and demanded that a new constitution declare "that equal pay and opportunities for women in industry shall be assured".[9]

Ryan had originally planned to return to Spain in late April. Possibly because his sister Catherine, Sister Aquin in the Mercy Convent in Tralee, was dying of tuberculosis, he was open to the idea of a postponement. She was his favourite sister – as a child she had taught him how to smoke, one of his greatest pleasures – and he travelled down to Kerry to visit her a couple of times. "She's a great skin," he told Gerald O'Reilly, adding with pride that "She and two other nuns in that convent are known as – and call themselves – 'the Communists'. They burn the *Irish Rosary* and the *Irish Catholic* stories about us, and tell priests to mind religion, not politics."[10] On the last occasion of his visit before he left for Spain, as he bid her farewell, Ryan wept at her bedside.

With the advent of Nationalist victories in the Basque region, the welfare of his men had become all the more pressing for Ryan: "I worry more now for the outcome of the war. The new Four power [non-intervention] pact will give Germany and Italy more scope. The liberty of Spain is apparently the price to be paid for staving off a great war."[11] Furthermore, the fissiparous nature of the Spanish government seemed to preordain its implosion. The Nationalist bombing of Guernica in late April elicited some international sympathy, but Republican factionalism, progenitor of a civil war within the Civil War, irreparably crippled the Republican struggle. The tensions between the government, the communists, the socialists and the anarchists were strained beyond breaking point by early May, when open hostilities broke out in Barcelona. Fighting went on for a week, during which the fratricide claimed 500 dead and 1,000 injured.

In Ireland, however, it seemed as if the various strands of republicanism were melding back together, and the new concord enjoyed a public show of strength to protest the coronation of George VI in London on 12 May. A handful of republican and left-wing groups had already tried to snuff out any plans for the coronation's celebration in Ireland, writing, en bloc, for example, to the Film Renters' Society that "we trust that you will advise your members against the showing of any films dealing with ceremonies planned".[12] Yet the alliance, including Republican Congress and the IRA, faced more robust opposition than the Film Renters' Society in their plans for a protest march against the coronation of a King of Ireland on its eve, in the shape of P.J. Ruttledge, minister of justice, and the policemen at his disposal. The march was proclaimed.

Regardless, a sizeable Congress contingent joined the three hundred or so IRA men gathered at Liberty Hall, the meeting place having been changed to dodge the huge police presence near the original venue of St Stephen's Green. However, the police were not to be so easily eluded and were near by in large numbers when Ryan approached Tom Barry, now IRA chief of staff, supposedly on the run, and asked where he and his followers should fall in. Barry welcomed his comrade from years past and told the Congress leader to fall in at the head of the march beside himself and Tadgh Lynch, editor of *An Phoblacht*. Eyeing the arm in its sling, Barry warned Ryan that they were in for a rough ride.

Marching toward O'Connell Street right into the ranks of policemen with batons drawn, the protestors put up a "show of resistance until detectives around Butt Bridge produced their revolvers and fired over the heads of the crowd. The firing lasted only for about fifteen or twenty seconds. Mr Frank Ryan . . . was hit about the head and bled profusely." Ryan's nose was broken, and Tom Barry and Tadgh Lynch had been knocked unconscious. Still, Ryan managed to gain O'Connell Street, where he "mounted the base of a monument and began to address a gathering which had spread across the tram lines. He had spoken several sentences when police made their way through the crowd."[13] Ryan evaded arrest and, after some hours in hospital, spent the night at a friend's home talking to Tom Barry.

From the base of the monument, Ryan had taunted the authorities that the march had gone ahead in total contradiction of the minister's prohibition, and the following morning himself and Barry plotted another march for that evening. The authorities, obviously reluctant to be tainted by public beatings of republicans, which they professed themselves to be, backed down. There was minimal police attendance at the second meeting, led up O'Connell Street to Cathal Brugha Street by Ryan and Barry, both with their heads swathed in bandages. From a flatbed lorry, Ryan thundered that the gathering was to "repudiate any connection with the ceremony that took place in England and to repudiate any legislation putting any foreign king in a position of authority either internally or externally". He went on to tell his listeners that, had the proposed new Constitution been truly republican, "there would have been celebrations and demonstrations all over the nation, but there was not a single bonfire or demonsration of joy, because it was not the Constitution that Tone and the men of 1916 died for".[14] Other speakers followed, but one IRA attendant claimed later that "it is only right to say now that Frank Ryan got the loudest cheer from the people, a lot more than Tom Barry, who was Chief of Staff".[15] After the speeches, a Union Jack was produced and burned.

The previous night Tom Barry had asked Ryan would he not remain in Ireland to work at strengthening the apparent cohesion of labour and republican groups in the country. It was clear that neither de Valera nor his new Constitution had the enthusiastic support of the electorate, and the very existence of the *Irish Democrat* and the fraternity that had protested the coronation both indicated that separatist and labour unity was in the offing. Ryan was even printing off copies of a revived, albeit short-lived, *An Phoblacht*. The possible overhaul of the constitution and the government could provide fertile ground for Ryan's cherished united front. Among those who would listen, the returned hero would be the obvious man for the job of leader. The sling on Ryan's arm was admired as a red badge of courage, and he was still a "most popular speaker on a platform", well-liked personally and his talents highly regarded. On a more personal level, Barry considered that "Frank was no more a communist than I was. He was a patriotic Irishman with left wing sympathies."[16] But Barry was to be disappointed.

Ryan told Barry of the men he had left behind in the XV Brigade and complained that the lack of unity amongst republicans in Ireland was as nothing compared to the fratricide in Spain. Why, then, Barry asked him, did he insist on returning? Ryan, referring to an ambush led by the IRA leader against the British, countered him with the question, "Would you have left your men to find their own way out after Crossbarry? I will go back and bring them home."[17] Paddy Byrne "pleaded with Frank not to return to Spain as the fall of the Republic seemed imminent, but he believed that his duty lay with the remnants of the Irish Battalion".[18] Indeed, Ryan thought their position, in light of the war's progress and the Spanish government's disarray, sufficiently precarious to discourage further recruitment for the cause. Four men in Christy Quearney's IRA company had gone, of whom one had been wounded and three killed, yet he presented himself to Ryan as a volunteer: "Frank said no; 'The Army is in a bad way and we are not winning in Spain. Stay behind and reorganise the Army. We may need it yet. We have enough IRA men in Spain, and they will gain experience and train you when they come home.'"[19]

Pessimism was equally fitting for the prospects of Ryan's causes in Spain and at home. The disintegration of Spanish Republican unity had an unexpected side effect: the atrophy of socialist/republican unity in Ireland. On the day the Republican self-destruction in Barcelona had finally ended, only days before the coronation solidarity in Dublin, Ryan had published, and was supposed to have written, an article impeaching a specific faction in Spain for its assault on fellow workers. He described the Partido Obrero de Unificación Marxista[20] (POUM) as "a Fascist force in the rear . . . The trouble originated with the numerically insignificant POUM, a Trotskyite body which has carried on a campaign of wrecking and disorganising against the war." The writer prescribed "crushing this pest once and for all".[21] The Northern Ireland Socialist Party, already drawing daggers with Irish communists over Spain, was outraged by the libel of its ideological cousins. Its support for the paper was soon afterwards withdrawn.

Ryan had already had difficulties learning to bite his tongue. Catering to the tastes of the paper's politically divergent subscribers, he had struggled to rein in his nationalist republicanism to avoid alienating Northern Protestants. He realised that the *Irish Democrat* had still to find a sound footing, and the caprices of the old printing machinery he struggled with prevented at least one issue from reaching the newsstands. The paper "will badly need help now", Ryan acknowledged. "To tell the truth, I've been so busy on the organisational side of it – and the mechanical too! – that for weeks past, I've been able only to slap together several issues. Spain is of minor news value in Ireland now. The furore of the Christian Front ramp has spent and wasted itself."[22]

Ryan clearly had his work cut out for him in Ireland, but his duty was in Spain. Notwithstanding that his priority lay with his men in the trenches, he perhaps suspected that socialist/separatist unity was living through yet another false dawn. With urgent domestic issues at hand, it was easier for militants to overlook their differences at least until a crisis had passed. It is unlikely that many in the IRA would have concurred with Ryan's assertion that "The 1916 Proclamation was always read to promise . . . a triumph of the poor over the small group of rich men who trafficked in their misery."[23] Furthermore, many republicans, Seán MacBride among them, had been seduced away from militancy by the new Constitution. By Ryan's logic, the hopelessness of his domestic causes only demanded increased effort rather than desertion, but he calculated that there was nothing so immediate for him to tend to that it superseded the welfare of his men in Spain. In which case, by remaining in Ireland, he was only "making time" before "resuming my trek back . . . What jails didn't teach me about patience, the eternal mañanas in Spain did."[24]

Ryan told nobody he was leaving, not even his sister, Eilís. She saw him for the last time at a party held by republican friends in Drumcondra, but when he arrived straight from the printing press, he was exhausted from working. He had a glass of Guinness and fell asleep sitting on the top of the stairs. The party evolved into a ballad session and Ryan was roused. One of the hostesses, Nora McGinley, was known to have a beautiful voice, and Ryan asked her to sing. She acquiesced and, as she recalls, whilst she was singing an old Irish air, "I happened to look out into the dark. There he was, with a light shining on him and a tear on his cheek. I never saw him again."[25] A few days later, on 4 June, Ryan slipped out of the country.

Travelling through London, Ryan took the opportunity to impress upon Communist Party officials the need for an Irish column existing alongside, yet distinct from, their British brothers-in-arms. His appeal was received coldly. He himself seems to have doubted the feasibility of such an enterprise in view of the war's attrition of both the Republican cause and the Irish contingent. Despite his uncharacteristic expectancy of defeat, Ryan remained inordinately proud of his men. This pride and his own position were conveyed in a London letter to Desmond Ryan.

> Here I am, the leader of a lost battalion, the remnants
> of which won't make a company. From Andalusia to
> Aragon, they fought and never once a panic. Windy?
> Yes, we moistened our pants awkwardly, but we
> never broke . . . I've no reputation to boast – or to
> seek – as an Internationalist. I came home three
> months ago more a Nationalist than ever. Whenever
> I yelled 'Come on the Irish', they came on. I wanted
> to bring out a few hundred men, I could get them, I
> could bring them. I didn't for I wanted them at home
> all the more. I go alone and I'll try to save the lives of
> the few that are left. That's my new role.[26]

A regular host of Ryan's in London was Sean O'Casey, the two having long since resurrected their friendship. The playwright remembered that Ryan's wound "was largely healed but still very ugly". O'Casey, too, was impressed by Ryan's iron code of duty: "I used all my eloquence to persuade him to stay at home, feeling in some way, that if he went back to Spain, we should never see him again. He refused to stay, saying that he 'couldn't think of leaving the boys by themselves'."[27] Ryan obviously shared some of O'Casey's apprehension regarding his possible fate; he left his pen and wallet with his friend Peter O'Flinn, telling him that he "might not be back".

In Dublin, after Ryan's departure, his colleagues decided to promote the united front strategy heralded in the pages of the *Irish Democrat* and to campaign against the new Constitution by entering a candidate for the election. It was decided to put forward Ryan, *in absentia,* in the Dublin South constituency. He had been the most vocal proponent of the united front and was a prominent veteran of anti-fascist conflict of a more substantial nature than street brawls. Ryan had not seemed to concern himself overly with missing the elections. An election meeting in Christchurch Place was visited upon by the inevitable hecklers hollering "Communist bastards" before harmonising for "Faith of Our Fathers". Next came not prayers but bottles and bricks. A short dash to an IRA meeting near by was rewarded by the return of a contingent weighty enough to see off the hecklers. The *Irish Democrat* foretold that "Ryan's election will be a victory for 'Government by the people, of the people, for the people,' a blow against coercion and a thump in the face for Fascism."[28]

Unfortunately Ryan could not deliver the thump, since he was neither in the country nor even knew he was a candidate. His sister Eilís and other volunteers knocked on doors and held meetings in his stead. The IRA, if inadvertently, further scotched Ryan's chances by ordering volunteers to abstain from the elections. In a poll of 57,011, Ryan won 875 first preference votes, climbing to 914 with the transfer of Seán Lemass's votes in the second count, after which Ryan was eliminated. Fianna Fáil's governance and the new Constitution were both approved by the electorate, but without enthusiasm. De Valera had to rely more than ever on Labour support.

Ryan was more upset that his departure meant missing the opportunity to welcome back to Ireland O'Duffy's Brigade. The Blueshirts returned in June after a near mutiny in Spain and bitter divisions had split their ranks. They had never engaged the enemy. They had first come under fire during the Nationalist advance in Guadalajara, during which a Dubliner and two Kerrymen were killed. Two of their number were then killed in a skirmish near Jarama, except against a different brigade on their own side. Subsequently, O'Duffy lost the confidence of the Nationalist command when he refused an order to advance without air cover, saying it was too dangerous.

O'Duffy was only very rarely seen by his men, whose tedium from doing little except guard duty behind the lines dragged down morale. That is not to say they enjoyed comfort or security; their lines were occasionally strafed from the air and were often the receptacle of enemy artillery and sniper fire. The meagre food and clothing allotted to the men was woefully inadequate during the wet and cold spring, and it was not unusual for 200 of the 600 men to be hospitalised at any one time. The men, in rain-flooded trenches, were rarely granted leave and had come quickly to the conclusion that they were only pawns serving O'Duffy's domestic political ambitions. By April, there was serious dissension among the officers, and it was clear that the brigade was not sustainable. O'Duffy wrote to Franco saying he wished to dissolve the *Bandera Irlandesa,* probably in anticipation of the *Generalismo* disbanding it. Upon their somewhat ignominious return home, they arrived as two conflicting factions.

As the Blueshirts had been preparing to leave Spain, Ryan was making his way there. He travelled with something of a heavy heart, driven by his compulsion to fulfil his obligation to his men. "So he went off," remembered Tom Barry, "never to return, which was Ireland's great loss. It was the only decision an honourable man could take, and Frank was certainly that."[29]

Notes to Chapter Nine

1. Marcel Acier, ed., *From Spanish Trenches* (London: Cresset Press, n.d.), p. 119.
2. *Irish Democrat,* 15 May 1937.
3. *Irish Democrat,* 24 April 1937.
4. Quoted in Seán Cronin, *Frank Ryan: The Search for the Republic* (Dublin: Repsol, 1980), p. 103.
5. Paddy Byrne, *Irish Republican Congress Revisited* (London: Connolly, 1994), p. 40.
6. Although support for the Spanish Republicans was quite strong in the North amongst Protestant workers and left of centre politicians not constrained by displays of reverence to the Church, by the same religious/political mores were Catholics in the North particularly ardent supporters of Franco. At least two Belfast IRA men had gone with O'Duffy to Spain.
7. *Irish Democrat,* 20 March 1937.
8. Ryan's stand-in was the valiant Father O'Flanagan, who, with Paddy Byrne, was to run a "Foodship for Spain" initiative. After opening their rented offices in Sackville Place, Brendan Behan arrived looking for the contract to paint it, which, though only fourteen, he was given by Byrne, who recalled that "every day for

a week he arrived, with a full holdall of stout". A bottle was offered to Byrne one morning, who refused, saying it was too early for him. "Behan was delighted with the fifty pounds payment he received for his first job. Years later, he came upon Byrne in a London pub: 'Paddy Byrne, the man who gave me my first fuckin' job, have a fuckin' drink.'" Peter Hegarty, *Peadar O'Donnel* (Cork: Mercier Press, 1999), p. 236.

9. *Irish Democrat,* 22 May 1937.
10. Quoted in Cronin, *Frank Ryan,* p. 112. The two journals were vigorous in their pillory of the Spanish government.
11. In a letter to Desmond Ryan, Desmond Ryan papers, UCDAD, LA 10/Q/19 (2).
12. Department of Justice files, NAI, Jus 8/471.
13. *Irish Press,* 12 May 1937. Paddy Byrne says that Ryan had been arrested at Liberty Hall, but that "the officer in charge acceded to his request to defer taking him into custody until he had dealt with some urgent unfinished business" – that being speaking on O'Connell Street. Byrne, *Irish Republican Congress,* p. 44.
14. *Irish Independent,* 13 May 1937.
15. Quoted in Uinseann Mac Eoin, *The IRA in the Twilight Years* (Dublin: Argenta, 1997), p. 769.
16. Quoted in Cronin, *Frank Ryan,* p. 108.
17. Quoted in Uinseann Mac Eoin, *Survivors* (Dublin: Argenta, 1980), p. 20.
18. Byrne, *Irish Republican Congress,* p. 44. See also Mac Eoin, *Twilight,* p. 770.
19. Quoted in Mac Eoin, *Twilight,* p. 769.
20. United Workers' Marxist Party.
21. *Irish Democrat,* 8 May 1937.
22. In a letter to Desmond Ryan, Desmond Ryan papers, UCDAD, LA 10/Q/19 (1).
23. *IrishDemocrat,* 22 May 1937.
24. Desmond Ryan papers, UCDAD, LA 10/Q/19 (1).
25. *The Irish Times,* 23 September 1992.
26. Desmond Ryan papers, UCDAD, LA 10/Q/19 (2).
27. Quoted in David Krause, ed., *The Letters of Sean O'Casey,* vol. 1 (London: Cassell, 1975), p. 875.
28. *Irish Democrat,* 26 June 1937.
29. Quoted in Cronin, *Frank Ryan,* p. 114.

CHAPTER TEN

Brunete to Burgos

I t took Frank Ryan ten days to return to his base camp in Spain. Travelling through France yet again, he made his way to the foot of the Pyrenees, which he crossed after a day and a half of hiking that sweated out any indulgences in Dublin. All the way he had been pondering his position, torn between two Republican causes, the one stalled and the other ill-omened. The Basque country, industrial machine of Spain, was bending to the Franco storm, its crucial naval port of Bilbao succumbing five days after Ryan had arrived back in the country.

He arrived in Albacete on 14 June 1937. The remnants of the Irish who had been in Jarama with the Abraham Lincoln Brigade, now part of a newly formed 20th Battalion, had just retired two days earlier to Albares, twenty miles to the east of the battle lines. There were no more than fifteen of them left. On 17 June, those serving in the British Battalion returned to Albacete after months on the rack of Jarama. The only relief from a trench life that had been tedious yet harrowing, thanks to the vigilance of their opposite numbers, had been when celebrations were held on Saint Patrick's Day and the anniversaries of the Easter Rising in late March and James Connolly's execution on 12 May.

After Jarama, both the initial battle and the ensuing stalemate punctuated by sniping and shell fire, the number of Irish effectives, supplemented by newcomers and others recovered from wounds, stood at a little under fifty. Ryan was soon busy working on a newspaper for the International Brigaders, *Nuestra Combate*,[1] but he also spent his time addressing the various grievances of his men and checking up on the wounded. At the same time, he was trying to consolidate his men in one unit and repatriate those he thought warranted it. That another offensive would not be long in coming was a dreaded certainty, so Ryan was working against the clock.

Both being in the XV Brigade, the two units of Irish were to fight alongside each other in the offensive, the ambition of which was to relieve the unceasing pressure on Madrid and distract the Nationalists from their onslaught of Santander in the north. The Brigaders were to be deployed as a shock force to punch a way through the Nationalist lines toward the town of Brunete, fifteen miles west of Madrid, and head south so as to give depth to the western and southern defences of the city. During the first days of July, Ryan travelled to Albares to join the Irish Lincolns.

> We left Albares on foot and travelled towards the Guadaramma mountains. After marching about twenty kilometres, we camped in a beautiful forest, with a river flowing close by. Johnny Power and Frank Ryan and I [Peter O'Connor] went for a swim. It was very refreshing, after which we moved on again. The big offensive began on 6th July, 1937, at 5.00 a.m. By 9.00 a.m. the fascists were being routed.[2]

Roughly 50,000 government troops were thrown into the assault, with effective aerial and artillery support. The full significance, tactical and psychological, of the thrust toward Brunete was not lost on Ryan; it was "an important step forward in the evolution of the Republican Army. At Madrid and Jarama, in previous months, it had been on the defensive. At Brunete, taking the initiative, it passed over to the offensive." The push on the fascist flank and rear would trap the besiegers of Madrid if it could link up with the government forces south of the city. "'Relieve the pressure on the Northern front!' was the slogan on which the offensive was initiated. 'Raise the Beleaguerement of Madrid!' was the most practical political and military interpretation," claimed Ryan. "For Madrid was, and is, the key to life and death for Fascism in Spain."[3]

The Lincoln and British Battalions were to take the village of Villanueva de la Canada as others swept around it on to

Brunete and a distant ridge, the high point of which was
known by the men as Mosquito Crest. The Brigaders moved
across the open plains toward the village under heavy
machine-gun fire. Urging his men forward, Ryan appreciated
the difficulty of their task. "They had to drive in outposts, capture a line of trenches strongly fortified with barbed wire,
break through a line of pill-boxes, and finally storm the trenches at the entrance to the town."[4] Under the murderous fire of
the defenders, there was hardly a blade of grass left on the
battlefield, and in the intense heat, the stench of fast-rotting
corpses was unbearable.

Breaching the town's defences, "a desperate affair", did not
take place until dusk. Ryan, the British and the Americans
"were trying to find cover in flat ground a few hundred yards
from the houses. Our aircraft and artillery had pounded the
place well, but the church kept standing. And from its tower,
machine-guns seriously hampered us." The Brigaders had been
pinned down all afternoon, under a scorching sun with no
water and little cover from either enemy fire or the heat. In the
fading light, the men, crouched in ditches and behind such
cover as they could find, saw a party of civilians walk out from
the town with their hands raised and calling, "*Camaradas.*"
Pat Murphy rose from behind the dunghill that gave him cover
and went toward the refugees to usher them from the firing
line.

> Just as he approached, a revolver barked then
> grenades started to fly. For five minutes there was
> pandemonium, guns cracking, grenades bursting and
> women and children shrieking. Pat, engaged in a
> hand-to-hand struggle, fell into a ditch with his oppo-
> nent, where he dispatched him. Beside him fell a little
> girl of about ten years who had been at the head of
> the group. "Lie quiet, girlie," said Pat, and she smiled
> as if she understood. A grenade burst in the drain and
> Pat was severely wounded in the groin.
>
> In five minutes it was all over; the last of the Fas-
> cists was accounted for. When the lads went round to
> collect their own and the non-combatants, they found
> the little girl, two old women and three old men dead.

The exodus of refugees had been covered by the machine-gun in the church tower, and about forty armed Nationalists had mingled with the civilians. Ryan drew consolation from the fact that "every single one of the Fascists who had driven them in front of them as cover was also dead", but his account is perhaps bowdlerised.[5] The use of the human decoy is even more horrific in the memory of *Brigadista* Sid Quinn, for whom it was

> . . . the worst incident of the war. A group of civilians were pushed out of the village, mostly women and children. We wondered what was happening until we saw they were being used as a living shield, they were screaming. It was ghastly to watch it. There were old men, babies, toddlers, and they were shot down by us because we couldn't stop. Every last one of them.[6]

From two directions the men stormed the town in the dark, getting their bearings from the flash of grenades they hurled before them. All night was spent mopping up, flushing out hidden defenders. Ryan came across them

> . . . dropping their guns and becoming innocent peasants in the cellars with the women and children. There were weird sights. In one house you went to talk to three men lolling in chairs. Not a scratch on them. They had all been killed by the concussion of aerial torpedoes. And every Fascist prisoner, if you could believe him, was either a Communist or a Socialist. It was the most People's Front town in all Spain![7]

Once the village was taken, the *brigadistas* advanced for two days. Rising over successive ridges and overcoming lines of defence, they ground to a halt at the foot of Mosquito Crest and the high ground around Romanillos that looked east to Madrid. There they came under heavy fire from above. At this stage, the aerial and artillery support clearing the way for the advance faltered. Peter O'Connor and his section advanced too far and, in danger of being cut off, were called back to the lower ground. Ryan recorded that "From July 9 to July 18, fierce battles raged for Mosquito Crest – key to the heights of Romanillos. Each day more troops were rushed down from the Santander front. Soon fascist aircraft and artillery out-numbered those of the Republican Army by three to one."[8] Replying to a communication from Ryan, O'Connor had to tell him that he was the only Irishman left with the Lincolns. Of the Irish altogether, nine had been killed and more wound-ed. Sid Quinn came across a wounded friend from Belfast: "I saw him lying down shot through the mouth and could do nothing about it. He was quite phlegmatic about it, he knew it was no good, so I just turned him over to make him more comfortable and he died."[9] The fire from the church tower had hit Bill Davis from Dublin. "He curled up, his fist shot out, clenched. 'Salud, camaradas,' he smiled and he died."[10]

"I wish I could give you certain pictures of the fighting," Ryan wrote home during the lull, "and there's some I try to forget myself. At times I saw it all like a panorama in front of me; then there were hours when my nose stuck further and fur-ther into the earth. Ludwig Renn says it was like the Somme, only a bit worse."[11]

Ryan was as well to keep his head down. The line of resis-tance had been stiffened, and despite the advance's petering out, the fighting continued in the form of counter-attacks, sniping and shelling. "One thing is, you never get inured to bombardment; used to it, certainly," he claimed. "But every time the torpedoes start to fall, you feel your guts contract, and the blood gets sucked up out of the body. Of all the read-ing matter, what should I have in my hand one such day but the story of Guernica. Then I really realised what it must have been for the women and children."[12]

On 17 July, the Nationalist counter-offensive started.

> That day we experienced the heaviest aerial and artillery bombardment yet received during the war . . . The scorching heat was unbearable. We held our advanced positions against heavy fascist counter attacks, in which they used aerial, artillery, anti-tank and anti-aircraft bombardments. The fascists made a fierce attack on the morning of July 20th on our right flank, using forty or fifty bombers, machine-guns and tanks. Our flank gave way and we began to

retreat slowly. The heat was intolerable. We were
parched from thirst. We had gone twelve hours at
that point without a drink . . . The bombardment
and machine-gunning from the air by Hitler's
Junkers was horrifying.[13]

On 24 July, the Nationalists recaptured Brunete. The losses
to the International Brigades had been atrocious, and the Lincoln and British Battalions were pulled out of the line. Half the
fighting men of the former had been lost, while only forty-two
remained in the British Battalion out of a pre-battle total of
300. The remnants of both "literally staggered to the rear past
the Spanish relief units. They had been in action for almost
three weeks with a minimum of food and water. On the way
to the rear, the bearded, filthy survivors stopped at a farmhouse (dubbed the 'Pearly Gates') to rest."[14] Although they
had captured and held enemy ground, if not Brunete itself, the
offensive had ultimately fallen short of its targets. The incursion neither linked up with *camaradas* south of Madrid nor
loosened Franco's fingers from the throat of the Basque country. Yet Ryan treated the readers of the *Irish Democrat* to a
happy ending:

> The more planes our fighters knocked down, the
> more kept coming on. And for all their bombardment
> – which was terrible in its intensity and duration –
> they only regained one village and a few square miles
> of territory. We hold a greater part of a wedge we
> drove into their lines. And we have plenty of man-
> power; the enemy relies on planes and artillery to
> make up for his poor-quality troops. The offensive is
> certainly a victory for us.

If Ryan seems never to have taken time off from propaganda, he at least did not descend to glorify the lot of the
Brigaders: "War's hell. There's little glamour in it when you're
there, especially when you see what's left – after shell and the
heat – of fellows that were joking with you a few hours
before." Rather, he explained that theirs was an ugly job that
they felt compelled to do, and if the Brigaders' motives were
idealist, they were at least commendable – and good copy for

the *Democrat:* "This one has got to be done and won, so that makers of war can never again cause Guernicas and Almerias and Bilbaos."[15]

As the fighting in Brunete ground to a halt during the closing days of July, Ryan travelled back and forth to Albacete. He instigated the repatriation of, among others, Frank Edwards, Joe Monks, Jack Nalty and Jimmy Prendergast. The last was supposed to be already en route to Ireland, but in the confusion had found himself at the front near Brunete: "You can just imagine how he felt," sympathised Ryan. "Dublin almost in sight and avions and artillery churning the ground around him. He won't forget it for a while."[16] On 27 July, the day the Nationalist counter-attack ran out of steam, Peter O'Connor was tracked down near Brunete by Ryan with orders for him to return home: "I felt like a deserter. But Frank said I must obey orders. He was afraid all of the Irish would be killed . . . He wanted some survivor or survivors to put the record straight about the Spanish War when we got back home."[17] In all, twenty Irish volunteers left Spain during August.

Meanwhile, Wexford's Peter Daly, just recovered from a wound, and Paddy O'Daire from Donegal were elevated to battalion commander and adjutant respectively. The promotions delighted Ryan, who had code-named the British Battalion "Elizabeth" in his letters: "You remember Elizabeth? Her new boss is Irish; and you remember how she hated the Irish? It's a great joke to be taking orders from what she used to call 'the pig in the kitchen' type. (Excuse my nationalism but she was a bitter person always and I can't help laughing at her.)"[18]

For those Irish who remained with "Elizabeth", a couple of sun-drenched weeks in Albacete were welcome respite from over six months of fatigue and poor nourishment, enemy shells and snipers' explosive bullets. Apart from rebuilding their strength, the men spent time repairing weaponry and renewing contact with home. Ryan wrote of his sorrow at not being near his sister Katie, as well as his hope that she might yet pull through. He gave assurances that he was in no danger, the weather was good and he was putting on weight.

Ryan also wrote that he was irritated by the treatment of the war in newspapers at home, in particular the *Irish Democrat,* "my own bloody rag, by the way". The arch-propagandist gave out strenuously about the tools of his own trade. American and Irish journalists threw stories together by chopping and mixing various sentences from interviews and letters, then topped off the concoction with a few "quotes" that they decided Ryan should have given. But his chief gripe, he wrote to Gerald O'Reilly, was that lazy writers should focus almost exclusively on himself, a recognisable figurehead, rather than give credit to the dozens of other Irishmen who had taken up arms against Fascism in Spain: "How many times have I asked that publicity be given to the lads that most deserve it? Why wasn't Gerry Doran's story of his adventures, and Goff's and Smith's in the *Democrat?* Go ask that of the editor. Now you'll have Nalty, Monks, Prender and Edwards – powerful stories, so get them to lay off me."[19]

The former editor also criticised the unattractive layout of the paper and the absence of articles penned by O'Donnell. Ryan's energy and purpose were missed by the paper, which had gone into decline, and in September, Ryan wrote an appeal to the readership that was given prominence on the front page.

> Here in Republican Spain, the *Irish Democrat* is very popular, and the news that it may have to cease publication causes great alarm . . . I am looking forward to hearing from my friends that the *Democrat* has overcome its difficulties. I will be hearing this good news if YOU, dear reader, subscribe every pound, shilling and penny that you can to the Democrat Defence Fund.[20]

As Ryan's appeal was winging its way to Dublin, the rest so welcomed by him and his men was abruptly curtailed: "We are on another push." The new push was centred on the plains south of the Aragonese capital of Zaragoza, astride the Ebro River. First by truck, and then by train, the XV Brigade were moved to the front, their immediate objective being the small village of Quinto and its commanding Purburell Hill. The inactivity of the anarchists, previously holding the line, had allowed the Nationalists to fortify their positions well.

Attempting to gain a foothold on the hill, the Irish came under fire from the positions atop it and the village's church tower. In the crossfire, Peter Daly received his third wound in Spain. This time it was fatal. O'Daire assumed command of

the battalion, which fell back at dusk, awaiting artillery support in the morning. O'Daire admitted that "to describe the
storming of Purburell Hill on the morning of August 26 is a
job for which I do not feel myself fitted. It was eight hours
fierce fighting on a bare hillside under a broiling sun. I must
admit, it was one of the fiercest battles in months of war
here."[21] Supposedly impregnable, the hill was captured, yield-
ing over three hundred prisoners. While comrade Brigaders
went on to storm Belchite, the key town to Zaragoza, the
British Battalion was detailed to hold the line against counter-
attacks, a task "less spectacular but equally gruelling".[22] They
held the line against immense pressure for three days, on one
of which they suffered no less than seven bombing and straf-
ing raids from enemy aircraft. Belchite fell on 6 September, but
the advance made no further progress. The resistance of the
Nationalists was superb. Again, an assault had ended in deadlock.

As summer declined and autumn came on, Ryan was still
dividing himself between field and staff duties. It was at about
this time that he was promoted to the rank of major. An English volunteer remembered him "working in the Albacete base
where he kept a watchful eye on the well-being of all the Irish
volunteers".[23] However, as the number of those volunteers
decreased, so did his purpose. There was even some talk of his
following, at the close of September, those he had already repa-
triated, but at the end of that month, he fell sick. When he
recovered, rather than leaving for Ireland, he went back to his
men, who were still holding the Aragon front. A number of
them

> ... went on a deputation to Frank to appeal to him
> to stay back, as he had been advised to do by the doc-
> tors. We pointed out to him the value he would be at
> home. We argued with him for over an hour, point-
> ing out the loss he would be in Ireland, where a few
> months previously he had been successful in uniting
> all sections of the people of Dublin in a mighty anti-
> Imperialist demonstration.[24]

Ryan returned to the front for the same reason that he had,
temporarily, forsaken the cause that moved him most, Irish

socialist republicanism. There were still sufficient numbers of Irishmen to keep him in Spain, and he had to be close to them. Ryan was still expecting to be back in Ireland for Christmas, followed by a trip to America, and, against the odds, he held on to hopes of seeing his sister Katie again. On 14 November, he received a letter from Éilis referring to their sister's death; she had obviously written previously with the details, but the letter had not reached him. It was a cruel way to hear of her passing, and the delivery of the news, void of dates or details, must have plunged Ryan into an agony of loneliness.

He was also detained in Spain by the greater demands made on his talents as a publicist, which at least limited his exposure to risk at the front. The greatest challenge for Ryan was probably having to strictly toe and propagate the communist line, a maddening task for one who was something of a loose cannon. As the communist hold within the Republican authorities tightened, dissent was correspondingly punishable, but Ryan considered himself communism's accomplice rather than its agent. He was too burdened by his need to voice his own opinions, and an anti-authoritarian streak that was not the narrowest, to be a truly consummate propagandist of others' ideas, but he managed to sufficiently discipline himself to avoid trouble.

Much of late 1937 was spent in either Madrid or Albacete, or, more precisely, on the road between the two. Ryan got used to sleeping in proper beds again, shaving regularly and wearing a uniform he was finally provided with after months of wearing an odd mixture of khakis. He attended November's anniversary celebrations for the International Brigades, along with the representatives of the numerous countries represented in the army. That same month he gave broadcasts over Radio Madrid:

> I recall that when we came here first, a leading Irish newspaper – in an effort not to be too harsh on us – depicted us as idealists who went to fight other people's battles, thereby implying that we are avoiding fighting our own. No interpretation could be more incorrect. We are realists.
>
> In the task of freeing Ireland in our generation, where was the initiative shown if not from men like

> Kit Conway, Charlie Donnelly, William Beatty, Peter
> Daly, and scores of other Irishmen whose graves are
> today on the battlefields of Spain? Just as these had a
> correct conception of a free Ireland – the conception
> of Tone, of Connolly, of Mellows – so they had a cor-
> rect conception of Ireland's place on earth.

A newspaper which printed an interview with Ryan had perhaps earlier featured an account of O'Duffy's expedition, as the
headline read "Ireland's Honour Redeemed – An Interview
with Frank Ryan". Articles composed by Ryan were subsequently translated for publication in the newssheet *Mundo
Obrero*,[25] and he helped the American communist poet Edwin
Rolfe edit an English-language paper for the *brigadistas*, *Soldier of Liberty*. He also started editing *Book of the XV Brigade*,
a compilation of narratives of the war written by brigade members. Its contributors were largely men from Ireland and Canada, the US and the UK, and Ryan was helped by Alonzo Elliott,
a Cambridge teacher, and a Scotsman, Alex Donaldson.

Part of Ryan's detail seems to have been to spend time with
various dignitaries who came to Spain to lend their support.
He met the writers Langston Hughes and Ernest Hemingway,
but the latter "doesn't want to be reminded of *A Farewell to
Arms* . . . He has no politics but is a real friend of the Spanish
people. Got ambulances sent here and it's since been found out
he used his own money on them. I'm due for a night in his
hotel." Ryan had a "few wild nights" in Hemingway's hotel,
despite the frequent shelling. The American remained untrou-
bled by bombardments, and he fashioned a dud shell that he
had retrieved into a reading lamp. For Ryan, however, being
shelled behind the lines was far more distressing than at the
front, for it, being all the more unexpected. Despite Madrid's
relative safety and his drinking whiskey with celebrities, it was,
after all, a city under fire. The front was only a tram-ride distant. Throughout, Ryan's disgust for war never flagged, only
intensified: "The more you see of war the more you hate it.
But this one has got to be seen through. When the pacifists
show me their way of beating Franco & Co., I'll be their first
recruit. Until then, this dirty way is the only way."[26]

Christmas of 1937 was particularly cold, and Ryan suffered
from chilblains in his fingers and toes. He spent the first two

months of the new year overcoming obstacles to collating and editing material for the *Book of the XV Brigade,* which, with an eye to going home, he was in a rush to be done with. The completed volume was dedicated to the Republic's President Manuel Azaña and concluded with a message for the "nameless heroes of the XV Brigade" from *La Pasionaria*: "You have shed your blood generously on the soil of Spain, Spain that is being redeemed for us and for you, by winning it for freedom and democracy."[27] In the foreword, Ryan pointed out that "it is not a history of the Brigade; its contributors are as yet making history".[28] Partisan undoubtedly, it is nonetheless an extraordinary achievement, realised under the most pressing conditions that ranged from bombardment to paper shortages. The articles, written at the front, on leave and in the hospitals, all had to be compiled and several translated within a very short time, yet the standard of writing is remarkable. Even had it been produced in peacetime, it would have been an impressive collection of insights and recollections yet fresh. Narratives complemented by several maps and scores of photographs, the book stretched to over three hundred pages. By the end of February, it was ready to be printed off. Ryan made preparations to leave for Ireland within a month.

On 23 February, the Nationalists had finally retaken the city of Teruel, east of Madrid. The triumph for Franco was of huge importance symbolically; Teruel had been held by the insurgents since the war's opening, a proud Nationalist salient thrusting into the Republican lines. It had withstood several assaults until early January when the defenders, after two weeks of bitter house-to-house fighting, had withdrawn only to mount a terrific counter-offensive. Having retaken the city, Franco prepared his forces for possibly the single most decisive offensive of the war, ranging along the Aragon front from Teruel east to the Pyrenees and driving toward the Mediterranean. Triumph would split the Republican territory in two. Nationalist superiority in arms and men was unequivocal. Defending the flimsy Republican lines were men who had yet to recover from Teruel, many of whom went into action without even rifles. The Nationalist advance along the Ebro River to the sea became a rout. Republicans were ordered to retreat and dig in at the village of Corbera to muster with *brigadistas* fresh from Madrid and Albacete. Frank Ryan was among them.

From Corbera, Ryan and the British Battalion were detailed to build up the defences at the town of Gandesa, perhaps ten miles to the south-west, which blocked the route to Tortosa and the sea. Gandesa had to be held. Little realising that the Nationalist line had since advanced and now blocked their route, the men trekked through an ill-starred night with such urgency that they caught up with their scouts. Near the village of Calaciete, the lead company of the British passed by small tanks along the roadside in the half-light of dawn. The political commissar, Wally Tapsell, called a question to an officer leaning out of one of them; he was shot dead. With confused horror, the men realised that the lettering on the tanks was not Spanish but Italian, and before they could move Italian soldiers had them surrounded, shouting at them to drop their guns and lie on the ground. The battalion had delivered themselves right into the welcoming embrace of a division of the crack Italian Black Arrows. The units to the rear tried to take to the higher ground and a fight ensued, but for those in the lead, Frank Ryan among them, resistance was futile. It was 30 March 1938.

Ryan and about 150 other prisoners were marched to a command post behind the fascist lines. Along the way, Italian tanks and trucks passed them, the soldiers leaning out to jeer and spit at the prisoners. Max Parker, an American volunteer, was already being held at the next post, watching captured Spaniards being shot out of hand, when Ryan and the others arrived.

> A fascist officer demanded to know who their commanding officer was. Captain Ryan immediately stood up. The English prisoners – all of them were in pretty bad shape, but fearing for Ryan's life, they all shouted "No, Frank! No! Sit Down!" But Ryan simply said "I am."
>
> We marched for some distance. Around 12.00 noon, we were put in an area off the main road. Captain Ryan then demanded loudly to know when we would be fed and given water. I acted as his interpreter, speaking Spanish to an Italian officer who approached us. Frank repeated his demands for food and water.

The Italian officer told us that Gandesa had fallen. Ryan didn't believe him and told him so. At this point, another officer joined us. He was German – Gestapo. He told us who he was. He got into a discussion in English with Captain Ryan about why he was in Spain. Frank told him, spelled it out for him; then asked the Gestapo officer *what he was doing in Spain*. The officer said simply: "You're a brave man". Then he turned around and left us.[29]

Ryan, in fact, held the rank of major, and captured Republican officers were normally executed on the spot. He reminded the men, who expected summary executions alongside their *camaradas,* why they were in Spain and told them not to lose sight of their purpose. Said Parker, "He was an inspiration." As the prisoners awaited their fate in the enclosure, they cheered at the sight of Republican planes flying overhead. The next morning they were moved on to another enclosure, where Dubliner Bob Doyle watched as an Italian officer

> . . . picked out Frank Ryan and asked him for details of the Brigade, its arms and complement. Ryan said he would give them any personal information they required but no military information whatsoever. With this the Italian reached up and slapped him across the face and we had to restrain Frank from retaliating.[30]

The Italian officer snapped at Ryan, "I suppose you are a Communist." "I am an Irish Republican," answered the prisoner, "but if I were a communist, I would be prepared to say so." Some time later, some of the Italian guards started booty-hunting. The helpless prisoners stood by as the foragers rummaged through their personal belongings, helping themselves to boots, clothing and whatever else took their fancy. Ryan objected to an officer commanding in what must have been the most forcible manner, since "the officer was so taken aback that he ordered the articles to be returned".[31] Ryan was soon led away. Italian soldiers later informed the Brigaders that their comrade had been court-martialled and was now under sentence of death. He was to be kept apart from the rest of the men. Upon his return, Ryan was placed out on the road in view of the prisoners and, with bayonet prods, ordered to give the fascist salute. He refused, whereupon an officer lined up a firing squad in front of him. Still he refused. Ryan was placed in a truck and driven off.

What Ryan and the others did not know was that the Italians were keen to hold on to their *brigadista* prisoners as chips in prisoner exchanges for Italians. However, Ryan was under sentence of his court-martial. One Brigader remembered that all the prisoners were housed for a night in an abandoned church, "except Frank Ryan, who returned in the morning after spending the night in a condemned cell with a Republican officer, and had once again been sentenced to death".[32] Ryan was segregated from the other prisoners as they were taken by truck and train to a prison in Zaragoza. As a propaganda exercise, the prison was opened to the pro-Franco press. Ryan was hidden away in solitary confinement where he could be quietly disposed of, yet, as an inmate later explained, some of the prisoners had engineered a way to bring the condemned man to the attention of the newsmen: "We have no story. See Frank Ryan," they replied to questions from the journalists.[33] An article by a respected Spanish journalist made reference to the exceptional case. It subsequently came to the attention of the solitary foreign journalist, William Carney of the *New York Times*, who was *persona grata* with the authorities.

Ryan hardly ingratiated himself with the one man who might save him. According to the journalist's account, visiting the prisoner was like being locked in a cage with a viper. Carney claimed that Ryan "glowered at and insulted" him, accusing him of "doing Fascist propaganda, and being in the pay of the Fascists". The dislike was intense and mutual. Carney claimed that the condemned man was "atheist and anti-religious, declares himself a separatist Republican just like Basques and Catalans". He even went so far as to imply that Ryan was in solitary out of concern for the other prisoners, alleging American Brigaders had told him, "Ryan was a 'tough guy', that nobody was safe in his company and he frequently killed other prisoners"![34] However, Carney's depiction of Ryan, rather than tying the condemned man's noose, saved him; his case became grist for the press mill and emerged as an international conversation piece – for which the Spanish journalist who first covered it was severely reprimanded.

Ryan was returned to his comrades, but his consistent
refusal to give the fascist salute earned him beatings from the
guards and caused much disquiet among his comrades, who
were divided on whether to follow his lead or not. Another
journalist noted Ryan's truculent attitude toward his gaolers,
claiming it was "enough to turn all sympathy from him . . .
Ryan was his own worst enemy."[35] The Brigaders, however,
admired his stand: "Frank Ryan . . . gave us a lead in respect
to giving the Fascist salute." In the end a compromise was
reached between the men and the guards, whereby a standard
army salute, of sorts, was given instead. Bob Doyle says of the
compromise that still "only Frank Ryan refused".[36]

After some days in Zaragoza, the men were moved on again
by train to San Pedro de Cardenas, near the Nationalist capital of Burgos, where an old monastery had been converted into
a holding pen for some 700 Brigaders and about 2,000
Basques. The men were roused at 5 a.m. and, around the
Nationalist flag, were expected to give some semblance of a
salute and sing the national anthem. Their one meal of the day
was then dished out, garlic soup and a little bread, the latter
often squirreled away for later on. Between breakfast and roll
call at night, the captives were left completely at the mercy of
their gaolers' whims. What clothing the men had was robbed
by the guards if it was of any worth, or else traded between
themselves for slices of bread. Many prisoners arrived wounded, and soon many more were sick, yet medical care was nonexistent. The number of prisoners' graves mounted.
Attendance at mass was compulsory, each prisoner's denomination, if he had one, being inconsequential. The guards
administered regular beatings, and after the frequent interrogations by German officers, their countrymen amongst the
incarcerated were usually taken away and not seen again.

To combat the deleterious effect of prison life on the minds
and bodies of the prisoners, the men organised committees to
instil order, solidarity and resistance to the regime. Ryan was
elected judge of a court that was held to try the offences of
prisoners against each other (stealing another man's bread
ration was a serious offence) and worked as a teacher in what
became known as the San Pedro Institute of Higher Learning.

New Yorker Lou Ornitz, whom Ryan had known earlier in Madrid and taught Irish songs to, remembered when the two were reunited in the diabolical San Pedro.

> Frank tried to console us. He was a tremendous man of courage. One night he was taken out and, as we said goodbye, he told us to sing the Kevin Barry song and we did as he was led away. He came back a few hours later and I thought he was a ghost.
>
> He said he thought the Spanish Republican government was doomed, that we had been sold out by the democracies, and that they would pay for it themselves, which they did. He was sick with fever and had a bad stomach. We were able to buy some medicine through friendly guards and some extra food. He recovered and started to teach his classes. They were always full.[37]

But being a pillar of prison society did not elevate the jurist and schoolmaster in the eyes of his jailers. Not unlike his times in Dublin years earlier, Ryan was being held while a case against him was being put together. Leopold Kerney, the Irish envoy to Spain, based in St-Jean-de-Luz just inside the French border, had been making enquiries regarding Ryan's plight ever since he'd learnt of his capture. That Ryan's rank placed him in greater danger and that his name was known in Ireland deemed that, of the half dozen Irish prisoners, it was Ryan who came foremost to the diplomat's attention. Kerney soon learnt that Franco's military judicial assessor in Burgos, a Colonel Jussett, was claiming that when he had been captured, Ryan had had on his person "documents of a compromising nature" concerning the shooting of prisoners in Belchite in September, as well as "jewellery from Fascist officers captured and executed at Brunete". He also learned that Franco himself "was very annoyed that there should be any interventions on behalf of such a man".[38]

Ryan's name was again making headlines in Ireland. His sister Éilis had heard on the news late one Saturday night that an Irish newspaper editor had been reported captured by the Nationalists. She knew immediately that it was her brother. With the help of friends of Ryan's, Éilis initiated a campaign to secure his release. By May, Kerney was in receipt of a petition ascertaining Ryan's good character to be presented to the Nationalist authorities on behalf of several cultural, academic and sporting bodies, such as the Gaelic Athletic Association and the Gaelic League. Others of the signatories were less likely: Cardinal MacRory was among the first to sign, as was Alfie Byrne. Prudently, revolutionary bodies such as the IRA, Republican Congress or the Communist Party of Ireland were not invited to provide character references.

A telegram from representatives of Irish American bodies belatedly urged de Valera to act. In fact, within days of Ryan's capture being known, the taoiseach had received the anxious Ryan family and had given advice on the wording of the petition.[39] Within two weeks of the disaster at Calaciete, de Valera had instructed Leo Kerney to inform the Nationalist authorities that the Irish government was "very disturbed to hear of the serious charge . . . The Irish government would greatly appreciate a lenient attitude towards Ryan's case. Public opinion here would be greatly incensed if punishment involves Ryan's life."[40]

At the instigation of Maud Gonne MacBride and son Seán, the papal nuncio in Ireland, Paschal Robinson, and the prominent Irish convert Sir Shane Leslie engineered a letter-writing campaign. The Irish legation in Paris approached a confidante of Franco's for an assurance that justice be done. The Vicomte de Mamblas was informed that the accused man, despite having objectionable political views, particularly in relation to Spain, was "an honourable and upright character . . . a courteous and gentle fellow but with very strong political convictions from which nothing would shake him".[41]

Leo Kerney, on 19 May, received confirmation from the Burgos authorities that Ryan faced a charge of commanding firing squads to execute insurgent prisoners. Rumours in diplomatic circles informed him that it would be claimed that Ryan had finished off those still living with his pistol. Kerney was not granted access to the prisoners at San Pedro, but worked through the British representative to the Nationalists, Sir Robert Hodgson, who assured him that Ryan was no worse off than the other prisoners, even if his future was that much more bleak. Hodgson had been appalled by the prison's regime on his first visit and used his considerable British diplomatic muscle with the authorities to have the conditions improved. He won for the prisoners changes in clothing and the occasional meal other than soup. Kerney, meanwhile, was pressing for Ryan to at least be allowed write more than the regulation ten words in a letter home. He advised Éilis Ryan to send clothes to him in the diplomatic bag from Dublin, and he received money from her, converted it and passed it on to her brother. Éilis also sent books and tobacco, but the prisoners were prohibited from receiving them.

If Ryan's immediate circumstances improved a little, his prospects did not. In London, the Duke of Alba wrote "it seems it has been proved that Mr Ryan has taken part in and actually directed the firing squads in the civilian red zone". Vicomte de Mamblas informed the Irish legation in Paris that Nationalist Foreign Minister Jordana, who had received pleas for Ryan from Hodgson, was unlikely to deport him because of his conviction that Ryan would only slip back into the country again. Ryan's life was in very real danger, said the Vicomte, not least because of the "difficulties he himself made by the attitude which he had adopted".[42] Monsignor Antoniutti, papal nuncio in Burgos, informed Paschal Robinson that he was powerless, that "in this case, the law must take its course".[43] He confided that the prosecution were to make much of Ryan's history in Ireland, including the fact that in the Irish Civil War he had taken up arms against the recognised government! The prosecution knew that he had gone on to "found a periodical which represented the extremist workers' opinion" before recruiting men for Republican Spain. In Ireland recuperating, Ryan had made "capital out of his wound to recruit a greater number of volunteers, not only in his own country but also among the Communists in London, Liverpool and Glasgow".[44]

Under the gaze of European and American journalists, the case against Ryan needed to be at least feasible, and the extra attention would give Burgos the opportunity to discredit not only Ryan but, by extension, all *brigadistas*. To help prove that he was a habitual cold-blooded killer well capable of executing prisoners, the authorities could draw from a fund of "circumstancial evidence". This was provided by Captain Thomas Gunning from Leitrim, some time journalist, ex-Blueshirt and right-hand man to O'Duffy. Gunning had since fallen out with his *commandante* and remained in Spain after his fellow *cruzadas* had returned home. He had the ear of the Burgos authorities and drunkenly bragged of his intercessions in the Ryan case, but was overheard by Kerney's secretary. Franco, claimed Gunning, was "too damn soft" on the prisoners, giving reprieves when execution would have been more just. Without naming names, he claimed: "There's one man, an International, that was captured in Gandesa, he had seven murders to his name outside the country and he was a scoundrel. For two months I've been trying to get him shot; I've gone to them with tears in my eyes to get them to shoot him. They *won't* shoot him."[45]

A day or two after his outburst, Gunning made an appointment with Kerney. Kerney deduced that the slanderer, without repenting the damage he had done Ryan, had perhaps guessed that his drunken broadcasts had been overly indiscreet and was now trying to make amends. His disclosures to the envoy whiffed of desperation. He alleged that he had told ministers in Burgos that the execution of Ryan, the purportedly notorious murderer in Ireland, would blacken Franco's name there. The Nationalists had let Gunning know that, until Ryan's name appeared in the newspapers, they had planned to "bump him off". Gunning also told Kerney that he had made enquiries into the evidence of Ryan, commanding firing squads but had been met with only evasive answers; he suspected there was none.[46] He concluded by saying that Ryan would probably be released, that there would probably be "no court-martial, because that would be putting a halo about his head". Gunning made no reference to the allegations of murders in Ireland and Kerney did not ask. If Gunning was doing penance for his public indiscretions, Kerney noted that he remained "hostile to Ryan" and had not wavered from his opinion that the prisoner "ought to have been shot".[47]

Gunning's attempts to salvage his reputation and ingratiate himself with the Irish minister were not a success.[48] Kerney wrote in reply to messages of concern from Hanna Sheehy Skeffington that "there is a damnable bloodthirsty scoundrel named Gunning who is well-known in Burgos and who himself boasts that he has done his utmost to get Ryan shot but laments the fact that they won't shoot him. To counteract this man's pernicious influence is my most immediate task."[49] The same day of his interview with Gunning, 3 June, Kerney contacted the authorities in Burgos to inform them that Ryan had never been held guilty of assassination in Ireland and that the accusation, if it was indeed being alleged by the Burgos courts, "*serait contraire à la vérité*".[50]

Kerney passed no judgment on Ryan in his communiqués with Dublin, except to note somewhat equivocally that "it appears that Ryan has a certain military reputation both on his own side and with Franco's people". His knowledge that the "American prisoners in San Pedro have a great admiration for Ryan" is not necessarily inconsistent with Carney's defamation, in Burgos' opinion, that Ryan "was looked upon as a dangerous customer and a sort of ringleader for others".[51] This would appear to be true. On 11 June, 100 British prisoners were prepared for departure from the prison, and Ryan was among them. The word had got out that they were to be transferred to Plasencia near the Portuguese border, where they would be used to haggle with in prisoner exchanges with the Republicans. Ninety-nine men were indeed taken away to be traded into freedom; the following day, alone, Frank Ryan was manacled and led by an escort of guards to a truck which brought him to Burgos Central Prison and trial.

Ryan later told the Red Cross that the day after his arrival in Burgos he made a declaration to a military judge. On 15 June, he was summoned for his court martial, conducted by a bench of three officers, with one prosecuting officer and one defending. Ryan met the defence counsel for the first time only a few minutes before the trial commenced. His limited comprehension of Spanish, compounded by his poor hearing, ensured that he remained largely ignorant of the proceedings as they unfolded before him. Ryan did not understand what the charges were, only that they "appeared to be grave and refer chiefly to my activities in Ireland, these latter figure in a letter from Ireland".[52] The prosecution referred to, but could not produce, the letter, purportedly from an Irishwoman. It declared that Ryan was "not a good Catholic" and was directly responsible for the murders of Kevin O'Higgins in 1927 and, more recently, Admiral Somerville. The IRA had shot the retired admiral in Cork in March 1936 after he had provided references for local men hoping to join the British navy. Ryan had, of course, left the IRA almost exactly two years earlier.

219

Ryan later claimed that "at my trial I wasn't interested much in my life, believing this was already forfeit". If such was the case, sheer Bolshieness was behind the considerable defence he presented. "I took up the attitude that I was a Prisoner of War. If they wanted to shoot PsOW, okay, but I objected to being shot on the evidence of an anonymous letter."[53] When Ryan challenged the claim that the Irish government also considered him a "bad man" by suggesting that Leo Kerney be summoned to the court, he was told that "the Irish government has no representative here". The accused told the court that his prime motive in going to Spain initially had been to "offset O'Duffy's propaganda". Ryan had been more concerned with Irish politics than Spanish and he had wanted to check the manoeuvres of the "British agent", O'Duffy: "I was first and foremost anti-British." Ryan went on to explain, truthfully, that he had, in fact, prevented many of his comrades in Ireland from going to Spain and that he had only returned to repatriate Irishmen. The task had proved lengthier than he had supposed, not helped by his personal pride which, especially after Teruel, ensured that he "didn't want to be considered a rat deserting a sinking ship".

In only one respect of his wartime service might Ryan be considered guilty of deceit. He had made no entries to his Military Book since July 1937, and the prosecution could not disprove his claim, when captured and questioned "with a rifle pointing at my chest", to have been at the front for only two days before being captured. The prosecution did not raise the matter, and Ryan prudently let it slide.

The court must have yawned its way through Ryan's monologue. Although the trial was little more than a charade for the press, albeit played out behind a closed curtain, Ryan could certainly not be further accused of skimping on his defence. If he was still listening, the judge would have heard Ryan's summing up: "In the end I told them I didn't want any clemency or mercy – as the Defender had asked – that I had observed the rules of war, such as they are; that I'd done nothing of which I was ashamed, and that I was a soldier in the Army of a govt. which the govt. of my country recognised."[54]

Knowing that he was under sentence of death before the trial, after his dismissal from it, he was none the wiser as to what his position was. He was not alone. As late as two weeks after the trial, Kerney, despite his constant tugging at the sleeves of the prison authorities, was still unaware that it had taken place at all. Overlooked by the authorities, Kerney sought a conduit through the superior clout of British representative Hodgson, "but even the British Agent in Burgos has never been able to ascertain what crimes are imputed to Frank Ryan".[55] The lack of any new information was ominous in that a sentence of death, Ryan learned, would have to be referred to a superior court for confirmation, and only then would he be informed of his fate. As the days then weeks passed, he could therefore take it that such confirmation being sought was the cause of the delay. He would at least have some breathing space before any order for execution was carried out. That so much was contingent on the war's course and the consequential diplomatic manoeuvrings was his only solace.

However, unbeknownst to Ryan, malevolent forces were at work against him. The Nationalist authorities claimed to be in receipt of several letters from Irish clergymen, particularly Jesuits, objecting to Ryan's release. Additionally, in tandem with Gunning's rantings were the far more discreet yet potent machinations of none other than Sir Robert Hodgson, under whose diplomatic cloak daggers were drawn for Frank Ryan. From ambassadorial murmurings, Kerney gleaned that "there is secret opposition [to Ryan] from another country than Ireland".[56] Hodgson had advertised to both his superiors in London and his diplomatic peers in Spain, including Kerney, his petitioning of the Nationalist authorities on behalf of Ryan. Yet word came to Kerney that Hodgson was simultaneously, but privately, denouncing the condemned man as "a gangster". William Carney assured Kerney that the story was true, that Hodgson had acted upon his defamation of Ryan by conspiring against his release. Further intelligence accounted for the curious claim that Ryan had pulled the trigger on Admiral Somerville. It so transpired, Carney revealed, that Sir Robert Hodgson was none other than the victim's son-in-law. Either Gunning had fabricated that specific charge to win the collusion of Hodgson, or else the slur had been a brainwave of Hodgson who was presumably familiar with the details of the murder. It is not too hard to imagine that the knighted blue blood had an innate detestation of Ryan and his militant Irish republicanism.

In his struggles to ensure that justice would be done, Leo Kerney, beguiled when he was not slighted, must have felt like a paragon stranded in the court of the Borgias. It was only in time that Kerney learned of the full extent of Hodgson's activities. The latter had tried to get a Colonel Martin, an Englishman in Burgos who had Irish connections, "to do some very dirty work" as regards Ryan. It was presumably not until Kerney met Ryan months later that the prisoner got to know of the intrigues against him. For the sake of his morale it was probably just as well that he only heard after the event that "a British diplomat tried to get him shot twice" out of "personal vengeance".

Yet Kerney uncovered some allies. A Captain Meade, son of an Irish emigrant to Mexico and formerly of O'Duffy's staff, contrived to help Irishmen regardless of their politics. It was he who alerted Kerney to Hodgson's bad blood toward Ryan. Meade also managed to obtain a promise by the Officer Commanding in Burgos, General Lopez Pinto, that he would never put his name to Ryan's death warrant. The general was persuaded by, paradoxically, Hodgson's skullduggery, Pinto telling Meade that he was "indignant at Hodgson's attitude regarding Ryan".[57]

Ryan himself had thought his defender in court and his interpreter, a cavalry lieutenant, were well-disposed toward him. Although Ryan's bases for optimism may have been tenuous, he was a man used to cherishing hope as his solitary tool against adversity.

Thus, in a relatively optimistic mood, he was able to write to his sister Éilis, at the close of June, that he thought often of the day when he would return to Ireland. He asked her to tell his parents not to worry for him and suggested that "Uncle Peter", as he code-named Peadar O'Donnell, would provide some money for clothes and cash that she sent. That the Spanish censors, unsurprisingly, had no Irish was awkward for Ryan in that he had to write in Spanish or, by his preference, French, but it also had its advantages. The letter closed in code: "*Je salue tous mes amis, et especiallement Deirile, Baolbás, et Silim.*"[58] Éilis gratefully understood that Ryan considered that he was, at least, in no immediate danger of death.

Even so, a week later, after still being told nothing, Ryan wrote to the Red Cross that "I am uneasy as I do not yet know

222

the sentence."[59] He was, in essence, living under a death sentence, feeding on the hope it might be repealed. It seemed that a penal purgatory was the best Frank Ryan could hope for.

Notes to Chapter 10
1. *Our Fight.*
2. Peter O'Connor, *A Soldier of Liberty* (Dublin: MSF, 1997), p. 26.
3. Frank Graham, quoted in Frank Ryan, ed., *The Book of the XV Brigade* (Newcastle upon Tyne: Frank Graham, n.d.), p. 129.
4. *Irish Democrat,* 28 August 1937.
5. *Ibid.*
6. Quoted in Judith Cook, *Apprentices of Freedom* (London: Quartet Books, 1979), p. 87.
7. *Irish Democrat,* 28 August 1937.
8. Ryan, *Book of the XV Brigade,* p. 130.
9. Quoted in Cook, *Apprentices of Freedom,,* p. 86.
10. *Irish Democrat,* 28 August 1937.
11. Ludwig Renn was a German writer and veteran of the 1914–1918 war.
12. *Irish Democrat,* 28 August 1937.
13. O'Connor, *Soldier of Liberty,* p. 28
14. Verle Johnstone, *Legions of Babel: The International Brigades in the Spanish Civil War* (London: Pennsylvania State University Press, 1967), pp. 119–120.
15. *Irish Democrat,* 28 August 1937.
16. Quoted in Seán Cronin, *Frank Ryan: The Search for the Republic* (Dublin: Repsol, 1980), p. 121.
17. O'Connor, *Soldier of Liberty,* p. 29.
18. Quoted in Cronin, *Frank Ryan,* p. 123.
19. *Ibid.*
20. *Irish Democrat,* 11 September 1937.
21. *Ibid.,* 27 November 1937
22. *Ibid.*
23. Bill Alexander, *British Volunteers for Liberty* (London: Lawrence and Wishart, 1982), p. 145.
24. Rosamond Jacob papers, NLI, 33/131.
25. *Workers' World.*
26. Quoted in Cronin, *Frank Ryan,* p. 125.
27. Ryan, *Book of the XV Brigade,* p. 306. *La Pasionaria* was Dolores Ibarruri, the well-known communist firebrand who had coined the rallying cry *No Pasarán!* (They Shall Not Pass!), referring to the siege of Madrid.

28. *Ibid.*, p. 9.
29. Quoted in Michael O'Riordan, *Connolly Column* (Dublin: New Books, 1979), pp. 119–20.
30. Quoted in D. Corkill and S. Rawnsley, *The Road to Spain* (Dunfermline: Borderline Press, 1981), p. 152.
31. International Brigades Association box, London: Karl Marx Memorial Library, 28/A/1.
32. *Ibid.*, 28/G/3.
33. Síghle Uí Dhonnchadha papers, UCDAD, 106/1711.
34. Department of Foreign Affairs, NAI, 244/8.
35. *Ibid.*, 244/22.
36. Quoted in Corkill and Rawnsley, *Road to Spain*, pp. 89, 153.
37. Quoted in Cronin, *Frank Ryan*, p. 145.
38. Department of Foreign Affairs, NAI, 244/8.
39. De Valera received a letter brimming with gratitude "for the extreme kindness and interest shown in poor Frank", from Vere Ryan, recovering from a stroke: "We know what you have done and will never be so ungrateful to forget even for a moment." Department of Foreign Affairs, NAI, 244/8.
40. *Ibid.*
41. *Ibid.*
42. *Ibid.*
43. *Ibid.*, NAI, 22/839.
44. *Ibid.*, NAI, 244/8.
45. *Ibid.*, 244/22
46. The only man who ever claimed to have witnessed Ryan's bloodlust was another Irishman, who rivalled Gunning in his slander of Ryan with dubious accounts of murders of civilians behind Republican lines. Brendan Moroney arrived at the Irish Embassy in Paris after deserting from the International Brigades. He claimed to have been sentenced to death for refusing to take part in firing squads against civilians: "When Frank Ryan, with whom [Moroney] had been on friendly terms, learned of his refusal to shoot Spanish civilians, he himself threatened to shoot him. Ryan was, apparently, not only in complete sympathy with the general campaign against God, Church and Fascism, but was an enthusiastic advocate of the measures being taken against those who were openly opposing the campaign. Moroney was unable to say whether Ryan had ever acted as a member of a firing squad or whether he had ever commanded one." For good measure, Moroney told his interviewer that he was "convinced that Ryan is a Communist" who "deserves to be shot". The deserter's yarn, full of self-praise and calumniation of his erstwhile colleagues, with which he hoped to bolster his appeal for funds to return

home, was disbelieved by the embassy official. Using diplomatic euphemism, he found "it difficult to form an opinion as to the amount of reliance that may be placed on this man's statements". Department of Foreign Affairs, NAI, Paris Embassy, p10/55.

47. *Ibid.*, NAI, 244/22.

48. Nor did Gunning make a good impression on an Irish priest in Spain, Father J.J. Mulrean, who reported to Kerney that when he had been serving under O'Duffy, Gunning had been regularly sent to Lisbon to post all letters from the men back to Ireland. After some time it became clear that the letters were not getting through; subsequently 5,000 unposted letters were found. While on his excursions to Portugal, Gunning had spent the monies given him by the men to cover postage. Mulrean also reported that Gunning had contracted venereal disease from his wife "whom he had induced to misconduct herself with Germans and Italians for money". Gunning's affairs were complicated, after his wife had left, by the presence of a lady friend, Ingeborg Lorenz, of whom he requested that no mention be made by the Irish legation when responding to enquiries from Mrs Gunning. Gunning's illustrious career continued in Germany working on the staff of William Joyce (Lord Haw Haw) until he died of tuberculosis in Breslau in June 1940. Department of Foreign Affairs, NAI, Madrid Embassy, 19/4 (87).

49. Hanna Sheehy Skeffington papers, NLI, 24/124.

50. Department of Foreign Affairs, NAI, 244/8.

51. *Ibid.*

52. *Ibid.*

53. *Ibid.*, A 20/4.

54. *Ibid.*

55. *Ibid.*

56. *Ibid.*

57. Military archives, Cathal Brugha Barracks, G2/0257.

58. Éilis would have translated the supposed friends' names thus: Deirile (deireadh le – end of), Baolbás (threat of death) and Silim (I think).

59. Department of Foreign Affairs, NAI, 244/8.

PART THREE

CHAPTER ELEVEN

Escape to Berlin

Frank Ryan spent the summer of 1938 in Burgos Central Prison living in the shadow of impending execution. For a while he was kept in a cell with seventeen other condemned men; each morning nine would be led out to be either shot or garrotted, and another nine would replace them. The psychological torture of Ryan included leading him out of his cell as if to deliver him to the firing squad or the noose, but then returning him. He came into possession of a comb on to which he scratched his name and nationality; he planned, should the morning come when he was called for sure, to throw the comb to prisoners not under death sentence, so that at least the Red Cross or British diplomatic service might hear of his fate.

Kerney's persistent enquiries on Frank Ryan's behalf and his suggestion that the captive be exchanged for Italian prisoners were met with no more enlightening response than that the case was still being examined. There was some resentment of Kerney within the Burgos regime, as the Irishman had been fêted by some of its ministers in early 1937 with a view to winning his country's early recognition of their government. However, this had not been forthcoming. Kerney hoped that the desire for such recognition, if not any tendency toward mercy, might prompt the Nationalists to look favourably on Ryan. At the instigation of Gunning, there was mooted in Burgos the idea of handing over the prisoner to the British envoy, Hodgson, a fate Gunning "supposed Ryan would resent more than shooting".[1]

In fact, within Britain a movement built up for Ryan's release. Meetings were held publicising his case, and Labour

MPs and trade unionists lent their names to the cause and various petitions. Pressure objecting to Ryan's predicament was applied on the Foreign Office to act through none else than that crusading knight Sir Robert Hodgson. In America, a campaign to publicise the case was formed, and letters were written to several embassies urging them to act on the captive's behalf. Articles and correspondence appeared in the newspapers. A letter addressed by his comrades in the Lincolns to the *New York Times* referred to the allegations of his having shot prisoners after the battle of Brunete.

> We who fought in that battle and were directly under the command of Ryan know that these charges are untrue. All the prisoners whom we captured were first questioned by the Brigade staff, to which Major Ryan was attached, and they were then turned over to the division command. Frank Ryan was with us all the time during the offensive and had nothing whatsoever to do with the prisoners.[2]

In Ireland various groups sustained pressure on the government to ensure that justice was done in Burgos. Eilís Ryan consistently sought, and was rewarded with, help from improbable quarters. She remembered when General Eoin O'Duffy "met me in Wynne's Hotel for a cup of coffee. He came with me to the GPO and he wrote a telegram to Franco from himself. He didn't pay for it but he did sign it, asking for Frank's release."[3] There were meetings held, leaflets posted, committees of action formed and speeches made in the Dáil, all focusing on Ryan's imprisonment. Over fifty deputies from the Dáil signed petitions. De Valera let it be intimated through Kerney that recognition of the Burgos government could be obstructed, dependent on the treatment of Ryan, yet the *Generalísimo* felt confident that he could call the bluff of the Chief. The Irish premier had a genuine personal interest in Ryan and was frequently in touch with his family; when a newspaper reported the execution of British prisoners, de Valera rang the alarmed Ryans to assure them that he had made investigations into the claim and had been reliably informed that it was erroneous.

Ryan's meagre contact with the outside world determined that he knew little of the activity on his behalf. All letters were censored, and their writers referred rarely to politics and knew better than to discuss the international agitation for his release. An anxious Hanna Sheehy Skeffington trumpeted the fact that "returned prisoners from Franco territory speak of the frightful conditions and constant efforts made to break the morale and even the physical health of Frank Ryan".[4] Yet fellow prisoner Fabricano Rojel remembered Ryan as a man who "not only in the armed struggle in Spain was an outstanding personality, but who also in the rigorous conditions of prison was a fighter of great integrity . . . It was a terrible testing place for men. Frank Ryan did not bow his head; the terror could not break his spirit."[5]

By the autumn of 1938, fresh prisoners were arriving, bringing news of the Republican retreat along the Ebro and a failed counter-attack. Soon there were over 5,000 prisoners, of whom hundreds shared Ryan's sentence, in a prison built for a tenth of that number. Their days, from seven in the morning to nine at night, were spent out in the prison courtyard. There the daily meal was eaten, wolfed down after being doled out to the cold and hungry men, their meagre blankets wrapped around them in an attempt to keep out the autumn chill.

The wretchedness of Ryan's existence was ameliorated somewhat after Leo Kerney was granted a first visit in mid-October 1938. Ryan was delighted to meet him, and Kerney was even able to wangle permission for the two to speak in English. They had, in fact, met before at the home of Budge Clissmann (née Mulcahy), and the envoy brought to the prisoner a Spanish grammar book sent over for him by their mutual friend. Despite the surroundings and the differences in their positions and politics – Kerney was a graduate of the de Valera school of Irish republicanism and favoured recognition of the Burgos government – there was an immediate compatibility between the two men. There was much to discuss, if not the advancement of Ryan's case about which both men remained in the dark. They spoke for an hour of events in Ireland and their shared acquaintances at home, after which Kerney left, promising to return when he could.

Kerney was true to his word to Ryan and to Hanna Sheehy Skeffington, to whom he wrote that he had "the earnest desire to be of real help to him".[6] He was able to win privileges for Ryan, and brought him parcels of food, tobacco and books.

On the French side of the border, Kerney converted money sent for Ryan's use at the best rates possible. He kept meticulous accounts of Ryan's income and ensured that the prisoner received a monthly allowance, often from his own pocket, which was then reimbursed by fund-raising in Ireland. Kerney visited every few weeks. His frequent presence, coupled with the pressure he brought to bear on the authorities and the amount of mail addressed to Ryan (even if he was not allowed to receive much of it), elevated Ryan's stature among the guards. One Nationalist official conceded that there had long been "a certain respect, if not for his attitude, for his truthfulness and bravery".[7] In time he became something of a dignitary, albeit a condemned one, and was granted some leeway. However, on one occasion, Ryan's cellmates were alarmed when he was summoned to the governor's office. They were then incredulous when, some time later, he returned "quite tipsy". The prison governor had in his office some bottles of whiskey that had been sent to Ryan from a supporter short of neither naivety nor optimism. The condemned man and the governor had shared a bottle in the latter's room.

Kerney occasionally brought with him another Irishman, Father J.J. Mulrean, long-time resident in Spain and one-time chaplain to O'Duffy's Brigade (by which he remained decidedly unimpressed). The three enjoyed conversations that continued as long as they were allowed and focused on their common interests in Ireland rather than their differences in Spain. Soon Kerney won permission for Mulrean to visit unaccompanied, and he became Ryan's confessor. Ryan had been refusing to accept communion from the prison chaplain, Father Marcelino Balinaga, who wore a pistol at his hip and, during one sermon, informed his congregation that they were no more than murderers and rapists. Two hundred among those who objected were beaten and put on half rations. Ryan was "appalled at the condition of these poor creatures at the end of their punishment. They were like ghostly zombies."[8] He mentioned the incident to Mulrean, who in turn mentioned it to the Vatican's representative to Burgos; the chaplain was replaced. Father Mulrean "would rob his Holiness if he thought he'd help me", Ryan told his parents.[9]

With the new year and the imminent surrender of the Spanish government to the insurgents, hopes were raised for Ryan's release. Despite rumours and the occasional nod and wink from sympathetic officials in Burgos, Kerney was only ever officially told, *in perpetua*, that Ryan's case was "being examined". February 1939 brought recognition of Franco on the part of the Irish government, the Civil War ended in March, and Kerney presented his credentials to Franco the following month. The Spanish ambassador in Ireland, J.G. Ontiveros, became the new focal point of pressure from Ryan's supporters, including representations from de Valera. Through its diplomats in Burgos, London and Dublin, the new government of Spain let it be known unofficially that there was no question of Ryan being traded for prisoners or released as a prisoner of war even once hostilities had ceased. He was considered a common criminal, a multiple murderer no less, and consequently would be treated as such, albeit with perhaps some leniency to expedite international diplomacy. Still, the close of the war and the repatriation of *brigadista* prisoners filled the Ryan family in Dublin with optimism, and a suitcase full of clothes was sent by diplomatic bag to Spain. However, the Ryans were to be disappointed. Frank Ryan's predicament remained unchanged.

The advent of peace in Spain eased somewhat the conditions in Burgos Central Prison. Ryan frequently suffered from pains in his muscles and joints brought about by rheumatism, and his heart, as had been predicted years earlier, was giving him trouble. However, the prison doctor was sympathetic, and his patient was excused from heavy labour duties.[10] Now able to receive books, Ryan became a schoolmaster again and taught prisoners Irish and English, both languages and literature. He built up quite a library of books *as Gaeilge;* by diplomatic bag Eilís had sent him works such as *An tOileánach* by Tomás Ó Criomhthain. His pupils were instructed to write and read out essays for him in English, often about Spain and their feelings for the country. Perhaps inevitably, the teacher felt a particular affinity with the Basques. As in San Pedro, a prisoners' committee was operating to maintain order and resolve, virtues Ryan had been able to instil in men for almost twenty years. A Burgos committee member recalled that the *camarada Irlandes* was

> an example of discipline. He took part in the work of
> this committee . . . and played a great part in creating

233

discipline and restoring morale. He was no sectarian. He was in contact with prisoners who were Communists, Socialists, Anarchists and Basques. He got a lot of support from the Basques and he got this because of his personality and simplicity.[11]

Ryan formed a particular friendship with Tom Jones, a Welshman who had been wounded and captured after the Ebro, then marched into Burgos during the final days of the war. A court had placed Jones under sentence of death but since had commuted it to thirty years within the walls of Burgos. Already having been held prisoner for some months, his physical condition was precarious: "Had I not received help from Frank, especially food, I would have become . . . a physical wreck." The two men, "both Celts in a foreign jail", sustained each other mentally.[12] "We were more like brothers than friends," recalled Jones, a miner from Wrexham. They spoke Welsh together, Ryan having studied the language as part of his Celtic studies at UCD. Jones remembered the two fervently speculating on what information they could glean of the developments in the outside world. The news of the Molotov-Ribbentrop pact between Germany and the USSR "shocked" Ryan: "He feared a mighty empire stretching from Europe to the Far East and he was horrified . . . For Frank Ryan, the anti-Fascist cause for which he was in prison and for which so many had died and suffered, had been betrayed."[13]

Closer to home and far more revealing, Jones remembered his comrade's furious reaction to news of the IRA bombing campaign in English cities in early 1939: "He was extremely angry . . . He classified them as irresponsible political lunatics who were doing the maximum damage to the Irish Republic and the future unity of the whole of Ireland. He claimed they would alienate British public opinion against all Irish people." According to Jones, Ryan had developed an affection for the British working classes after fighting alongside them, and by now he considered Irish unity would be won "not so much by force of arms, but through British and world public opinion and by agreement with the Protestant people of Northern Ireland". The Welshman even went so far as to say that "he was so angry that he requested me to pass on two or three names to the representatives of the British Embassy who came to the prison to see me". Jones does not add that he complied. It is likely that the request was made in the heat of Ryan's fury and frustration and that it came to nothing. Jones could not remember the names, but one – who "operated out of New York" – was without doubt that of Sean Russell, IRA chief of staff, last heard of in the States and instigator of the campaign.[14] Jones' remarkable claim suggests that even within the confines of Burgos, Ryan's political evolution continued apace.

Ryan, although hampered by his increasingly poor hearing, improved on his Spanish. He also seemed able to weather the frequent bouts of ill-health. In the autumn of 1939, the debility in his muscles and joints crippled his arms, which he could not move. He was laid up in hospital for a month, where he at least was allowed to lie in until 8 a.m. and he received a glass of milk each day. Kerney was impressed by the "gay, cheery, courageous Frank . . . whose equanimity I have come to admire". The demands on Ryan's teaching, when he was able, obliged him to request, via Kerney, textbooks of English literature for use in his filled classrooms: "His mind is fully occupied and time hangs less heavy on him than might otherwise be the case," Kerney told the Ryans.[15] He also passed on to Eilís a message from her brother to the effect that she was not to attempt to visit him as she planned, as Europe was on the threshold of war. The start of the war in September 1939 was taken by Ryan to be a further hindrance to any chance he might have of being released and returning home.

Yet, that autumn, another unlikely candidate volunteered herself to work for Ryan's cause, the Spanish aristocrat and fervent supporter of the *Generalisimo*, the Duchess of Tetuan. Of noble lineage, the Duchess' family name was O'Donnell and she was a descendant of the Wild Geese who had fled to Spain upon the collapse of the Irish Gaelic order in the seventeenth century. More recently, Peadar O'Donnell, while visiting Spain in 1936, had used his influence with a Republican clique to which he had become attached, to secure a safe passage out of Madrid for a relative of the Duchess. She was a frequent visitor to the Irish legation in Paris and, upon hearing of Ryan's dire circumstances, had left a parcel of food and clothing for him in Burgos. He never received it, but she persisted, and later parcels were handed over to him. She then composed, with Kerney, a petition to Franco which she dispatched, although she was unable to get a private audience with him.

Less prosaic than hampers of food from a Duchess, but more practical, was Kerney's hiring of Baron Champourcin, a respected lawyer who took on to fight Ryan's corner and hopefully negotiate his release. Ryan's letters home, customarily more upbeat than he was himself, at Christmas 1939, were full of good cheer. He reported being healthy, well-fed and optimistic about his chances of a discharge. Praise was expressed for Kerney, and Burgos was compared favourably with Mountjoy. He admitted that he had had a few scares for his life, particularly early on, but by now was living on the assumption that Franco would spare his life to facilitate relations with the world's democracies.

In early 1940 Ryan thought he saw in the sky above Burgos the first swallows of his freedom. His expectations were elevated by a further spate of releases and a general revision of sentences. Tom Jones was told he was free to go. Ryan was neither pardoned nor released. His death sentence was commuted to thirty years imprisonment. He "was extremely glad for me", recalled Jones, "but he became quite depressed". Although he appreciated the efforts that de Valera and others were making, Ryan was beginning to despair of them bearing fruit, and he had started to think of alternative means to gain his liberty. Along with some Spaniards, Ryan and Jones had already plotted routes of escape which had proved implausible. The experience gained from clambering over ivy-clad walls around St Colman's counted for little at Burgos Central Prison. Ryan now asked Jones to visit his family upon his release – but not to mention his ill-health – and, while in Dublin, to make contact with the IRA. Jones was to ask the IRA on Ryan's behalf to demand his release, and should that not be forthcoming within six months, his old comrades were to start bombing Spanish embassies wherever possible. It was a tall order that exhibited both the prisoner's desperation and his faith in Irish republican loyalties. Upon leaving in March 1940, Jones was distressed by the sight of those friends doomed to remain,

> . . . but it was leaving Frank Ryan behind that hurt the
> most. My instincts told me that most of the prisoners

would not see their families again, and I felt that Frank was one of them . . . Tears were rolling down his cheeks when I said goodbye, and smiles and tears were not easily evoked at Burgos penitentiary.[16]

Decades later, Jones still considered the friend he left behind to be "the bravest and most honourable man I have ever known".[17]

Franco's obstinacy in detaining Ryan after granting repatriation to the other *brigadistas* remains something of a mystery. At one point he had sent an aide to interview Ryan and received the subsequent report advising that the Irish *brigadista* "should have been shot within the first 24 hours of capture as he was a very dangerous anti-Fascist".[18] Franco ordered one of the military commanders to ensure that Ryan served the full thirty years. The dictator may have been keeping promises made to Spanish clergymen acting on behalf of their brethren in Ireland. Perhaps he sincerely believed Ryan had murdered unarmed Nationalists. Franco's wrath must have been aggravated by the knowledge that Ryan had returned to resume fighting after being invalided home. Not known as a man to welcome opposition, he must have been further incensed by Ryan's insubordination while incarcerated. But just as Ryan's reprieve of execution was probably prompted by consideration of international politics, so was his continued detention likely to have been the result of Ireland's poor bargaining power. It was not rich enough to buy out prisoners as America had and could offer little in the way of potential as a trading partner or diplomatic ally.

Leo Kerney suggested to his superiors in Dublin a likely source of Franco's intransigence regarding Ryan. The *Generalisimo*, Kerney had learned, "had given orders that nothing should be done in the Ryan case without his express permission – it appeared that some commitment had been entered into, perhaps with Hodgson, by General Franco, which prevented the latter from releasing Ryan".[19] Franco's appreciation of international opinion informed him that he could not shoot Ryan, but neither was he obliged to release him. De Valera had already recognised the *Caudillo*. There was nothing to be gained by freeing his token *brigadista* with the rank of major. Ryan was a prized scalp from the despicable alien reds who had presumed to take a hand in the shaping of Spain, cherished by Franco as "my most important prisoner".[20]

In fact, the dictator and his prisoner had something in common. Baron Champourcin, Ryan's legal representative, was a member of Franco's secret service who also found time to work for the German intelligence, the Abwehr. He regularly supplied information to the head of the Abwehr in Berlin, Admiral Wilhelm Canaris. Appropriate intelligence was passed on to Abwehr II, a department dedicated to fomenting discontent behind enemy lines, particularly in regions and countries subject to those enemies. To that end, Abwehr II had on its books Ukranian, Flemish, Welsh, Indian and Breton nationalists. Also on its payroll were Jupp Hoven, who had lived in Ireland and studied at Queen's University, and Helmut Clissmann, husband of Budge Mulcahy. The two friends were among the intelligence service's experts on Ireland and the IRA.

On the wall in Admiral Canaris' office was a portrait of a predecessor of the admiral's, a Colonel Nicolai, who, over twenty years earlier, had overseen Roger Casement's gunrunning expedition to the Banna Strand. Ireland was a lode with obvious potential for the designs of the Abwehr. It was considered a back door into Britain by which sabotage and spying by the IRA might facilitate Hitler's plans for Operation Sealion, the invasion of Britain planned for the summer or autumn of 1940. There was much speculation in Berlin regarding de Valera's position. Steadfastly neutral though he declared Ireland to be, he might endorse action against the British in Northern Ireland, particularly if under pressure from a republican lobby headed by the IRA. The possibility that the taoiseach might be overthrown and replaced by a leader more antagonistic to Britain, and therefore, so went the logic, more sympathetic to the Germans, was investigated. The fact is, German intelligence was woefully ignorant about the strength and capabilities of the IRA, and it underestimated Irish popular support for the allies, which came second only to a desire for the maintenance of neutrality.

This ignorance was manifest when, striving to make contact with the IRA, German agents approached, as a suitable conduit, none other than Eoin O'Duffy! However, contacts were established with, and a transmitter delivered to, the IRA before the outbreak of the war. The Irish writer Francis Stuart subsequently arrived in Germany to teach English and literature, but also brought messages from the illegal organisation. However, the transmitter was soon seized by the gardaí after it had been used recklessly and an agent captured. Canaris and the head of Abwehr II, Major-General Erwin von Lahousen, were fast accumulating doubts about the worth of the IRA, which appeared ill-organised and far too cavalier in its attitude to operations.

Clissmann and Hoven were probably well aware of the obstacles to Ireland's being used as a springboard for exercises against England. As exchange students in Dublin, they had much interest and many friends in the republican movement and theirs had been familiar faces at the offices of *An Phoblacht* when Ryan was its editor. Clissmann had studied at Trinity, writing a doctoral thesis on the Wild Geese in Germany, and later worked in Ireland for the German Academic Exchange student initiative. Although he, with Budge, had returned to Germany at the outbreak of the war, Clissmann still had insights into the IRA possessed by very few in Germany. Joven informed his superiors in the Brandenburg Regiment, attached to the Abwehr, of Frank Ryan, his predicament and how his release might be advantageous to Germany. Although Ryan had been out of the IRA for over five years and had had many a verbal scrap with them since, he had formidable contacts in the movement and was an old colleague of de Valera. He might not work with the IRA or for the Germans in Ireland, but in America he would surely advocate Ireland's neutrality, rousing Irish America against, if not American intervention, American pressure on Ireland to serve the allies. It was a very persuasive case, and Clissmann's and Joven's superiors were finally persuaded.

At around the same time, an IRA agent arrived from Ireland with plans for a revival of IRA activity in the North aided by German paratroopers. The agent, Stephen Held, also requested German intervention in the imprisonment of Frank Ryan. Following orders from Canaris, the German intelligence agent in Burgos, Wolfgang Blaum, sought and was granted an audience with Franco, who promised to consider handing Ryan over to the Germans. Two days later, he agreed to do so in what must have been a rare drop of his guard, for within a week he reneged. He suggested, however, that some way might be found to hand over the troublesome Irishman without his having to succumb to actually signing the order for his release. Negotiations proceeded between the Germans and the Spanish over the liberty of Frank Ryan. It was decided that, as Franco refused to lose face by granting a pardon, Ryan would be given a chance to escape whilst being moved from one prison to another.

Champourcin then contacted Kerney and told him that Ryan would be given the opportunity to leave Spain via German-occupied France and thence to try to make his way to either America or Ireland. It seems that Dublin subsequently endorsed the plan as the only means to free Ryan; Irish citizens were considered neutrals in Germany, therefore at liberty. The Spanish secret service demanded only that Ryan give his word that he would never again return to Spain, and the Abwehr insisted that their only desire was that he be free to work for Irish republicanism in whichever way he saw fit. On 12 July 1940, Kerney visited Ryan and told him what was afoot. Champourcin then brought a German named Wizner to see the prisoner, who reported that his visitor had been very "fair-minded and had asked no commitments of him". Ryan informed Wizner that he had "been waiting for this visit for two years".[21]

The apparent transfer of the prisoner duly took place, but when the opportunity came for Ryan to flee, he either did not realise it or else calculated that being on the run in Spain would be worse than hopeless. He had not been informed that the transfer was a ruse. Consequently, after confusing the guards at the second prison where he was duly presented, Ryan was soon back in Burgos.

A few days later a Spanish police car stopped at the bridge in the town of Irun on the French border where it was met by a German intelligence agent named Kurt Haller. In the car following it were Wolfgang Blaum and Frank Ryan. Champourcin was in a third car, and Leo Kerney, unknown to the authorities, was some distance behind to make sure Ryan left Spain alive and safe. He suspected the Spanish might exploit the situation to dispose of the red menace; it would not be the first or last time a prisoner was "shot while trying to escape". Kerney watched as Ryan crossed over the bridge from Franco's grasp into the open arms of the Third Reich. From his embassy in Madrid, he wired a message to Dublin that the "case of Frank Ryan continued to receive close attention with the result that he was allowed to escape from prison and Spain".[22]

Ryan was driven by Haller to Paris. Shabbily dressed, sickly and reeking of dungeons, he was put up in a large house on the outskirts of the city where he was kitted out with new clothes. The next day himself, Haller and another German officer ate at the luxurious Tour D'Argent restaurant. "Ryan was completely flabbergasted by the whole thing," remembered Haller, "and thought he was dreaming".[23] Ryan's bewilderment was understandable. Sprung from the cave of Burgos, he emerged blinking into a world he could neither recognise nor comprehend. After over two years of a dangerous and dismal life as a prisoner of Spanish fascists, he was being courted by the Nazi regime in great splendour, a red republican diehard being fêted by ideological adversaries against whom he had campaigned and fought for nigh on ten years. The Paris he knew was now under the subjugation of a triumphant German army that seemed to hold Europe in the palm of its hand. This remarkable turn of events would have spun the head of the most robust republican socialist, but for added measure Ryan was a sick man, almost deaf, surrounded by men in uniforms speaking a language he did not understand.

A degree of relief arrived in the shape of Helmut Clissmann, who met Ryan a few days after his arrival in Paris. Shocked by the appearance of his Irish friend, with rotting teeth and a gaunt face and body aged beyond its years, Clissmann tried to answer Ryan's incessant stream of questions and soothe his agitation. Compounding his disorientation, Ryan was prey to a multitude of suspicions regarding his hosts' motives. Clissmann reiterated that Ryan was a free man, that the Abwehr only hoped that the free exercise of his Irish radicalism might, however indirectly, hamper Britain's capacity to uphold German progress. Few in the Abwehr were sincere Nazis, and Ryan's violent opposition to Fascism in Spain would be overlooked. What Ryan did was entirely up to himself. First they must travel to Berlin to review the options open to him. The two men left Paris on 4 August 1940.

In Berlin the following day, Ryan was introduced to Dr Edmund Veesenmayer, a special adviser on Ireland to the

Foreign Office. With Veesenmayer was a man that the Germans wanted Ryan to meet – IRA Chief of Staff Sean Russell. Ryan had not been told of the planned reunion, and the Germans were sufficiently informed to wonder was it wise to bring together representatives of two antagonistic factions within Irish republicanism. The Germans' caution was wiser than they knew. A heavily coded letter from Gerald O'Reilly in New York to Burgos had informed Ryan that Russell was supposed to be in Europe. Ryan's fury with Russell's bombing campaign had been sincere, and an Irish intelligence memo even alleges that while he was in Burgos, Ryan "wondered if Russell was working against him".[24] Yet that had been eighteen months prior to their reunion, and since then the onset of the war had changed things dramatically. The German gamble was rewarded. The two men were delighted to meet each other again, their differences overwhelmed by being thrown together in such unforeseeable circumstances.[25] "They embraced one another like brothers who had not seen each other for many years," remembered Kurt Haller.[26] The Germans were heartened and touched by the sight, as Russell, his arm around Ryan, told him that he was leaving for Ireland on the morrow; would Ryan like to accompany him? The answer was a most definite "yes". After the hell of Burgos and the confusion of Paris, it must have seemed as if all his prayers were being answered. The two sat up until late, catching up on each other's news and no doubt swapping stories; they both had plenty to share and, until now, precious few people to share them with.

Shortly after the IRA campaign in Britain that had so incensed Ryan, Russell had sailed for America to argue his strategy's merits and raise funds to sustain it. Throughout all the splits, recriminations and flirting with politics that had marked the IRA in the 1930s, Russell had remained the personification of the conservative, physical force mentality and, as such, had received the sponsorship of Joe McGarrity of Clan na Gael. A devout, ascetic Catholic void of pretensions or indulgences, Russell's interest in politics was non-existent and his ideology minimal. The role of the IRA, from his perspective, was to win for Ireland a thirty-two-county republic ; how Ireland then managed it was up to the politicians. Although a respected and long-serving quartermaster for the organisation, unauthorised fundraising in America in 1937 for the bombing campaign had led to his suspension upon his return. Electioneering chicanery on the part of his supporters had seen him returned as chief of staff and so paved the way for the campaign of 1939. Returning to the US, Russell had run into trouble with the law, but after jumping bail, the influence of the Clan along New York's docks had enabled him to secure passage, in April 1940, to Europe, ostensibly working as a stoker.

Arriving in Genoa, Russell was soon in the care of the Abwehr. He was taken to Berlin and, after settling in at a country villa, was sent on sabotage and explosives instruction courses. Plans were drawn up for Operation Dove, Russell's return to Ireland. His sponsors would give the IRA man a free hand, and a red flower pot would be placed in a window of the German Embassy in Dublin to let him know that the invasion of Britain was under way. Russell would be able to draw on funds from the ambassador, Eduard Hempel. He had several meetings with Veesenmayer and the foreign minister, Joachim von Ribbentrop, who were impressed by his determination and *gravitas*. The two Germans considered Russell to be intense and sensitive and were careful not to give the impression that they were ordering Russell to do anything. Veesenmayer was so taken by Russell that, years later, he had his portrait painted from photographs he had kept.

However, the attempts by his Nazi admirers to indoctrinate Russell with their philosophy and politics failed spectacularly, and Russell resented them bitterly for their efforts. Instead, he formed a bond with the Austrian Catholic Lahousen in whom he confided

> I am not a Nazi. I'm not even pro-German. I am an Irishman fighting for the independence of Ireland. The British have been our enemies for hundreds of years. They are the enemy of Germany today. If it suits Germany to give us help to achieve independence, I am willing to accept it, but no more, and there must be no strings attached.[27]

It was after a final meeting with Canaris, Lahousen and Veesenmayer representing Ribbentrop, that Russell met Ryan.

The following morning Russell, but not Ryan, met Ribbentrop who filled him in on the transport arrangements which were to take effect in foty-eight hours. The Abwehr had gone to no small amount of effort persuading Admiral Dönitz of the German navy to spare a U-boat and one of his most trusted officers. Russell was provided with what would be his only luggage, a transmitter with which he was to maintain contact with the Abwehr. He was given a specific code for the purpose. There had been plans to send two Glasgow Irishmen, captured in France and since trained in radio transmission, with Russell, but there would not be room enough for four travellers in the cramped confines of a U-boat. It was agreed that the place beside Russell would be granted to Ryan, code-named Richard I and Richard II respectively. The Germans thereby fulfilled the promise made to Ryan in Burgos. Furthermore, Russell had lobbied for Ryan's inclusion, and the Germans probably calculated that what the mission would lose in communications expertise, it would gain in republican cogency.

On 7 August, the two men were taken to Wilhelmshaven, and the following morning they set sail under the command of Hans-Joachim von Stockhausen. The delivery of the two Irishmen was only part of Stockhausen's detail: he was to land them in Smerwick Bay, near Ryan's beloved Dingle, and then go on to attack allied shipping in the Atlantic. The voyage was rough, but the U-boat stayed well below the surface and broke the Royal Naval blockade to head north around Scotland and then south to the Irish west coast. On board, conditions were cramped and noisy, and the two Irishmen had little scope to do much other than keep out of the way. They were deprived of fresh air and there was no opportunity to enjoy comfort or exercise.

On only the second day out, Russell started vomiting violently. He had complained of stomach pains when in Germany, but there was only a medical orderly on board, trained to dress wounds, who tried to diagnose and treat his complaint. Russell took laxatives but to no effect. Ryan watched helplessly as the pains increased until, after four days of agony, Russell died in his arms.

The remaining passenger was in a quandary unlike any he had faced before, and he had faced many. Similarly, von Stockhausen, clueless as to the details of Operation Dove but still with anti-shipping orders to carry out, was impatient to know what was to be done next. He undoubtedly wanted to unburden his craft of surplus passengers, dead and alive. He asked Ryan if he would land with Russell's body or remain on board until they returned to Germany. Ryan had been present at none of the meetings between Russell and the operation's architects in Germany, and the two Irishmen had not discussed its aspirations. They had spent little time together before setting off, and once on board the conditions and noise prevented conversation. In any case, Ryan had thought it imprudent to ask.[28] Russell, and more likely the Germans, perhaps did not trust Ryan, the renegade republican and democratic socialist, with the details of how the IRA/Nazi alliance was to be put into action. The details of who was to meet Russell and where were beyond Ryan's ken. Even had he landed with the transmitter, the code to be used for IRA contact with the Abwehr had gone the way of Russell.

Further, Ryan had to consider the wider scope of his options. In the summer of 1940, it seemed certain that Germany would soon be invading Britain. It also seemed likely that Britain, providing it was able, might invade the Free State for the use of its naval ports, which Britain had handed back to Ireland in 1937. In either situation, a man in Ryan's position, linking Dublin (both the IRA and the government) and Berlin, would be indispensable to Irish interests. Two further scenarios, that Ireland would remain neutral and unmolested or that Germany would invade Ireland, would leave Ryan in either an awkward position or a damnable one. However, Ryan probably, and not unreasonably, thought that of all the predictions, these two were the least likely to come to pass.

Presented with yet another fantastic turn of events, Ryan had to act, and immediately. It was a most pressing dilemma for the Irishman, already reeling from the shock of his friend's death. Ryan struggled to make a decision. As it stood, he was under no obligation to the Germans. They had, he later stressed, "insisted from the start that the trip was to be taken unconditionally".[29] He must have weighed up the fact that by returning to Germany he could no longer claim that he had just used his enemies to spring him from prison and deliver him home. If, in an attempt to salvage something of Russell's mission, he delivered himself to Russell's conspirators, he was presenting himself as a willing accomplice of the Third Reich. Nonetheless, he soon concluded that, despite being within reach of the Irish shore, he was compelled to return to Germany. The psychological palliatives Ryan concocted to soothe his conscience were a mixture of the pragmatic – his present worthlessness to Irish republicanism – and the politically opportunistic – that he might be of infinite use to his cause should the dice of the war roll the way he predicted. A hundred miles from Galway Bay, Russell was buried at sea with full honours, and Ryan was ferried away from the coastline he had waited three torturous years to set foot on.[30]

Budge Clissmann says that Ryan "felt it was his duty" to return and try to recover the ground lost by Russell's death. This sense of duty evidently overwhelmed the abhorrence that Ryan held for Nazism. "He was first and foremost an Irish republican," she says. "Everything else came second." Nonetheless, his decision, according to his friend, was made "very reluctantly". Despite the calamitous and traumatic circumstances, he retained an awareness that "although he could not do Sean Russell's job in Ireland, he could do it in Germany".[31] The new circumstances wrought by the war had lessened the distance between the socialist and the dynamiter; Operation Dove, regardless of how much Ryan knew of its objectives, was far removed from bombing English railway stations and city centres. Perhaps he suspected that the mission was of greater import than it actually was, and that if he did not substitute himself for Russell, a unique opportunity for Irish republicanism would thereby be lost. Or it might stem a British invasion of Ireland. As it was, landing in Ireland with Russell's transmitter but neither code nor plan of action, Ryan would be of no use to anybody. Merely having been able to return home was now evidently not enough for Ryan, however much he yearned to do so. He later explained it to Francis Stuart.

> After some hesitation, he asked the submarine commander to return with him to Germany. I think he later regretted this decision, but being in the dark as to the plan behind the voyage, he was reluctant to land in Ireland and meet his old comrades with nothing to tell them but the news of Russell's sudden

death. Expecting, as they were, long awaited news
from America . . . and also from Germany, Frank was
loath to return from his own exile on a German sub-
marine with only a tale of disaster.[32]

Optimist that Ryan was, he probably figured that he need
only return to Berlin for a few briefings before he would again
be shipped back to Ireland, only with knowledge enough to
satisfy the aspirations of Operation Dove. Even should he
decide not to shoulder Russell's task, he could at least play the
part of a once-off envoy between the Germans and the IRA.
The U-boat submerged to commence its hunt for allied shipping but soon developed engine trouble and returned to dock
at L'Orient. After less than two weeks, Ryan was back in
German-occupied territory.

Notes to Chapter 11

1. Department of Foreign Affairs, NAI, 244/22.
2. *New York Times,* 30 May 1938.
3. Aodh Ó Canainn, "Eilís Ryan in Her Own Words" *Saothar* 21,
    1996.
4. Hanna Sheehy Skeffington papers, NLI, 24/126.
5. Quoted in Michael O'Riordan, *Connolly Column* (Dublin: New
    Books, 1979), p. 147.
6. Hanna Sheehy Skeffington papers, NLI, 24/124.
7. Department of Foreign Affairs, NAI, A 20.
8. Tom Jones, International Brigades Association Box, London: Karl
    Marx Memorial Library, 28/G/13.
9. Quoted in Seán Cronin, *Frank Ryan: The Search for the Repub-
    lic* (Dublin: Repsol, 1980), p. 152.
10. The good doctor must have overly advertised his sympathy for
    the prisoners; an investigation found him to be a Republican of
    long standing, and he immediately joined his patients in their
    cells.
11. Quoted in O'Riordan, *Connolly Column*, p. 148.
12. Tom Jones, International Brigades Association Box 28/G/13.
13. *The Irish Times,* 10 April 1975.
14. Tom Jones, International Brigades Association Box 28/G/13.
15. Quoted in Cronin, *Frank Ryan*, p. 153.
16. Jones did as Ryan had asked him, visiting the Ryan family and
    making contact with the IRA. After being taken to a secret loca-
    tion, blindfolded, Jones was cross-examined before his interroga-
    tors assured him that they would "do everything necessary" for

his friend, their ex-comrade. Jones thought the men "sincere". Tom Jones, International Brides Association Box 28/G/13.

17. *The Irish Times,* 10 April 1975.
18. Military Archives, Cathal Brugha Barracks, G2/0257.
19. Department of Foreign Affairs, A 20/4.
20. *The Irish Times,* 19 June 1979.
21. Both Tom Jones and Leopold Kerney had noted that Ryan had started to learn German some time earlier. Military Archives, Cathal Brugha Barracks, G2/0257.
22. Department of Foreign Affairs, NAI, Madrid Embassy, 19/4 (49).
23. Quoted in Enno Stephan, *Spies in Ireland* (London: MacDonald & Co., 1963), p. 160.
24. Department of Foreign Affairs, NAI, A 20/4.
25. Lahousen later claimed that there was "immediate friction between the two". *The Irish Times,* 6 June 1958.
26. Quoted in Stephan, *Spies in Ireland,* p. 162.
27. *The Irish Times,* 6 June 1958.
28. Another Irishman in the service of the Germans, one W. J. Murphy, claimed Francis Stuart told him that Russell and Ryan had gone to Ireland to prepare the way for a shipment of guns for the IRA. Once arrangements for the delivery had been made on the Irish side and contact established with the Abwehr, Stuart was to follow with the cargo. See Eunan O'Halpin, *Defending Ireland: The Irish State and Its Enemies Since 1922* (Oxford: Oxford University Press, 1999), p. 197.
29. Department of Foreign Affairs, NAI, A20/4.
30. The historian Michael McInerney claims Ryan had no choice: "Against his wishes, Ryan who wanted badly to return to Ireland, was taken back to Germany on instructions from Berlin." *The Irish Times,* 6 April 1968. The recollections of Helmut Clissmann, however, qualify this claim. If indeed the decision to return Ryan to Germany did emanate from Berlin, according to Clissmann, that was only because Ryan "requested von Stockhausen to cable Veesenmayer for fresh instructions before proceeding to Ireland". Quoted in Carrolle J. Carter, *The Shamrock and the Swastika* (Palo Alto: 1977), p. 118.
31. Interview with the author.
32. Francis Stuart, "Frank Ryan in Germany", *The Bell,* vol. XVI, no. 2 November 1950, p. 38.

CHAPTER 12

An Irish Republican Socialist in Nazi Germany

When the U-boat carrying Ryan sputtered back into
L'Orient, it was greeted by a dismayed Veesenmayer
wanting to know what had happened, as contact
between the ocean depths and Berlin had been only intermit-
tent. Ryan and members of the crew were interviewed, and
their accounts of Russell's sickness were passed on to two
physicians who, independently, concluded that Russell had
died of a perforated ulcer.

The only man who suspected there was something amiss
was Russell's friend Lahousen, who had taken a dislike to the
"wild Irishman" Ryan: "Russell was an idealist and a gentleman, the other was nothing but a gangster." When news came
through of Russell's death, Lahousen decided "there had been
some sort of dirty business. Right away I suspected that man
Ryan, who was a ruffian."[1] It can only be supposed that
Lahousen still harboured anxieties about introducing the red
Ryan to Russell, but mutterings of the latter being poisoned
persisted for some years. Eighteen months after the event,
Ryan still felt compelled to inform Leo Kerney that "the
rumour about my part in an alleged assassination doesn't
worry me. He and I were always good personal friends – and
never more so than during his last days. He died in my
arms."[2] Veesenmayer and Ribbentrop grieved for the failure
of Operation Dove, but they did not hold Ryan responsible.
According to Kurt Haller, "There was not the slightest shadow of suspicion on Frank Ryan after his return."[3] Veesenmayer drove the Irishman back to Berlin, where he was given

comfortable accommodation and privileged rations but little to do.

Almost immediately after his return to Berlin, Ryan wrote to Leopold Kerney to thank him for all he had done. His gratitude for having his freedom, of sorts, is evident, but so also are his frustrations: "Although it's liberty, although I can at last do what I like and only what I like, it is unfortunately impossible for me to get home until this war is over. I can only hope that my folks won't worry too much, and that's about the only worry I have left in the world." He asked would Kerney, "in the discreet way of which you are capable . . . assure all whom it may concern that I'm safe and sound".

The letter, brief and partly coded, made no mention of Russell or Operation Dove. Posted in Lisbon, with no return address or mention of Ryan's location, the note may have been sent by a third party.[4] However, a later letter to Kerney from Ryan refers, in a roundabout way, to the letter and to an attempt by Ryan to get to Gerald O'Reilly in New York, possibly from Lisbon.

> When I arrived here, I had hopes of getting home, but they were short-lived. Later, all was fixed and ready for me to go to Gerald's. Practically on the eve of departure there was a crux, due to an unforeseen circumstance, so I had to come back. I had written to you just when I was sure all was OK. (Did you get the letter?) Anyway, that route to Gerald's is closed. There is now much talk of making the journey in a longer way. I'm hoping it comes off.[5]

After Ryan's failure to reach Ireland, America was the obvious second choice of destination for a man whose mettle had yet to be gauged by his beneficiaries. Understandably, his hosts viewed Ryan with some ambivalence. Sections of the Abwehr were antipathetic to Nazi ideology, but Ryan's reputation as a communist firebrand hardly recommended him to those with whom he was supposed to work. On the other hand, his recovery after the malevolence of Burgos and his apparent vigour to act against British interests in Ireland impressed upon them that, could he be dropped home in the right circumstances, he might prove a force to be reckoned with.

More importantly, the Germans had a somewhat inflated view of Ryan's relationship with de Valera. Quite probably the Abwehr knew of de Valera's appeals to Franco on his prisoner's behalf, and although theirs were two greatly contrasting shades of republicanism, the two men did indeed respect each other. Despite occasional flights of IRA *coup d'etat* fancy, the Germans appreciated that the most they could hope for was that Ireland would remain neutral. The crucial question was whether de Valera would resist pressure to support Britain's war effort and thereby deny her access to the "treaty ports", now keenly missed in the battle for the Atlantic. Assuming that the taoiseach remained as steadfast as he had been thus far, the Germans then had to calculate the likelihood of Churchill is taking the ports and the Free State by force.

In the instance of a British invasion from the North, the IRA must be united with de Valera to put up a maximum resistance. German guns would support it. At weekly meetings, Ryan was asked his opinion on all matters relating to Ireland, North and South. His presumably somewhat speculative views on de Valera's resolve to remain neutral, Irish public opinion regarding the war, the influence of the Irish in America and the capacity of the IRA to engage in guerrilla warfare were all noted down and mulled over. He was a supporter of de Valera's policy of neutrality and counselled the Germans accordingly. As a contingency measure, however, they drew up plans for Operation Green, which would, in the event of a British incursion into the Free State, facilitate the closing of Irish ranks and enhance their military capacity. Ryan, with a foot perceived to be in each camp, was seen as the man who could make possible the unity of the Irish government and the illegal army that it was currently suppressing.

British dominance of the skies over the English Channel, succeeding the Battle of Britain a month after the venture to Ireland, put paid to any immediate execution of Operation Sealion. There was no immediate use for Ryan evident. Veesenmayer, predictably, had always had his reservations about the red Irishman. The two men appreciated each other's capabilities and had a civil working relationship, while at the same time sharing a mutual dislike personally. Each, of course, had an abhorrence of the other's politics, but it was never discussed. However, as the months passed, the German noticed that the Irishman was getting restless, and he was anxious to use his charge in some capacity before any disillusion set in. He described Ryan (possibly charitably, since it was for Kerney's ears) as "a fighting man . . . an active man forced to lead a life of inactivity and he felt that very much and would like to return to Ireland. [Veesenmayer] would like to help."[6] The Nazi's philanthropy aside, Ryan's republican contacts were too good to neglect, and Veesenmayer was determined that his potential as a contact man between the Abwehr and the IRA bear fruit. All the Abwehr could do at the moment was to keep Ryan content until needed, and he was largely left to his own devices.

Those devices were precious few. Ryan's closest friend in Berlin, Helmut Clissmann, was away on a trip to England via Ireland. The Irish republican socialist certainly avoided the company of Nazis. "In Germany, Ryan regarded himself as a stranger," recalled Clissmann. "He hardly came into contact with Nazis."[7] Conversely, Francis Stuart, whether he enjoyed a moment of *schadenfreude* or felt sympathy for Ryan, was struck by a later occasion when the compatriots met two of Ryan's friends. "One was wearing his party Swastika badge on a little gold plaque. I thought it was funny – because these were rare and extremely influential people – that Frank Ryan, who had come from the international Brigade in Spain had such a friend."[8] He enjoyed spending time with Breton nationalists, with whom he lived for a while on the Steinplatz. Although he had studied some German in Burgos, Ryan's limited knowledge of the language, coupled with his deafness, by now severe, meant that communication with others was virtually non-existent.

Further, Ryan, living under the pseudonym of Frank Richard, did not want to advertise his presence in the country in any way, to those either within or without it, undoubtedly appreciating how it might be viewed from abroad. Already many of his closest republican friends in Ireland, particularly Peadar O'Donnell and George Gilmore, had spoken out against IRA collusion with the Third Reich. If the persecution of others was the price to be paid for exploiting Ireland's opportunity, then they wanted no part of it. Furthermore, Churchill was perceived to be looking for any excuse to invade Ireland to recapture the ports. Ryan's, and by extension Irish republicanism's, complicity with the German war effort might serve Britain's interests more than anybody else's by giving Churchill the very excuse he needed.

Another reason for the normally extrovert Ryan's secreting himself in the shadows was more personal. He was still very wary of his circumstances in Germany. He and his past were well-known to Edmund Veesenmayer, a dedicated Nazi not remembered for placing great value on the lives of others. Yet how effective were his pseudonym of Frank Richard and the shield of the Abwehr against the zeal and vigilance of the Gestapo should the uncertainties of wartime render his situation more precarious? One Irish historian has claimed of Ryan's time in Germany that he was "never *persona grata,* at least in the political sense . . . he remained also under the supervision of the Gestapo".[9]

With no friends and only bundles of newspapers to entertain himself, Ryan soon got word through to Francis Stuart to call round to the house where he was living as Francis Richard. When he arrived at the address, Stuart was surprised to meet his compatriot, whom he vaguely recognised. "I saw that he had something to tell me, to unburden himself of, I might say, to a fellow country-man in his own language." Ryan told the writer, who himself was in Germany for reasons more complex and personal than Ryan's, of his escapades. Stuart became "aware, as he spoke, of the conflict of feelings he had when, somewhere off the Irish coast, after Russell's burial at sea, he had decided to turn back". Clearly, Ryan was still distressed by recent events and his present predicament. "Later, I remember we went out and sat on the terrace of a cafe. The unburdening himself of the story had been a relief."[10]

By this time, Stuart was augmenting his university lectures with work for the Ministry of Propaganda, writing pieces that were broadcast to Britain and Ireland by William "Lord Haw Haw" Joyce. He met Ryan for lunch regularly during the autumn of 1940, and the two seemed to relish each other's company, exchanging opinions on the war or, more often, memories of Ireland.[11] Restless and homesick as Ryan doubtless was, he knew he had much to be grateful for. He kept his opinions of his Nazi saviours to himself. He may have thought it hypocritical to denigrate those he had opposed for years, having since gratefully walked into their embrace. Perhaps he thought his opinions of the regime would offend Stuart, who was working for it directly, whereas he himself only hoped to use it to suit Ireland's needs.

By the close of 1940, Ryan could be forgiven for thinking that those needs might yet be met. Germany had not yet invaded Russia, which Ryan must have considered to be a potential bolthole, and it would be a year before Pearl Harbor and the conflict in Europe evolved into a truly world war. Ryan clearly thought the war could only advance Irish republicanism, as he explained in a coded letter to New York. Ryan depicted Britain as a businessman in competition with several other firms, the IRA and Clan na Gael included: "I hope that everyone will work together against him, and as publicly as possible. I would like to be informed of the progress of such efforts. I have no doubt that in trying to bankrupt ours, and other rival firms, ours is the one that will emerge best out of the mess."[12] Appalled by Hitler's megalomaniacal rampage, Ryan, according to Stuart, nonetheless thought the upheavals caused by his benefactors' aggression allowed for some light of optimism:

> He was free after years of imprisonment . . . the war had not yet become the horror that it did later (or maybe its full horror was not yet manifest to us), he was still in good health and his relationship to the German authorities had not become strained to the degree it became later.
>
> I think in these early days of the war, he still had some faith. Faith, I mean, in the kind of world in which he believed might still, just possibly, emerge when the war ended; a kind of freedom which had been the hope with which he had set out in the morning of his pilgrimage to Spain.[13]

Further, of his status in Germany, Ryan could not have been more pleasantly surprised: "I enjoy the status of a 'gentleman at large'. . . . I remain my own master . . . nobody can make me do anything I don't want to do. (Incidentally no-one has even (or ever) tried here – a thing which surprised me at first but no longer does.)" In a more personal sense, however, Ryan felt keenly the pangs of a downcast heart. He was a man whose oxygen and sustenance were activity and sociable company. True, he had Stuart's ear to fill and opinions to debate for a few months, and he was sharing a house with Helmut Clissmann, whose mission to England had been aborted. Yet, writing to Leo Kerney, Ryan admitted that he was "not so cheery as I'd like to be. I have absolutely no news, personal or otherwise, from home or abroad. I heard last month, from the bearer [Budge Clissmann], that, a year ago, my mother had been periodically ill. I wish I could get news of her, and the rest of my family."[14] The frustrations and boredom that constituted the life of Frank Richard were perhaps among the greatest foes Ryan had yet faced.

He refused to be drawn into the German propaganda machine as Stuart had. Stuart occasionally discussed his work with Ryan, whose comments made him realise "that all this is not my work, and I must not become too involved".[15] On another occasion, the two chatted about the content of weekly broadcasts that Stuart had assented to give: "He agreed that they must not be propaganda in the sense that the flood of war journalism on all sides has become, and that of course, they must support our neutrality. He suggested, and I fully agreed, that there must be no anti-Russian bias."[16] Propaganda, in either oratory or writing, was of course where Ryan's foremost talents lay, and if the Abwehr knew anything about Ryan, they surely knew that. Yet he would not allow himself to be seduced into selling those talents. All collusion on Ryan's part had to unambiguously advance Irish republicanism rather than serve German Nazism.

It was only with great reluctance and against his better judgement, therefore, that Ryan let himself be drafted into speaking to Irish prisoners of war who had shown an interest in working for the Germans. Presumably he was inspired by an empathy for Irishmen in foreign prison camps. Something short of a hundred men purporting to be Irish had answered the call, and they were being held in a special camp, apart from other prisoners, near Friesack. Only a handful of officers were among them, and they insisted that they would only fight alongside the Germans if the Free State were invaded. Ryan's reluctance to involve himself derived not so much from the fact that he and his colleague Clissmann "were both very sceptical as to whether our mission could have any possible success". Rather, Ryan was anxious that he might be recognised by some of his countrymen. He still held that public knowledge of his being in Germany would smear both the name of Frank Ryan and Irish republicanism as well as be detrimental to Irish neutrality. He was perhaps persuaded that no one would make the connection between the Irishman last heard of in Spain and a visitor to a German prison camp. "As a matter of fact," recalled Clissmann, "Frank Ryan was immediately recognised by several of the prisoners and greeted with a friendly 'Hello Frank'".[17] Ryan was devastated and refused to have anything more to do with the formation of an Irish Brigade.

It was already too late. Unbeknownst to him, among the recruits was a certain Major McGrath, who had been told by his British army superiors in the prison camp to volunteer himself to work for the Germans and report back, which he did. Ryan couldn't have known for sure, but probably guessed that his fears had been realised.

The spring of 1941 was uneventful for Ryan, tedious, but not intolerable: "Looking on at a war is rather a novel experience for me, and – for a change – not a disagreeable one."[18] The threat of a British invasion of Ireland to secure her ports receded, and with it the likelihood of demands on Ryan by the Germans. The shadow of Hitler's dominance over continental Europe lengthened after mopping up around the fringes of the Balkans and Greece. Keeping a watchful eye on Britain, he was only pausing to gather his strength to remove from the European chessboard the Russian piece. The conquest of her bountiful, menacing vastness hovering over the Führer's eastern flank would provide Hitler with the linchpin to world domination and eternal glory. The means to this end, Operation Barbarossa, was launched in late June 1941. The course of the war and Ryan's fortunes, equally unpredictable, were immediately transformed. Clissmann and Ryan were together when the news broke of the campaign's thunderbolt kick-start. The Irishman turned to the German and told him: "Your war is lost".[19]

Simultaneous with the assault on Russia, the German Foreign Office was planning another venture in Ireland, named Operation Osprey. Hitler had bragged that European Russia would fall within six weeks. Initiatives in western Europe were, therefore, not to be neglected, particularly as there were rumours of American engineers in Northern Ireland surveying sites for future military and naval bases. The prospect of an invasion of the Free State from the North was revived, only now given further gravity should America become combatant.

The plans and dates for Operation Osprey were repeatedly changed, the only consistent factor being that it would be executed by Ryan, Clissmann and a radio operator, Bruno Reiger, to counter allied invasion. Originally, according to Kurt Haller, it was proposed to establish "a sort of listening post or telephone exchange in Southern Ireland. This listening post should be brought into use in the Irish people's struggle against the intruders . . . [it] would also have contacts with de Valera's government. Frank Ryan and Helmut Clissmann were nominated for liaison duties." Essentially Ryan was to unite strands of republicanism and position them behind de Valera, leaving the contacts with Germany to his colleague. Contrary to von Ribbentrop's earlier idea put to the Fuhrer, "that this action be under the sole control of the Foreign Office", by late August the Abwehr war diarist was recording that "he now attaches importance to the Armed Forces. It is of particular importance to the Armed Forces to have wireless contact with the IRA, and thereby receive wireless reports for the Luftwaffe." The role proposed for Ryan had acquired a decidedly military dimension. Clissmann concurred that he and Ryan were to "act as military contact men between the Irish government and the German Army in the event of Anglo-American occupation of Ireland and to help organise guerrilla warfare against the aggressors".[20] A seaplane was to land the three men in Lough Key, Roscommon.

How much of all this Ryan was privy to is not known. Presumably he would have consented, if only to get home, but it is likely that he would have enjoyed little further success and equally likely that he knew it. Although they may have welcomed his German contacts, many in the IRA would have been wary of him, whilst de Valera would have been outraged by any approach from Ryan. It can only be speculated on; Hitler's six weeks in Russia had passed, and as summer closed, the strident German advance across the endless Russian steppes slowed. The preparations for Operation Osprey similarly ground to a halt. "The situation has changed a lot since I last wrote you, hasn't it?" Ryan wrote to Leopold Kerney in September 1941, adding that he had deduced, "I'm here for quite a while!"

With the abandonment of Osprey, Ryan was getting increasingly impatient. Rather than waiting for an opportunity to arise that might see him homeward bound, he took the initiative to press for his transportation. However, it was not long before the Germans started to consider that his arrival in Ireland, via Germany, would only further embitter the allies toward the Free State. Ryan wrote that he had "recently raised very strongly the question of my going home. The answer I received was that if I went, the respective governments of the greater and lesser islands might (without cause) get nervous. Whence, I conclude, *inter alia,* that the winter will be very mild."[21] Presumably, had he arrived in Ireland, Ryan would have been shrewd enough not to tug at the British lion's tail, but his arrival from Germany would be considered antagonistic toward Britain. Furthermore, Hitler's increasing preoccupation with the eastern front determined that he remained confined to Berlin acting in a "consultative capacity". It seems that he had little to do, as the Germans hoped for nothing more from Ireland than that she remain neutral. Ryan's position was the same. In November 1941, he wrote to Kerney:

> There is a very definite hands-off policy with regard to the little island . . . The office is apparently dominated by the fear that Sam or John would find an excuse to step in there . . . The office appears very satisfied with your Boss' unyielding attitude to Sam and John. They look upon him as a potential future friend.
>
> My view – it will be a quiet winter in the West. What the New Year will bring them, helluva-lot-more'n me don't know. So far as I am personally concerned, I can only guess. There are many guesses! There might be a situation in which I might go as a liaison to your Boss!

Ryan's letter went on to touch upon the debilitating rivalry that existed in the various German departments – such as the Abwehr and the Foreign Office – whose remits overlapped. By this stage Ryan obviously had some insight into the mechanics of the German war machine, implying that he was something of an insider. This renders questionable his claim that his status as a "distinguished guest", or, officially, a "non-party neutral is established". As does the revelation of his discomfort at the prospect of being "asked to do something I don't like. Such a situation is – soberly speaking – highly improbable. But if the unlikely should ever happen, sit yez down aisy! For I won't do the dirty."[22] Many, of course, would say he was already doing "the dirty", but whatever the war had deprived Ryan of, it had obviously left with him his belief in his own integrity.

On 7 December 1941, a month and a day after writing to Kerney, Japanese aircraft and submarines attacked Pearl Harbor. On 26 January 1942, American troops arrived in Northern Ireland. The prospect of an Anglo-American invasion of Ireland once again took centre-stage, and Ryan saw it as his responsibility to "ensure that Germany didn't do anything rash that might provoke them", says Budge Clissmann.[23] He was puzzled as to why other Irish republicans were not aligning themselves solidly with de Valera. So far as he was concerned, "In a time of national crisis like this, there must be a unified command. The country comes before party. So, in his neutrality policy – which is the only sane policy under the circumstances – Dev should get 100% support."

Although he conceded that the two might be incompatible, he saw a second task for republicans opposed to de Valera: to "organise and fit ourselves to be eventually that government which alone would succeed his – in his own words 'a more extreme Republican government'". Although he was willing to act as a channel between Berlin and the IRA and the Dublin government, he made it clear that he represented none of the three. He would not act in the interests of factions but of Ireland only. Among Ryan's primary anxieties was that, should the "black day" of invasion come, "I'd hate to be stuck here. I want to get back – so that I can play a part (and I really believe I could do a little) in unifying my friends to support Dev in his foreign policy, while reserving our rights to differ on other matters."

Frank Ryan's hopes for Ireland rested with the attrition of both the allied and axis powers rather than the victory of either. The ideal prospect, by his thinking, was that Ireland "be left in peace until Bull is weak enough for us to get our own. It's a slim chance." He thought it more likely that the ports would be held for an indefinite period by one or the other of the combatants. He remained remarkably non-partisan and still regarded both the swastika and the Union Jack with disgust. However, should the occupation of Ireland come to pass, he considered a German victory to be the most propitious for ending partition. Second only to the war concluding in an exhausted stalemate, such a victory would sufficiently shake up the pre-war status quo in the British Isles and give Ireland her chance for reunification.

Incredibly, Ryan, who had previously disabused his readership of the notion that England's enemy was necessarily Ireland's friend, seems to have thought that a victorious Hitler would have respect for Irish self-determination. Pondering German dominance of Ireland, he claimed "even that wouldn't be so bad as to what would happen us ultimately if Sam and Bull were to win".[24] The devil Ireland did not know could be no greater enemy to Irish reunification than the devil it did. Francis Stuart remembered that Ryan "speculated very much" on the German domination of all Europe. The writer, possibly hoping his Nazi collaboration would thereby be eclipsed, even claimed Ryan went so far as to say that "when Germany wins the war, I will be a member of the Irish government".[25]

Conversely, what few redeeming features he had found within the Third Reich – personal gratitude for saving his life, a measure of antipathy toward Nazism – were gradually overwhelmed. His slow-burn hatred of Nazism had evolved gradually from flaming declamations in the streets of Dublin to a white heat whilst he was its guest in Berlin. "He grew to hate the regime," according to Francis Stuart. The writer, who hadn't seen Ryan since late the previous year, recalled that the "months of the latter half of 1940 when I saw Frank nearly every day had one atmosphere, and after this, all my memories of him have another".[26] His initial wariness of his patrons degenerated into a disillusion that had truly started to ferment with the invasion of Russia. "He was extremely sensitive about German propaganda", remembered Helmut Clissmann, "and after the outbreak of war with the Soviet Union, sneered at newspaper reports which spoke of hundreds of thousands of prisoners taken."[27] The propaganda was not the half of it. "He detested the arrogance and contempt shown by officials towards foreigners and even towards their own people . . . To survive, however, he had to hide his real attitude toward most officials. He did not like Veesenmayer but played along in the hope that some day he would return to Ireland."[28]

It is hard to believe that Ryan had a sudden epiphany regarding Hitler's Third Reich. For sure, he had suffered from political delusion before to the extent that it was almost a character trait. Yet the obliteration of his political idealism was not the sole source of his mounting disgust. It is likely that Ryan had been willing to turn a blind eye to the ethos of Nazism so long as it served the interests of the homeland that he loved. He was doing little for the Germans and could therefore claim in May 1942 that, thus far, "my conscience won't have any serious problems to grapple with". Yet, that same month he was coming round to the idea that victory might not reward Germany and his aspirations for Ireland: "It looks like that, doesn't it? England will hang on, fighting to the last Russian and Chinaman, losing all the battles in the hope of winning the peace."

Returning to Germany on the U-boat in 1940 had been a gamble he'd been forced to make under great pressure, and it was starting to look as if his bet was lost. He passed censure, probably unfairly, on the reasons given for not being able to return him to Ireland: "They raise the objection that my appearance at home, now, would make Bull think I was coming home with 'orders of the day' and that a crisis would be precipitated. I don't think I'm so almighty important."[29] The IRA was being vigorously suppressed by de Valera, and by late 1942, the Abwehr's Irish department had effectively shut up shop. Ryan's trip home or to America "as a free agent" was forgotten as soon as it was considered to serve no purpose to the regime. Riding on the high tide of optimism in 1940, "Frank had been taken up very much by the Germans," remembered Stuart. "But later he was dropped."[30] The promises made in Burgos and Paris had vaporised.

As it gradually became apparent that he was trapped in the belly of a duplicitous beast that would profit Ireland nothing, Ryan's own useless culpability was borne in upon him. Had Irish republicanism been served he was, by his own logic, to a degree exculpable insofar as in that movement lay his premier hopes and dedication; at its altar he had sacrificed his socialism and egalitarianism. He had even denied himself a return to the bosom of his comrades and his ageing parents. As the war hung decidedly in the balance and the prospect of his repatriation receded, he was faced with the diabolical reality that he had sacrificed all for nothing. The man who prided himself on his integrity had colluded with his enemy to no purpose, and he was left with nothing but a debt to the devil. Therefore, it is hard not to suspect that, added to his growing revulsion of the Third Reich as the war's ravages heightened and he appreciated better its methods, he possessed a deeply personal resentment of the regime.

Francis Stuart thought that, for a man like Ryan,

> . . . with a deep love of country in the old and romantic sense, and an equally deep faith in the possibility of a reign of social justice and equity, the war must have been an even greater horror, as it grew plainer daily that it was not going to serve any of these things. And no one of us saw more plainly than he did that when it ended nothing would be left but ruined towns and endless bitterness.[31]

Ryan still refused to do anything more than advise the Germans on how best to ensure Ireland's neutrality and continued to maintain his low profile. He spent Christmas 1942 with Helmut and Budge Clissmann at their home in Copenhagen. Drinking wine, talking of the war and Ireland, Ryan was moved to propose sending a telegram to de Valera congratulating him on his staunch resistance to pressure to support the allies. Neutrality was, for Ryan, sacrosanct. When Roosevelt's re-election campaign started up in 1943, a plan was mooted to stir up "ethnic" votes against him. It was proposed to broadcast anti-Roosevelt propaganda to Irish-Americans from a station purporting to be in Ireland but, in fact, in Holland. Ryan was alarmed, and his strenuous objections, supported by the Clissmanns, on the grounds that it would only inflame Roosevelt further against the Free State, shelved the idea.

Ryan's insight was sought on a proposal made to the German Embassy in Dublin to raise a Green Brigade to fight alongside the Germans against Bolshevism on the eastern front, and on its instigator, Eoin O'Duffy. As if Stalingrad was not trouble enough for Hitler in Russia. Ryan was quizzed, too, about Charles Bewley, the ex-Irish ambassador to Germany fired by de Valera for being too pro-Hitler. He was still loitering on the fringes of the Third Reich, trying to involve himself in various intrigues, and had returned for a visit to Berlin in 1942. The Indian nationalist, Subhas Chandra Bose, told Bewley he had met Ryan on the street, "but he seemed in a hurry and went away without giving me his address". Bewley was not a man to let well enough alone: "I went to everyone I knew who might have influence. But my efforts met with the same results as Bose's: a meeting between us was out of the question. Ryan was being held by the Army authorities for a secret mission and was bound to avoid contact with the outside world."[32]

The truth was slightly less dramatic. He was still living in comfort compared to most Berliners in a large shared flat in the Nymphenburgerstrasse. The naturally gregarious Ryan, at times as lonely in crowded Berlin as he had ever been, enjoyed having friends round. Stuart's girlfriend Madelaine Meissner was a regular at his occasional small parties, which "were lively and there was no shortage of food and drink". He had a small coterie of friends, mostly colleagues of Clissmann's with vaguely left-wing sympathies. There was also, much to his delight, Gretel, Madelaine's sister, "but it was not really serious on either side. Frank was highly romantic and his chivalry naturally impressed my sister. He spoiled her with presents."[33]

The only other highlights in Ryan's life were Budge Clissmann's visits from Copenhagen and contact with home. He had intermittently corresponded with Eilís through Kerney, to whom he also wrote, giving his impressions of the war viewed from Berlin. De Valera may have disowned Ryan once he was in Germany, but Kerney could have served as a conduit of useful information from the engine room of the Third Reich to the taoiseach. Kerney had visited the Ryan family during a trip to Ireland, and had returned to tell Ryan that his father was well despite having undergone a prostate operation. His mother had been recovering from a coronary. Familial anxieties therefore compounded the exile's homesickness. "How I wish I could be with them, but it can't be done!" he wrote to Eilís. "I see no prospects. We must be patient."

His letters to family made minimal mention of the war and only in the vaguest terms. As had been the case when he was in Spain, Ryan painted a rosy picture of his life for his family. Despite his resentment of his guardians' not allowing him home, it must be said that he was continually treated with respect and generosity. Ryan wrote, truly enough, that any suffering he had to endure was primarily due to homesickness. He claimed to be living in more comfort than most in Ireland, and let them know he enjoyed an embarrassment of rations: "Every time I stick a fistful of tea in the pot, I think of your half ounce and wish I could send you some."[34] He insisted that his health was good and had only ever been bad as a result of the privations of Burgos. The war presented no dangers to him, he had for months only witnessed ineffectual air raids, and the whole conflict was, for him, little more than an inconvenience. Ryan gave the impression that, held up in Germany, he was merely putting his feet up for a while until he could travel back to continue his life as before. There was certainly no cause for alarm.

That same summer, 1942, Ryan struck up a close friendship with Christian Nissen, a fifty-year-old captain of the merchant marine who had been a blockade runner during the Great War. The two men certainly had one thing in common – Irish prison camps. After being captured, Nissen had spent the Great War years interned in Oldcastle, County Meath. The Abwehr had since employed him to sail small fishing boats to Ireland to drop off German spies, something which undoubtedly drew Ryan to him initially. Francis Stuart considered Nissen "the one hope left to Frank of being able to return to Ireland. For by now, although he almost never spoke of it, I believe that was the thought constantly at the back of his mind."[35] In a letter to Kerney more candid than those to his family, Ryan admitted that loneliness and frustrated homesickness were eating away at him: "Time hangs heavily on my hands . . . Partly from the necessity of maintaining an incognito, and partly from choice, my range of friends is very small. For instance, I avoid most people who have ever been in my country as well as most who hail from it. I get everything I ask for – except a deportation ticket!"[36]

The Irishmen at large in Berlin were, as a whole, not among the finest specimens of their race, undoubtedly another reason Ryan avoided seeking their company. Those claiming to be Irish patriots commonly had ulterior motives and mercenary hearts. Among the dozens who had put their names forward for Friesack, only ten or so had been thought suitable to form the so-called "Irish Brigade". Among these worthies were two men named Codd and Stringer, to whom Ryan, whether with his prior consent or not, was introduced in a cafe. Presumably because Codd, ex-sergeant in the British army, could speak Spanish and knew something of the country, "Frank Richard" invited them to visit him at his home. They did so and were impressed by the comfort in which he lived – although they thought it odd that he employed a Russian woman as a housekeeper.

John Codd was subsequently trained in sabotage and radio transmission, but his womanising was so incessant and indiscreet, Abwehr considered that his pillow talk might endanger security. He was consequently transferred to Dusseldorf, where he found a fresh supply of women to court. Court them he did, and during one night of carousing he hit a policeman. The exasperated Abwehr threw him in jail. There he was visited by Kurt Haller and a man named Moloney – whom he recognised instantly as Frank Richard. Ryan informed Codd that he had "friends in high places" and could get the errant sergeant set free.[37] Codd was soon at liberty to walk the streets of Berlin and marry a local fraulein.

Ryan's efforts on behalf of Codd were not the norm and presumably, as before, were prompted only by sympathy for an Irishman languishing in jail. He had remained one step ahead of Bewley, and when an Irishman named Mulally had recognised and greeted him, Ryan pretended not to understand him before fleeing. He steered clear of William Warnock, the Irish representative in Germany, who likewise declined to seek out Ryan. Just as the Germans thought it would be inappropriate to send Ryan home, so did de Valera want Ryan to stay where he was – so long as nobody found out. His arrival back in Ireland might have implicated de Valera in a German conspiracy that he was innocent of. The British government had already unearthed Ryan anyway, thanks to his visit to Friesack and the reportage of Major McGrath. Ryan's closer friends also had an idea he was safe and in Germany. When Jim Larkin Jr. and Roddy Connolly went to see J.P. Walshe, secretary at the Department of External Affairs, the two parties conceded they knew that Ryan was in Germany in some capacity other than a prisoner. The three agreed not to disclose the fact, "according to the wishes of Frank Ryan and his family", which of course also accorded with the wishes of the government and Ryan's republican and socialist colleagues.

Therefore, the only people who didn't know were the general public. Writing to Kerney of his abundance of rations and privileged life at the fountainhead of all he despised, Ryan had asked, "Who'd have forecast this for me a few years ago?"[38] Who indeed? Certainly not those who recalled the incorruptible republican socialist from his days in Ireland and Spain. Petitions and headlines asking "Where Is Frank Ryan?" were still commonplace. Rumours abounded: he was living incognito in America or else travelling there via either Mexico or Siberia, where he had gone before Germany invaded the Soviet Union. Both *Reynolds News,* an English co-op paper, and the *brigadista* veterans' journal, *Volunteer for Liberty,* claimed he had been murdered in Spain.[39] The *Irish Democrat* reported that the *Canadian Tribune* had announced Ryan's murder in Germany.[40] In London, the *Irish Freedom* newspaper constantly demanded answers from J.W. Dulanty, the Irish high commissioner, regarding Ryan's whereabouts – if he was alive at all.

The public curiosity concerning Ryan's fate was considered to be a well-meaning but embarrassing nuisance by the man himself. In a brief telegram to Gerald O'Reilly in New York, Ryan had, as far back as June 1941, asked that news be passed on to certain people that he was well. Touched though he may have been, he also expressed the wish that Peadar O'Donnell "will stop making a fuss pressing for information" about him.[41]

The only information that Ryan wanted imparted was to his friends and family: that he was safe. It was true, but the complete truth was more bleak. There was little for him to do in Ireland as the population was steadfastly in support of neutrality, while in Germany he had essentially outlived his usefulness. To both countries he had become something of a political liablility; the Germans did not want to return him, and de Valera did not want to receive him. Ryan must have surmised as much, and his inherent optimism had taken a cruel battering. Still, his family were to know nothing of all this: "I feel sure enough that some day I'll go back and start again

where I left off. I regard this period as an interruption and
nothing more . . . I'll survive to become sick of being at home!"
he wrote in summer 1942.[42] For the present, he told them, he
was haunted in his sleep by dreams of childhood days spent in
Kilfenora. It was to be his last contact with his family.

Notes to Chapter 12

1. *The Irish Times*, 6 June 1958.
2. Department of Foreign Affairs, NAI, A 20/4.
3. Quoted in Enno Stephan, *Spies in Ireland* (London: Macdonald & Co., 1963), p. 166.
4. The Abwehr would have appreciated that Lisbon port was conducive for travellers hoping to dodge wartime restrictions. A few weeks after Ryan's letter was sent, Margaret Daly, an Irishwoman living in Spain, travelled through Lisbon to Ireland to deliver messages and thousands of American dollars from Germany to the IRA.
5. Department of Foreign Affairs, NAI, A 20/4.
6. Department of Foreign Affairs, NAI, A 47. The quote is taken from a report from Kerney of a secret meeting he had with Veesenmayer, during which they discussed Ireland's position in the war. The meeting was arranged by Clissmann, disapproved of by de Valera, and led to a severe rebuke for the diplomat.
7. Quoted in Stephan, *Spies in Ireland*, p. 223.
8. Quoted in David O'Donoghue, *Hitler's Irish Voices* (Belfast: Beyond The Pale Publications, 1998), p. 58.
9. Desmond Williams in *The Irish Times*, 11 July 1953.
10. Francis Stuart, "Frank Ryan in Germany", *The Bell*, November 1950, p. 38.
11. Stuart's recollections of Ryan are often contradictory. He either changed his opinion of his colleague as the years went by or else his occasional snipes at Ryan's character were designed to deflect from himself the post-war execration he suffered for his own collusion with the Nazi regime. It could also simply be that as the novelty of the each other's company wore off, he realised, "I never liked Ryan . . . we didn't really get on." Quoted in Geoffrey Elborn, *Francis Stuart: A Life* (Dublin: Raven Arts Press, 1990), p. 15.
12. Quoted in Seán Cronin, *Frank Ryan: The Search for the Republic* (Dublin: Repsol, 1980), p. 199.
13. Stuart, "Frank Ryan in Germany", p. 38.
14. Department of Foreign Affairs, NAI, A20/4.
15. Quoted in Elborn, *Francis Stuart*, p. 156.

16. Quoted in O'Donoghue, *Hitler's Irish Voices*, p. 99.
17. Quoted in Stephan, *Spies in Ireland*, p. 236.
18. Department of Foreign Affairs, NAI, A 20/4.
19. Quoted in Stephan, *Spies in Ireland*, p. 122.
20. *Ibid.*, p. 223.
21. Department of Foreign Affairs, NAI, A 20/4.
22. *Ibid.*
23. Interview with the author.
24. Department of Foreign Affairs, NAI, A 20/4.
25. Quoted in Elborn, *Francis Stuart*, p. 157.
26. Stuart, "Frank Ryan in Germany", p. 39.
27. Quoted in Stephan, *Spies in Ireland*, p. 223.
28. Francis Stuart in an interview with Michael McInerney, *The Irish Times,* 11 April 1975.
29. Department of Foreign Affairs, NAI, A 20/4.
30. Quoted in Cronin, *Frank Ryan*, p. 220.
31. Stuart, "Frank Ryan in Germany", p. 40.
32. Charles Bewley, *Memoirs of a Wild Goose* (Dublin: Lilliput Press, 1989), p. 196.
33. Madelaine Stuart, *Manna in the Morning* (Dublin: Raven Arts Press, 1984), p. 26.
34. Department of Foreign Affairs, NAI, A 20/4.
35. Stuart, "Frank Ryan in Germany", p. 39.
36. Department of Foreign Affairs, NAI, A 20/4.
37. Codd remained in Germany until the end of the war when, disguised as a French POW, he managed to get himself and his German wife into France and from there back to Ireland. Military Archives, Cathal Brugha Barracks, G2/0257.
38. Department of Foreign Affairs, NAI, A 20/4.
39. 6 August 1944 and Spring 1944 respectively.
40. August 1945.
41. Military Archives, Cathal Brugha Barracks, G2/0257.
42. Quoted in Cronin, *Frank Ryan*, pp. 222–3.

CHAPTER 13

The Final Lonely Road to Dresden

On 15 January 1943, Frank Ryan collapsed in an apoplectic fit brought about by a stroke. Remembered by most of his Irish friends as a tall, strong-looking man, he had habitually worked himself to fatigue at the expense of his well-being, and heart trouble and some two years of imprisonment in Spain had corroded at the weaknesses in his constitution. While staying with the Clissmanns in Copenhagen in January 1942, he had been knocked unconscious in a car accident and bled profusely. After a few days in hospital he had been released, but the shock to his system had demanded he visit his own doctor for some time afterwards. A general examination by a Dr de Crinis had revealed that he was suffering from "organic disease of the heart and vascular system, and of the central nervous system".[1] Later that year, Francis Stuart noted that Ryan tended to "stagnate in conferences", that he was "obviously tired, isolated".[2] The mentally and physically robust man of Dublin days had withered dramatically in little over five years. Ryan's fighting days were over and his own body, once such an asset, was becoming his greatest enemy. At the time of his stroke he was still only forty.

Francis Stuart and Madelaine went to visit him in the Charité Hospital on 27 January 1943. Stuart's diary entry for that day records: "He was pretty ill still, eyes veiled, left arm partially paralysed. A terrible place this; locked, re-locked. Other patients in uniform like convicts. The food, he said, very bad. He lies there day after day, can't read much, and that till the end of February perhaps." Stuart spoke to him of the Belfast IRA man, Hugh MacAteer, a prison escapee on the run, thinking it would cheer him, "but I saw F. was far from all this and the world".[3] Madelaine agreed that the hospital "was a horrible place . . . more like a prison".[4] As to what had brought Ryan there, Francis Stuart gave his own, perhaps fanciful, diagnosis: "It was, I believe, as much the strain of struggling against the evil and confusion that he saw overshadowing all his hopes, as a physical malady that affected him finally." Stuart went to visit Ryan again ten days later, after which he noted: "He is very patient and has great power of resistance. Gave me a shirt and a piece of soap that he had brought back from Denmark at Christmas."

Ryan slowly made a recovery of sorts; although he was able to leave the hospital, he was frequently back in with various complaints. Years later Stuart still remembered "the hospitals in which we used to visit him, the look of his long face and dark hair on the pillows, his humorous greetings and grimaces at the strange places I found him".[5] Germany's fortunes in the war were far from conducive to the poorly receiving the medical attention and rest they needed. The frequency and intensity of the allied air raids was on the increase, the hospitals were over-subscribed and understaffed, and food was becoming more scarce. For all that, a doctor who examined Ryan in May "expresses gratification at my progress. He has ordered more massage. I can drink anything but Schnapps and smoke a little. He expects in mid-July I'll be quite cured."[6]

At the end of that month, Ryan changed address and moved to a flat in Grunewald. Few of his Berlin friends were around any more except Stuart. Helmut Clissmann had been with the Afrika Corps in Tunisia, Hoven was with a parachute regiment in France, and the others had either been scattered or killed. A woman who lived in the same building, Hildegard Lubbert, became acquainted with Ryan. She soon realised how impaired his existence was by his deafness, and she became a source of great succour to the sick man. That she worked in a pharmacy had its obvious, if illegal, advantages, but she also spent many of her free hours taking care of her new friend, partially paralysed and in low spirits. Yet he still wasn't too sick not to get excited by Irish politics. In June he was writing to Clissmann his analysis of the recent Irish general election after which de Valera had had to form a coalition to get his majority.

While the state of Ryan's health rose and fell, the conditions under which he and other Berliners lived were in steady decline. The lives of civilians were increasingly under threat. Incendiary bombs struck Ryan's own building, and though it remained undamaged, a fire raged in the garden. The house on the corner of his street was burnt out, and he went without a gas supply or telephone line for some days. Having no coal, he had to boil the kettle by burning old newspapers. As if it stood as a memorial to happier and safer days in Berlin, he told Helmut Clissmann that their old drinking haunt, "the Ratskeller, survives in the midst of an awful wilderness".[7]

Ryan was still suffering the effects of the stroke when, in mid-September, he was returned to hospital for another lengthy stay. This time it was a stomach ulcer, and he was told that he would have to remain for at least four weeks, living on a strictly supervised diet. As it consisted, for at least the first week, of only tea and porridge, there was not much of a diet to supervise. The hospital's puritan regimen and his not being allowed to smoke were both irritants, but he was grateful to be there at all. He considered it his good luck that the Charité, where he had been previously, had not been able to take him in. Still, he was always starving and his dreams at night were filled with solid foods – hams, turkey and chicken – to eat.

He knew well that the dreams of cornucopia would continue once he had been discharged. He had had to surrender all his ration books and privileges upon entering the hospital and anticipated being strung up by red tape to retrieve even normal rations. Mundane bureaucratic wrangles made a dangerous life harder to bear for a sick man. It aggravated a novel tendency toward irascibility in Ryan. His lively sense of fun dissipated, replaced by a grim sense of humour. Over the course of four weeks, his health improved and his release was a relief, he told Gerald O'Reilly in New York. "I'm out of hospital at last. The last X-ray showed no sign of the ulcer. I'm on a diet of course: chicken, eggs and other such unobtainable things." Ryan's black humour couldn't disguise the effects of the attrition inflicted upon his being by the war and his failing health. "I've lost 12 kilos. In all 1943 has been a tough year for me." He was not the same man he had once been when he served as the personification of optimism in the face of adversity: "The news gets no more cheery; I need about a barrel of Faith and Hope extract to face up to it!"[8]

Ryan was still at a loose end, more so than ever, only now his tedium was accompanied by discomfort and a certain amount of peril. His friends were concerned about his ability to endure the afflictions and privations they all suffered. He was still under somewhat limited medical supervision and receiving a course of injections. For a retreat, he had access to his "funkhole", presumably a friend's place out in the country, removed from burnt-out buildings and air raids. He was not, however, always well enough to travel there. It was perhaps for the same reason that he was unable to take up the Clissmanns on their invitation to spend the Christmas of 1943 in Copenhagen.

Instead he spent the festivities in a new apartment building where Hildegard Lubbert had also moved. The air raids became ever worse and more frequent. They were hazardous for Ryan particularly, since he lived on the top floor of his building and was unable to hear the sirens wailing. Fraulein Lubbert would rush up to his flat to alert him whenever the alarm sounded. Even then, rather than descending into the shelters, he often remained above ground watching the bombers passing overhead. Stuart remembered that "Life in Berlin was now becoming an ordeal even for those in good health. For Frank it was in many ways a nightmare." Fraulein Lubbert looked out for him in the evenings, "but in the mornings if neither I nor a friend could be with him, he would sit in a cafe with a cup of *Ersatzkaffee* in front of him, or, as I remember him once remarking with one of his grimaces, line up in a queue at the hairdressers simply in order to know what was happening".[9] Budge Clissmann remembered that "his main occupation at the time was foraging", undertaken not merely for food but for comfort, information and trustworthy company.[10]

Stuart and Madelaine went out on picnics with him when possible, and the two Irishmen would concoct ways of escaping from Germany and returning to Ireland – Ryan would marry Madelaine and thereby make an honest Irish citizen of her, after which they would be speedily divorced. More realistically, Kurt Haller suggested that Ryan take himself off to Slovakia to fully recuperate, but nothing came of the idea. Veesenmayer claimed he could arrange for the debilitated

Irishman to go to Switzerland, presumably on the grounds of his ill health and Ireland's neutrality. "He said, 'No – that would be my death,' " remembers Budge Clissmann. "He'd be cut off, he felt, from everything that counted at that time to him, especially news. He had access to the latest news. And he would have no friends."[11]

Yet Ryan's desperation is apparent by his willingness to consider two options that he earlier would have ruled out. The first idea was Stuart's.

> In the chaos we foresaw coming, I was wondering how, in his ill state of health, he could survive all the inevitable hardships and find some way back to Ireland. This thought was in both our minds . . . I suggested to him that he should get in touch with the Irish Legation. I saw he did not like the idea, but, all the same, he promised to consider it and asked me, if he decided to act on it, whether I would inform the Irish *chargé d'affaires* of his position, as he himself thought it inadvisable to go.[12]

Stuart said he would do as Ryan asked.

Ryan's only other chance to escape Germany, if not the war or the Germans, was more sinister and a source of some anxiety to him. The Gaelic scholar Hans Hartmann supervised the Luxembourg-based Irland-Redaktion, from which propagandist broadcasts were sent to Ireland, and there was yet some lingering faith in the idea of broadcasts to Irish-Americans. Hartmann was having a hard time coping alone and was on the lookout for an informed, preferably Irish, aide. Ryan's preparation of a "top secret" memorandum on the subject had led the Foreign Office to believe, mistakenly, that "a suitable person for the Irish station was now available".[13] Stuart and Haller told Ryan that Hartmann was on his scent and wanted to bring him to Luxembourg to act as an adviser on the Irish in America. Ryan, dismayed at the flimsiness of his cover and resentful of being hounded, tried to transfer to Hartmann the misinformation that plans for an Irish-American Geheimsender (secret radio station) had been dropped. He complained in a letter to Clissmann on 13 January 1944 that, despite his efforts, "the matter has gone further – more so than I like".

However, he had obviously not dismissed the enterprise: "I see just one possible good point in the affair. If Hartmann can give me good translation work in Luxembourg I've no objection to giving him my opinion whenever he wants it. So far as I can see, he is the last hope for me to find something for me to do." The bait was obviously tempting – he possibly thought Luxembourg would be more conducive to finding a route home – but he approached it with some trepidation. "[Veesenmayer] and Haller are enthusiastic about the proposal and say it would be very nice for me there in Luxembourg. (When I hear that, I begin to have doubts, naturally)."[14]

Would "advising" Hartmann on his broadcasts merely serve to entangle Ryan further into the web of the Third Reich from which he was already trying to extricate himself? He would not himself have been broadcasting to Ireland, but it is possible that his input would have meant he effectively wrote those broadcasts. Counselling the Abwehr had placed him in a nuanced position, one that would be even more acute should he become employed by Irland-Redaktion. Whereas bolstering German respect for Irish neutrality could be explained away as Ryan's serving only his homeland, working for Hartmann in propaganda, however reluctantly or cynically, would be viewed far more gravely. He may have felt that, with Germany's defeat now clouding the horizon, he had nothing to lose. Perhaps, blinded by the desperation of his circumstances, he may have opted for a relatively salubrious life and a revived chance of getting home.

We will never know. At the end of January 1944, the allies launched an enormous bombing raid against Berlin. As if challenging, or even tempting, death to find him, Ryan stayed above ground, in the open, assailed by the freezing cold. He collapsed and lost consciousness. Help arrived, but it was some time, in the midst of terror and confusion, before a doctor could be found and longer still before he could be revived. He was taken to a dilapidated hospital in Schinagendorf staffed by nuns. There his misery was only exacerbated. The windows were fastened and blacked out, the nuns panicked at the sound of the air raid sirens, and the stench was awful. Diagnosed with pneumonia, Ryan had to spend the first few days in the basement with the wounded from the bombing, all of them untended and deprived of air. Patients with festering wounds sat or lay in the corridors and wherever else there was space for them. He had been moved upstairs when Budge Clissmann came to visit, cheering him immensely. Still, she noticed in him a streak of self-pity foreign to his nature. He made it quite plain what he thought of his surroundings, grubby and stinking, employing his most bitter invective against the fact that no one in the hospital knew how to make a proper cup of tea. Budge was dispatched to the kitchen to do just that.

By now accomplished in deploying ruses to wangle whatsoever he needed, Ryan was able to procure a certificate from Dr de Crinis that entitled him to recuperate at a sanatorium in Loschwitz, a suburb of Dresden. After two wretched weeks in "the terrible hospital in Schinagendorf", he was delivered there by Kurt Haller. From there he wrote that he was "getting better already but won't be allowed up for some more days. It's a posh place and will probably be very expensive. It seems very well staffed. Very good service. I'll be here at least six weeks." Again he fretted over the minutiae of daily life. All his things remained in Berlin, and he asked the Clissmanns to send him shirts, pyjamas and a dressing gown, "Now practically indispensable, alas! as I expect to be sick or ready to be sick for a year or so!!"[15] What few clothes he had brought from Berlin were now no good to him. His frame was so shrunken that they no longer fit.

Francis Stuart and Madelaine Meissner made a trip down to Loschwitz to visit their friend on St Patrick's Day.

> He had everything that could be wished for. The contrast to the cold, broken, windowless rooms in Berlin was a vivid one. He had a warm room high over the Elbe. There was a library, sitting-rooms, comparatively good food, medical care. I had never seen him so miserable. They had kept his papers in Berlin. Even had he become well enough to leave, he was a prisoner.[16]

Madelaine Stuart was equally troubled by the visit. "It was a very beautiful place . . . The park where we strolled for a while was immaculately kept, and yet all the luxury could not hide the mortuary in the grounds, which we passed on our walk with him. He showed us his pulse throbbing in his wrist and said, 'We'll be in Ireland next year!'[17] Later, however, the friends were eating precious bread and sausage washed down with a glass of wine, when Stuart proposed a toast

> "To the next St Patrick's Day in Ireland." I forget what he answered. I know he did not believe in the possibility any more. It was a very sad afternoon. I had a feeling that for Frank, this was the worst time of all, worse than the years in Burgos prison under the shadow of execution; worse than the return voyage in the submarine within sight of the Irish coast.[18]

Stuart had tried to carry out his promise to Ryan to approach the Irish Legation on his behalf, but found that the building had been bombed and its occupants had abandoned Berlin altogether. Kerney had told Ryan to let him know of any plans to return home so that he might approach his superiors in Dublin on his behalf, but contact between the two seems to have ceased. Budge Clissmann visited Ryan in March and let Kerney know how things stood with him. She wrote supposedly out of concern for the health of a lady friend who was "looking very badly and was very depressed. ..[Although she] will probably recover sufficient health to lead a fairly normal life, she will never be the same again." Kerney sent a telegram, accompanied by a copy of Budge Clissmann's letter, to F.H. Boland at the Department of External Affairs in Dublin appealing for Ryan's repatriation: "My purely personal wish for some time has been to get her home again . . . I think the question should be raised on humanitarian grounds."[19] The sense of urgency in the despatches from both of Ryan's friends was severely undermined by wartime delays in communications.

Whether or not Ryan was aware of Budge Clissmann's raising the alarm and furthering the cause of his return home, he was leaning towards Hartmann's offer of a job in Luxembourg. He agreed to at least meet the linguist to talk the proposal over. Ryan reasoned, rather feebly, that he had no friends in Berlin or Loschwitz. Further, if nothing else, Hartmann, a respected translator of Irish texts into German, "has books – especially in my own language". He also maintained that it must be "clearly understood" that he would only be there temporarily and he wanted to ensure that "there'd be no cause for misunderstandings on business or political matters".[20] Ryan implied that he merely sought a few weeks in Luxembourg, particularly as he was unsure where he would live once discharged from the sanatorium. Occasional tips to Hartmann and some translation work, if that was indeed all that would be asked of him, was worth it to him.

Ryan could paint his cooperation as once again merely acquiescing to suit his own ends because, unlike his physique and his optimism, his other notable characteristic – recalcitrance – had not withered. Indeed his malevolent desires for the Third Reich were almost suicidal. Francis Stuart remembered that his friend "never, to the day of his death, abandoned his beliefs. He rejoiced at the Red Army victory at Stalingrad."[21] Budge Clissmann asserts Ryan never came under the sway of the Swastika to even the slightest degree. Stuart knew well that Ryan's hatred of Nazism had only deepened, because the man himself wrote Stuart countless letters enunciating, explaining and justifying his abhorrence of the hand that fed him. Ryan did not risk sending them by post; the loyal, if foolhardy, Hilda Lubbert delivered them into Stuart's hand personally. They were sufficiently incriminating that Stuart would destroy them as soon as he had read them.

In fact, the contents of Ryan's vituperative missives should not have surprised the authorities at all. For all of his purported anonymity outside of a closed intelligence circle, the German civil police, for whom the name Frank Richard, let alone Frank Ryan, should have meant nothing, knew of his existence in Germany. Although they knew little, what knowledge they possessed was damning enough. A query was addressed to the police concerning the mysterious Irishman in April 1944. The reply was that "all that is known of him is that he is a Communist and stood in the Dáil elections of 1937".[22] It is astonishing that Ryan, perceived and freely described thus, survived unmolested as long as he did. Although he was no longer under the aegis of the Abwehr (dissolved two months earlier, and during the spring of 1944 he became increasingly anxious that the Gestapo had him in its sights), evidently there was somebody still looking after him.

Ryan's stay at the sanatorium was extended because its director was away and, consequently, the patient could not be discharged. He was grateful for the breathing space it gave him to sort out where he would go next. His ailments came and went – fevers, a blood clot agonisingly pressing on a nerve in his ankle – as did the dates for his release. At the close of May 1944, four months after his collapse during the air raid, he was discharged.

Ryan returned to Berlin and the building shared with Hildegard Lubbert. For the first couple of days he seemed recovered and glad to back at the centre of activity. Luckily enough, during those early days of June, the German skies enjoyed a full moon that precluded the incursion of allied bombers. Working on the assumption that he would soon be going to either Luxembourg or Copenhagen, he had passport photographs taken that show a grim expression in a face gaunt and tired. He soon relapsed and within days was diagnosed as suffering from pleurisy. Hildegard Lubbert, Francis Stuart and Madelaine Meissner took turns keeping vigil over the bedridden Ryan. He possessed no strength and was still suffering from paralysis on his left side. Madelaine cared for him through the nights.

> I was often terrified during those vigils as Frank looked ghastly. When Francis [Stuart] came in the morning he would shave him and the two men would make plans to go to Switzerland and from there to Ireland . . . His homesickness was heartbreaking to watch. I have never seen anyone long so much for his homeland.[23]

At the dawn of 6 June, an armada of allied shipping landed troops, tanks and guns on the beaches of northern France. The news appeared to stir the embers of Ryan's will to live. He studied maps and discussed with Stuart the options open to the allies once a foothold in continental Europe could be secured. "But", recalled Stuart, "he was no longer, I knew, deeply involved in it."[24] Respiratory problems worsened. Ryan had to be helped from bed to chair, where he would sit with his head on the back of another chair in front of him so as to facilitate breathing. After some frenetic wrangling with the health authorities on the part of Fraulein Lubbert, it was conceded that Ryan could return to the sanatorium in Loschwitz. A car was to pick him up and deliver him to the station on 9 June. "The last painful and saddening help that Francis could give him", wrote Madelaine, "was to help him dress, putting on his socks and shoes for him."[25] Ryan asked his friend to shave him. When this was done, Ryan told Stuart to take the rest of his razor blades, which were very hard to come by. He probably guessed he would not need them much longer.

The car duly arrived, and the driver helped the derelict Ryan down the stairs. Hildegard Lubbert was to travel with him in a special compartment on the train reserved for their use. Stuart and Madelaine said their goodbyes. Reflecting on a minor incident of a few days earlier, Stuart knew that the end was near and suspected that Ryan did too. The writer recollected "arriving one evening and seeing him from the doorway before he had noticed me. It was clear to me then by the expression on his face that he was very near death. But I saw something else, too, that I should find it hard to define. I thought he had left a great deal behind him and was glad of it."[26]

In Loschwitz the faithful Hildegard Lubbert stayed by his bed all night. In his sleep, Ryan became delirious and returned to the conflict in Spain, roaring out orders in Spanish. The following day, during the afternoon of Saturday, 10 June 1944, he died.

Ryan died without pain, consciousness or awareness of his sickness. The post-mortem revealed that his heart had been unable to bear the strain of an inflammation of the lungs, caused by pleurisy. One heart valve, handicapped by fairly advanced arthritis, had been unable to close properly.

On the fourteenth of that month, a handful of Ryan's friends travelled to Loschwitz for his funeral. Hildegard Lubbert and Budge Clissmann did the organising. Francis Stuart's diary records an "intense sense of loneliness, leaving F.'s body there in that place, far from everyone. A feeling of final and utter aloneness."[27] Budge Clissmann realised that, for Ryan, "the most that could be hoped for was a life of semi-invalidity and continuous taking care . . . Frank was the last person who would ever find happiness under such conditions." She notified Leo Kerney that Ryan's burial was "preceded by a Mass for the dead and held in full accordance with the rites of the Catholic church . . . The grave lies on a beautifully quiet cemetery on the banks of the Elbe, and the ceremony was simple and sincere and, for us Irish, very lonely."[28] Budge Clissmann would later return to the cemetery to erect a small cross she had had made. On it were inscribed Ryan's pseudonym, Frank Richard, the dates of his life and the name he preferred to go by – Proinnsias Ó Riain.

Three weeks after the funeral, on 8 July 1944, Leo Kerney's and Budge Clissmann's petition to the Dublin government to approve Frank Ryan's repatriation finally landed on a desk at the Department of External Affairs. The appeal was refused.[29]

Notes to Chapter 13

1. Department of Foreign Affairs, NAI, A 20/4.
2. Quoted in Geoffrey Elborn, *Francis Stuart: A Life* (Dublin: Raven Arts Press, 1990), p. 156.
3. Francis Stuart, "Frank Ryan in Germany", *The Bell*, November 1950, p. 40.
4. Madelaine Stuart, *Manna in the Morning* (Dublin: Raven Arts Press, 1984), p. 39.
5. Stuart, "Frank Ryan in Germany", p. 40.
6. Quoted in Seán Cronin, *Frank Ryan: The Search for the Republic* (Dublin: Repsol, 1980), p. 224.
7. *Ibid.*
8. Stuart, "Frank Ryan in Germany", p. 40.
9. *Ibid.*
10. Interview with the author.
11. Quoted in Cronin, *Frank Ryan*, p. 228.
12. Stuart, "Frank Ryan in Germany", p. 42.
13. As David O'Donoghue has pointed out, this conclusion must have been drawn after Ryan had agreed to advise on the project but before he had denounced it. David O'Donoghue, *Hitler's Irish Voices* (Belfast: Beyond the Pale Publications, 1998), p. 145.
14. Quoted in Cronin, *Frank Ryan*, p. 229.
15. *Ibid.*, p. 231.
16. Francis Stuart, "Frank Ryan in Germany Part II", vol. XVI, no. 3, *The Bell*, December 1950.
17. Madelaine Stuart, *Manna in the Morning*, p. 39.
18. Francis Stuart, "Frank Ryan in Germany", p. 38.
19. Department of Foreign Affairs, NAI, A 20/4.
20. Quoted in Cronin, *Frank Ryan*, p. 231.
21. *The Irish Times,* 11 April 1975.
22. Department of Foreign Affairs, NAI, A 20/4.
23. Madelaine Stuart, *Manna in the Morning*, p. 39.
24. Francis Stuart, "Frank Ryan in Germany Part II", p. 40.
25. Madelaine Stuart, *Manna in the Morning*, p. 40.
26. Francis Stuart, "Frank Ryan in Germany Part II", p. 39.

27. *Ibid.*
28. Department of Foreign Affairs, NAI, A 20/4.
29. F. H. Boland wrote to Dan Bryan in Military Intelligence that "We don't intend to reply to this telegram, for the present at least. Repatriation would hardly be feasible in present circumstances." *Ibid.*

Works Cited

Acier, Marcel ed. *From Spanish Trenches*. London: Cressett, n.d.

Alexander, Bill. *British Volunteers for Liberty*. London: Lawrence and Wishart, 1982.

Andrews, C.S. *Dublin Made Me*. Cork: Mercier, 1979.

Andrews, C.S. *Man of No Property*. Cork: Mercier, 1982.

Banta, M.M. *The Red Scare in the Irish Free State, 1925–37*. Unpublished M.A. Thesis, University College Dublin, 1982.

Bewley, Charles. *Memoirs of a Wild Goose*. Dublin: Lilliput, 1989.

Bell, J. Bowyer. *The Secret Army: The IRA*. Dublin: Poolbeg, 1998.

Bell, J. Bowyer; Klaus, Gustav ed. *Ireland and the Spanish Civil War in Strong Words, Brave Deeds*. Dublin: O'Brien, 1994.

Boyce, D. George. *Nationalism in Ireland*. London: Croom Helm, 1982.

Brome, Vincent. *The International Brigades*. London: Heinemann, 1965.

Byrne, Paddy. *Irish Republican Congress Revisited*. London: Connolly Publications, 1994.

Carroll, Denis. *They Have Fooled You Again: Michael O'Flanagan (1876–1942)*. Dublin: Columba, 1993.

Carter, Carrolle J. *The Shamrock and the Swastika*. Palo Alto, CA: Pacific Books, 1977.

Connolly O'Brien, Nora. *We Shall Rise Again*. London: Connolly Books, n.d.

Coogan, Tim Pat. *De Valera: Long Fellow, Long Shadow*. London: Arrow, 1995.

Coogan, Tim Pat. *The IRA*. London: Fontana, 1980.

Cook, Judith. *Apprentices of Freedom*. London: Quartet, 1979.

Copeman, Fred. *Reason in Revolt*. London: Blandford, 1948.

Corkill, D. and Rawnsley, S.J. eds. *The Road to Spain*. Dunfermline: Borderline, 1981.

Cronin, Mike. *The Blueshirts and Irish Politics*. Dublin: Four Courts, 1997.

Works Cited

Cronin, M. and Regan, J.M. eds. *Ireland: The Politics of Irish Independence 1922–1949*. London: Macmillan, 2000.

Cronin, Seán. *Frank Ryan: The Search for the Republic*. Dublin: Repsol, 1980.

Cronin, Seán. *Irish Nationalism*. Dublin: Academy Press, 1980.

Cronin, Seán. *The McGarrity Papers*. Tralee: Anvil, 1972.

de Vere White, Terence. *Kevin O'Higgins*. London: Methuen, 1948.

Donnelly, Joseph. *Charlie Donnelly: The Life and Poems*. Dublin: Dedalus, 1987.

Doyle, M. *The Republican Congress: A Study in Irish Radicalism*. Unpublished M.A. Thesis, University College Dublin, 1988.

Duggan, John P. *Neutral Ireland and the Third Reich*. Dublin: Lilliput, 1989.

Elborn, Geoffrey. *Francis Stuart: A Life*. Dublin: Raven Arts, 1990.

English, Richard. *Radicals and the Republic Socialist Republicanism in the Irish Free State*. Oxford: Clarendon, 1994.

Fallon, Gerard. *Sean O'Casey: The Man I Knew*. London: Routledge & Keegan Paul, 1965.

Fanning, Ronan. *Independent Ireland*. Dublin: Helicon, 1983.

Feeley, Pat. *The Gralton Affair*. Dublin: Coolock Free Press, n.d.

Fisk, Robert. *In Time of War*. Dingle: Brandon, 1983.

Foley, Conor. *Legion of the Rearguard*. London: Pluto, 1992.

Foster, R.F. *Modern Ireland 1600–1972*. London: Penguin, 1988.

Garvin, Tom. *1922: The Birth of Irish Democracy*. Dublin: Gill & Macmillan, Dublin, 1996.

Gilmore, George. *The Republican Congress*. Dublin: Dochas Co-Op. Society, n.d.

Gurney, Jason. *Crusade in Spain*. Newton Abbot: Readers Union, 1976.

Greaves, Desmond. *Liam Mellows and the Irish Revolution*. London: Lawrence and Wishart, 1987.

Greaves, Desmond. *The Life and Times of James Connolly*. London: Lawrence and Wishart, 1986.

Hanley, Brian. *The IRA 1926–1936*. Dublin: Four Courts, 2002.

Hegarty, Peter. *Peadar O'Donnell*. Cork: Mercier, 1999.

Hoar, Victor. *The Mackenzie-Papineau Battalion*. Copp Clark Publishing, 1969.

Works Cited

Hobsbawm, E.J. *Nations and Nationalism Since 1780*. Cambridge: Cambridge University Press, 1990.

Hopkinson, Michael. *Green Against Green: The Irish Civil War*. Dublin: Gill & Macmillan, 1988.

Johnston, Verle B. *Legions of Babel: The International Brigades in the Spanish Civil War*. University Park, PA: Pennsylvania State University Press, 1967.

Keogh, Dermot. *Twentieth Century Ireland: Nation and State*. Dublin: Gill & Macmillan, 1994.

Keogh, Dermot. *Ireland and Europe 1919–1948*. Dublin: Gill & Macmillan, 1988.

Lee, J.J. *Ireland 1912–1985*. Cambridge: Cambridge University Press, 1989.

Levine, Maurice. *Cheetham to Cordova*. Manchester: Neil Richardson, 1984.

Litton, Helen. *The Irish Civil War: An Illustrated History*. Dublin: Wolfhound, 1995.

Lyons, F.S.L. *Ireland Since the Famine*. London: Fontana, 1979.

Macardle, Dorothy. *The Irish Republic*. London: Gollancz, 1937.

Manning, Maurice. *The Blueshirts*. Dublin: Gill & Macmillan, 1970.

Mac Eoin, Uinseann. *The IRA in the Twilight Years*. Dublin: Argenta, 1997.

Mac Eoin, Uinseann. *Survivors*. Dublin: Argenta, 1980.

McGarry, Fearghal. *Irish Politics and the Spanish Civil War*. Cork: Cork University Press, 1999.

McGarry, Fearghal. *Frank Ryan*. Dundalk: Dundalgan Press, 2002.

McHugh, James P. *Voices of the Rearguard: A Study of An Phoblacht – Irish Republican Thought in the Post-Revolutionary Era*. Unpublished M.A. Thesis, University College Dublin, 1983.

McInerney, Michael. *Peadar O'Donnell: Irish Social Rebel*. Dublin: O'Brien, 1979.

McManus, F. ed. *The Years of the Great Test 1926–1939*. Cork: Mercier, 1967.

Milotte, Mike. *Communism in Modern Ireland*. Dublin: Gill & Macmillan, 1984.

Monks, Joe. *With the Reds in Andalusia*. London: John Cornford Poetry Group, 1985.

Works Cited

Murphy, John A. "The New IRA 1925–62", in Williams, T. Desmond ed. *Secret Societies in Ireland*. Dublin: Gill & Macmillan, 1973.

Murray, Patrick. *Oracles of God: The Roman Catholic Church and Irish Politcs 1922–37*. Dublin: University College Dublin Press, 2000.

Neeson, Eoin. *The Civil War in Ireland 1922–23*. Cork: Cork University Press, 1969.

Nevin, Donal. "Radical Movements in the Twenties and Thirties". In Williams, T. Desmond ed. *Secret Socities in Ireland*. Dublin: Gill & Macmillan, 1973.

O'Carroll, J.P. and Murphy, John A. eds. *De Valera and His Times*. Cork: Cork University Press, 1986.

O'Casey, Sean. *Autobiographies*. London: Macmillan, 1963.

O'Casey, Sean; Krause, David ed. *The Letters of Sean O'Casey*, vols. 1, 2. London: Cassell, 1975.

O'Casey, Sean. *Three Plays*. London: Macmillan, 1970.

O'Connor, Joseph. *Even the Olives Are Bleeding: The Life and Times of Charles Donnelly*. Dublin: New Island, 1992.

O'Connor, Peter. *A Soldier of Liberty*. Dublin: MSF, 1997.

O'Donnell, Peadar. *The Gates Flew Open*. Cork: Mercier, 1966.

O'Donnell, Peadar. *Monkeys in the Superstructure*. Galway: Salmon, 1986.

O'Donnell, Peadar. *Salud: An Irishman in Spain*. London: Methuen, 1937.

O'Donoghue, David. *Hitler's Irish Voices*. Belfast: Beyond the Pale, 1998.

O'Donoghue, Florence. *No Other Law*. Dublin: Anvil, 1986.

O Drisceoil, Donal. *Peadar O'Donnell*. Cork: Cork University Press, 2001.

Ó Duinnín, Eoghan. *La Niña Bonita agus An Róisín Dubh*. Baile Atha Cliath: An Clóchomhar, 1986.

Ó Faolain, Seán. *Vive Moi!* London: Sinclair-Stevenson, 1993.

O'Farrell, Padraic. *Who's Who in the Irish War of Independence*. Dublin and Cork: Mercier, 1980.

O'Halpin, Eunan. *Defending Ireland*. Oxford: Oxford University Press, 1999.

Ó hEidirsceoil, Seán. "A Personal Memoir of the Thirties", in Klaus, H. Gustav ed. *Strong Words, Brave Deeds: The Poetry, Life and Times of Thomas O'Brien, Volunteer in the Spanish Civil War*. Dublin: O'Brien, 1994.

Works Cited

O'Loughlin, Michael. *Letters from the New Island*. Dublin: Raven Arts, 1991.

O'Riordan, Manus. "Communism in Dublin in the 1930s", in Klaus, H. Gustav ed. *Strong Words, Brave Deeds: The Poetry, Life and Times of Thomas O'Brien, Volunteer in the Spanish Civil War*. Dublin: O'Brien, 1994.

O'Riordan, Michael. *Connolly Column*. Dublin: New Books, 1979.

O Síocháin, P.A. *Ireland: Journey to Freedom*. Kells: Kells Publishing Co., n.d.

Patterson, Henry. *The Politics of Illusion: Republicanism and Socialism in Modern Ireland*. London: Hutchinson Radius, 1989.

Preston, Paul and Mackenzie, Ann. *The Republic Besieged: Civil War in Spain*. Edinburgh: Edinburgh University Press, 1996.

Regan, John. *The Irish Counter-Revolution 1921–1936*. Dublin: Gill & Macmillan, 1999.

Rumpf, E. and Hepburn, A.C. *Nationalism and Socialism in Twentieth Century Ireland*. Liverpool: Liverpool University Press, 1977.

Ryan, Frank ed. *The Book of the XV Brigade*. Newcastle upon Tyne: Frank Graham, n.d.

Sheehy Skeffington, Andrée. *Skeff; The Life of Owen Sheehy Skeffington*. Dublin: Lilliput, 1991.

Stephan, Enno. *Spies in Ireland*. London: Macdonald, 1963.

Stradling, Robert. *The Irish and the Spanish Civil War*. Manchester: Mandolin, 1999.

Thomas, Hugh. *The Spanish Civil War*. London: Penguin, 1990.

Stuart, Madelaine. *Manna in the Morning*. Dublin: Raven Arts, 1984.

Ward, Margaret. *Hanna Sheehy Skeffington: A Life*. Cork: Attic, 1997.

Ward, Margaret. *Unmanageable Revolutionaries: Women and Irish Nationalism*. London: Pluto, 1995.

Works Cited

NEWSPAPERS

Daily Express
Irish Democrat
Irish Freedom
Irish Independent
Irish People
Irish Press
The Irish Times
Kilkenny People
Limerick Leader
The Nation
New York Times
An t-Óglach
An Phoblacht
Republican Congress
The Worker

JOURNALS

Ó Canainn, Aodh. "Eilís Ryan in Her Own Words", *Saothar* 21, 1996.

Hammill, Jonathan. "Saor Éire and the IRA: An Exercise in Deception", *Saothar* 20.

Staunton, Enda. "Frank Ryan and Collaboration: A Reassessment", *History Ireland,* vol. V, no. 3, Autumn 1997.

Stradling, Robert. "A War of Ideals? Irish Volunteers in the Spanish Civil War", *Cathair na Mart,* no. 15, 1995.

Stuart, Francis. "Frank Ryan in Germany", *The Bell,* vol. XVI, no. 2, November 1950.

Stuart, Francis. "Frank Ryan in Germany, Part II", *The Bell,* vol. XVI, no. 3, December 1950.

ARCHIVES

University College Dublin
Moss Twomey
Sheila Humphries (Síghle Uí Dhonnchadh)
IRA Southern Command
Eithne Coyle
Ernest Blythe
Mary MacSwiney

Works Cited

Richard Mulcahy
Sean O'Mahoney
Caitlín Brugha
Seán MacEntee
Desmond Ryan
National Library
Hanna Sheehy Skeffington
Rosamund Jacob
Joseph MacGarrity
Anne O'Farrelly
National Archives
Department of Justice
Department of the Taoiseach
Department of Foreign Affairs
Archives of the Labour History Museum
Paddy Byrne
Karl Marx Memorial Library (London)
International Brigade Archives
Imperial War Museum (London)
Sound Archives: Spanish Civil War Collection

Acknowledgements

The list of people to whom I owe heartfelt thanks for their help and encouragement in the writing of this book is far longer than I would have imagined before I started it. Certainly, the kinds of demands I have made upon them exceeded my expectations, and no doubt theirs. I only hope they can draw consolation from the facts that they have made this book possible and are now the subject of my sincere gratitude. For myself, I was not only helped inestimably by the contributions of others but like to think that I have found and secured friendships in the process. Beth Nunan did more for me than I could have possibly expected – or can possibly list – and herself and James were paragons of hospitality. Stephanie Boland was especially supportive, as well as resourceful and patient. The encouragement and interest shown by my family in Ireland and England were as beneficial to me as the more practical chores they volunteered on my behalf.

Thanks must go to Kieran Hoare of the NUIG Archives Department for setting me on the right road in the first place and giving me inspirational advice ever since. For labourious translation work, I am grateful to Trish Burke, Seán Ó Flathar-ta and Enda and Katherine Rohan. Budge Clissmann, Tommy Cooke, Catherine O'Brien and Packy and Lou Earley were particularly generous with their time and memories of Frank Ryan. Ita Killeen thought of my efforts at crucial times, while Imelda and Pauline Robinson showed consideration and generosity. Katherine Duffessy at NUIG Computer Services repeatedly got me out of trouble, and Michael Donnelly was similarly generous with his computer password. Paul (O) Donovan and Christina Pysik certainly have to be thanked for something or other, and Mr P.J. Kelly of Galway and Hi Many provided freely and graciously of his technical support. My landlord Charles was a surprising patron of Irish socialist republican research, being more than merely accomodating, and I sincerely thank him.

Seamus Helferty and the staff at the UCDAD were never less than friendly and informative. I must also thank the staffs of the Labour History Museum, the Cathal Brugha Barracks' Military Archives, the National Library, the National Archives and, in London, the Karl Marx Memorial Library and the Imperial War Museum. Aodh Ó Canainn was generous with his insights and sharing his research. Manus O'Riordan, Emmet O'Connor and Joost Augusteijn helped in whichever way they could, while the camaraderie shown by Fearghal McGarry, author of a fine book on the same subject, kept up my own spirits. I was further shown great kindness by Fathers Cunningham and Stirling at Rockwell College and Fathers Kelleher and Forde of St Colman's College. Niall Andrews, TD, was prompt and helpful with his recollections of the reinterment of Ryan's remains. I am indebted to Eugene at Connolly Books in Temple Bar, while Des Ryan in Limerick and Sean Ryan in Kildangan were particularly considerate. Lastly, my thanks must go to all of those, including most of the above, who were not only polite enough to feign interest but sustained my endeavours despite my boring them to tears with tales of research woe and Frank Ryan trivia.

Index

Please note that Mac and Mc are treated as if spelled the same

Index

Index

Index

Index

Index

Index

119, 134, 140–1, 148, 149, 151, 152, 153, 154, 190, 206, 222, 235, 252, 266
  harassment of 49, 52n
O'Donoghue, Donal 41, 108
O'Duffy, Eoin 60, 75–7, 82, 109, 126, 149, 152, 153, 155, 156, 161, 163, 167, 168, 169n, 183, 196, 197, 209, 217, 220, 225n, 230, 232, 238, 262
Ó Duinnín, Eoghan 35, 51, 106, 122, 132, 142
Ó Faoláin, Micheál 70
Ó Faoláin, Seán 20
O'Farrelly, Annie 85, 152
O'Flanagan, Father Michael 43, 59, 197n
O'Flinn, Peter 187, 195
O'Hannigan, Donnachadha 23
O'Higgins, Kevin 44, 73n, 219
O'Leary, Arthur 113
Ó Máille, Padraig 25
Ó Maoileoin, Tomás 35–6
O'Reilly, Donal 159–60, 170n
O'Reilly, Gerald 73n, 115, 133, 149, 156, 163, 183, 190, 206, 242, 250, 266, 271
O'Riordan, Michael x, 110, 152, 170, 224, 247
Ontiveros, J.G. 233
Orange Order 57–8, 93
Ornitz, Lou 215
O'Sullivan, Tadgh 75

Paris 155, 187, 216, 217, 235, 241–2, 261
Parker, Max 211–12
Partido Obrero de Unificación Marxista (POUM) 193
Patton, Tommy 170n
Pearl Harbor 254, 259
Pearse, Pádraig 17, 32, 40, 48, 49, 52, 53, 57, 63, 66, 69, 114, 115
  Éire Saor Gaedhealach 17, 32
People's Rights Association 88
Pinto, General Lopez 222
Popular Front Coalition (Spain) 147

Power, Johnny 153, 164, 181, 183, 200
Power, Paddy 164, 181, 183
Prendergast, Jimmy 153, 166, 173, 205
Price, Michael 103, 111, 112, 113, 120, 125
Proclamation of Independence (1916) 82, 194
Progressive Publications Society 189
Public Safety Act (1923) 26
Public Safety Bill (1931) 82

Quearney, Christy 110, 113, 193
Quill, Mike 73n, 149
Quinn, Sid 202, 203

Randall, Lesley 78–9
Reiger, Bruno 257
Renn, Ludwig 203, 223n
Republican Congress 112–121, 124–40, 149, 150, 151, 152, 189, 190, 191, 216
  ASU plan 136
  Athlone conference 113–14
  Athlone Manifesto 114, 115, 119
  Bodenstown parades 116–17, 131–2
  first congress 120–1
  Rathmines fissure 125, 129, 133
  Savoy Cinema stormed 130–1
Republican Congress 115, 116, 117–19, 125, 126, 128, 129, 130, 131, 133, 134, 135
Republican File 86, 88
Republican Press Ltd 48
Revolutionary Workers' Groups (RWG) 93–4, 97n, 103, 106
Reynolds News 266
Rising (1916) vii, 17, 18, 36, 37, 54, 65, 66, 67, 170n, 192
Robinson, Paschal 216, 217
Rockwell College 15, 16, 19, 28
Rojel, Fabricano 231
Rolfe, Edwin 209
Roosevelt, Franklin D. 262

297

Index

Russell, Sean 77, 149, 235, 242–5, 246, 249, 250, 253
Ruttledge, P.J. 191
Ryan (née Slattery), Ann 13, 16, 108, 255, 263
Ryan, Ann (sister) 42
Ryan, Catherine 42, 190, 208
Ryan, Des 59
Ryan, Desmond 188, 195
Ryan, Eilís vii, x, 14, 16, 17, 23, 28, 42, 90, 108, 122, 154, 156, 170, 194, 196, 208, 215–16, 217, 222, 225n, 230, 233, 235, 247, 263
Ryan, Frank
  "*An Phoblacht Abú*" 80
  arrested in France 107
  Book of the XV Brigade 209, 210
  breaks strike at Knocklong creamery 18–19, 128
  candidate for Dublin North-West 137–9
  childhood 13–18
  at Clan na Gael Convention 65–8
  deafness 14, 47, 103, 107, 155, 219, 235, 241, 252, 270
  detained in Germany 241–4, 247, 249–67, 269–80
  Easter Week and After 48–9
  "Easter Week message to Republicans" 90
  editor of *An Phoblacht* 49–50, 53, 55–60, 69, 70–1, 80, 85, 90, 91, 92, 102–3, 106–7, 110
  elected to Army Executive of the IRA 50
  Emancipation 49
  escapes from Spain to Germany 240–1
  fights Free State army 21–5
  Frank Richard pseudonym 252, 253, 255, 265, 277, 280
  hatred of Nazism 260–1, 262, 277
  "The Ideals of the Young Men of Ireland" 66–7
  imprisoned in 1932 86–7, 88–9

  imprisoned for sedition (1931) 78
  interned in Hare Park 26–7
  IRA documents charge 46, 53
  Irish language promotion 30–2, 46–7, 53, 56, 85, 119–20
  leaves the IRA 112–13
  "The Men and Women of the Orange Order" 93
  Radio Madrid broadcasts 208–9
  reactaire of An Cumann Gaedhealach 30–1
  reinterment vii, ix
  returns to Germany on U-boat 245–7, 261
  "Revolutionary Organisations" 76
  Seachranaidhe (Wanderer) pen-name 48, 49, 92, 108
  skill as an orator 31, 35, 47, 65, 76, 77–8, 90, 119, 120, 130, 189, 192
  and Spanish Civil War 151–2, 154–69, 172–85, 197, 199, 199–211
  in captivity 211–23, 229–41
  stroke 269–70
  talks to Irish prisoners of war 255–6
  teaches at Cúig Cúigí 32, 46, 47
  tramples the tricolour 127
  at UCD 19, 21, 30, 32, 120, 130, 234
  "The Ulster Question" 92
Ryan, Jeremiah Joseph 42
Ryan, John (brother) 42, 67, 97n
Ryan, John (nephew) vii
Ryan, John 77, 78
Ryan, Mary 42
Ryan, Maurice (Moss) 14, 17, 42
Ryan, T.J. 96n
Ryan, Vere 13, 16, 108, 224, 263
Ryan, Vincent 14, 42, 107, 135

Saor Éire 54, 60, 65, 68–71, 80, 81, 84, 86, 90, 91, 92, 94–6, 97n, 99, 102, 104–5, 113, 137, 140
  1931 convention 82

298

Index

Index